CONFESSIONS OF
a Mediocre
WIDOW

Or, How I Lost My Husband
and My Sanity

CATHERINE TIDD

Published by Sourcebooks, Inc.

P.O. Box 4410, Naperville, Illinois 60567-4410

(630) 961-3900

Fax: (630) 961-2168

www.sourcebooks.com

Library of Congress Cataloging-in-Publication Data

Tidd, Catherine.

Confessions of a mediocre widow : or, How I lost my husband and my sanity / Catherine Tidd.

pages cm

1. Tidd, Catherine. 2. Widows--United States--Biography. 3. Widowhood--United States. 4. Grief. 5. Loss (Psychology) 6. Adjustment (Psychology) I. Title. II. Title: How I lost my husband and my sanity.

HQ1058.5.U5T49 2014

306.88'30973--dc23

2013018386

Printed and bound in the United States of America.

POD 10 9 8 7 6 5 4 3

To Brad
When in doubt…I look up.

Contents

*"Life does not cease to be funny when people die
any more than it ceases to be serious when people laugh."*

—George Bernard Shaw

Author's Note

L ife can change in the blink of an eye."
    As a mother of three, I've seen those changes in action.
One day a kid is barely walking and talking, and the next she's
tripping over her Stride Rite shoes and yelling "Shit!" just before
her head hits the corner of the coffee table. One day she's running
away from the boys on the playground, and the next she's waiting
by the phone for them to call. And any mother will tell you that
one day your son is in one size, and then the next morning when
you're dressing him for school, his pants are an inch too short.

I've figured out that the most obvious kind of change seems
to happen "in the blink of an eye." That's the type of change that
other people can see and are comfortable with (even if it's an
"uncomfortable change") because it can be labeled and categorized.

"It's a growth spurt!"

"It's hormonal."

*"Her husband just died. Give her time. She'll be back to her old self
in a few months."*

The other kind, the deep-down kind, takes more time and
more patience. That's the kind of change that you don't realize

has happened until you look back a few years later and think, "Was that *me*?" And you're stunned to realize that you and the person you abandoned years ago without giving her a second thought are one and the same.

All of my big changes were gradual. Oh, sure. You could say that my husband's death was "in the blink of an eye," and I wouldn't argue with you. You could say that that moment, that blink, was what changed my life forever. You could say that the second I heard the words, "He's not going to make it," I became an entirely different person.

And you'd be right.

But the change into the person I became didn't happen in that moment. It didn't happen as I was riding in the passenger seat of my mother's minivan on the way home from the hospital after hearing those words. And it didn't happen at the funeral.

In a way it happened all at once. And in another way it took years.

As with all life changes, at some point you have to own who and what you are. You have to accept it so that you can move forward and become who you are meant to be. So here goes.

I'm Catherine. And I am a widow.

No one says when they're ten years old, "Hey! You know what? I've decided to become a doctor when I grow up. No wait! An astronaut. Better yet...I'll be a widow! That will amaze *everyone!*"

But I'm betting that through this unwanted education, I've learned more about life—*my* life—than I would have as a doctor or an astronaut. I've learned about loss, love, and how to truly pursue happiness. I've learned how to look at someone who may not be making the decisions I would and say, "Why does it matter? Their journey is all their own." I have a master's in grief with an emphasis in empathy. And I'm not afraid to use it.

And like all widows out there, I've got a story that is in some ways completely my own.

And in some ways, it's the story of millions.

Widowhood

when normal becomes a fantasy

1

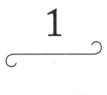

I spent my eleventh wedding anniversary planning my husband's funeral.

If I could figure out how to make that rhyme, it would be the beginning of a great country song.

I'm not sure if I'll ever be able to forgive Brad for suddenly leaving me with three children under the age of six, no job, and a mortgage on a house that we bought because *he* liked the location.

Oh, I know it wasn't his choice. It's not like I sit around picturing him up on a cloud in a chaise lounge, fruity beverage in hand, waving down to me and saying, "Have fun down there!"

But there have been moments of deep darkness—as I figured out the bills, health insurance, and child rearing alone—when I have wondered if he didn't get the better part of this deal.

The first time I saw Bradley Tidd, I was in Colorado Springs where he was a cadet at the Air Force Academy. He was laughing as he threw a football, completely unaware of my stare. The grass in the field where everyone was tailgating was dry and crunchy, just begging for the first snow of the season. The grounds overflowed with sports cars, a purchase that seemed to be required of every cadet the moment they made it to their junior year.

And in the middle of all of that macho testosterone stood Brad, his arm cocked above his shoulder, ready to throw a spiral to another classmate, laughing as if his internal joy couldn't be contained and was just bubbling out of him.

A little shorter than I was, he had the all-American looks of a soon-to-be Air Force officer, with his light brown hair cut as close as it could be and his frame suggesting that he worked out but still had a good time. Four years my senior, he had a mischievous grin that reached all the way up to his green-hazel eyes and matched his irresistible laugh, which would eventually teach my heart how to stop and then keep right on going again.

The last time I saw Bradley Tidd, thirteen years later, he lay motionless in a hospital bed not five miles away from that spot in the field. Those hazel eyes were shut, and the infectious laughter that had gotten us through moves, job changes, and childbirth had stopped. His hair was still short, now due to the battle he'd had with a receding hairline that started in his midtwenties and eventually won when, at thirty, he decided to start shaving his head completely bald.

We were just so damn *normal*. He was the breadwinner; I was the homemaker. We grilled on the weekends with our neighbors, had occasional date nights where we tried our hardest to talk about anything other than the kids, loved a lot, and fought a little. There were times when I'd ask myself, "Is this *it*? What life is supposed to be like? Do I want more?" and almost always answered myself, "Nope. I'm good."

We were partners in every way. And while our relationship wasn't perfect (whose is?), we seemed to function as well as we could, given the fact that we had three young children and almost no time to ourselves. Like most couples who have been together for a long time, I felt like I knew Brad better than anyone else in the world.

And like most people who have been through an unimaginable loss, I've wondered, since he's been gone, if I knew myself at all.

July 16, 2007.

Picture a normal Colorado summer morning, with blue skies and the perfect breeze floating through two open windows. At the crack of 8:30 a.m., I was still in my bed, half asleep, enjoying that gentle wind, waiting until the last minute to emerge from the cocoon I had created with the six pillows. I'm not the early riser.

My kids figured out at a young age that, until their stomachs were audibly growling, they should *not* wake Mommy up. Even then, my oldest, Haley, who was five, would gently come in, rub my arm, and try to rouse the slumbering beast in the calmest way possible so as not to anger it. Sarah, who was eighteen months old at the time, must have gotten my sleeping gene, because she rarely woke up before 9:00 a.m. And my son, Michael, who was three and stuck in the middle of a bunch of estrogen, just tried to do whatever he could to blend into the background so that none of the crazy females surrounding him would strap him down, force a Cinderella costume on him, and take pictures to show future prom dates.

He would pretty much go with the flow.

As I slept with my pillow over my head (which I did every night because my dog snored like an Irishman on a bender), I slowly came out of my princess-like dream world, thinking, "Was that the phone ringing?"

I checked my caller ID, which read "Penrose Hospital," with

a Colorado Springs area code. I dismissed it, thinking that it was probably someone looking for a donation, and wasn't I lucky to avoid that call? I mean, that's why I had this, my *favorite* piece of technology. How did people avoid solicitors (and their extended family) in the '80s?

But then I remembered that Brad was driving south of Denver that morning for work and that I'd better call back just in case.

"Penrose Hospital."

"Yes, I wanted to make sure that no one there called me. I just missed a call and I wanted to double-check that it wasn't about my husband."

"Name?"

"Brad Tidd."

"Please hold."

After holding for about five minutes, I felt my heart begin to pound in my ears. It should have taken that receptionist a minute to check her computer, see that he wasn't there, and get back on the phone with me, annoyed that I had wasted her time.

"Ma'am?"

"Yes?"

"I'm transferring you to a nurse right now."

Damn.

A voice came on the line that was entirely too cheerful for the mood I was sinking into.

"Hello? Mrs. Tidd? This is Joanie," she said over the noise of trauma in the background. "I have your husband here with me."

"What happened?" I said frantically, running down the stairs from my second-floor bedroom and starting to pace. "What's going on? Is he okay? Why is he there?"

"Now, don't worry. He's fine," she said in a way that I knew was supposed to calm me but just made me more impatient.

"He's talking. He was in an accident, but you'll have to talk to someone when you get here about what happened. We're going to take him in for some x-rays and you can meet him in the ER. Right now it just looks like he has a dislocated knee. Don't rush. Take your time getting down here. I promise that he's okay."

Right, lady. Don't rush. If he's so fine, why isn't he calling me?

At that point I couldn't get off the phone fast enough. I couldn't trust some stranger to tell me that my husband was "fine." I needed to see for myself. I sat down on the recliner in the TV room for a minute and looked around wildly, trying to decide what to do next. Haley sat on the couch, her eyes focused on *The Wiggles*. Michael sat on the floor, fiercely concentrating on constructing a castle out of blocks. And I could hear the sounds of Sarah in her crib, babbling away to a stuffed animal.

Crap. I can't take them with me. Now what?

And I immediately started dialing my parents' phone number.

My parents had moved to Denver six months earlier from Louisiana, something that I couldn't have been happier about. Those poor people had made it through Hurricanes Katrina and Rita, only to move north during one of the worst series of snowstorms on record in Colorado. Not only that, but they had brought along my extremely asthmatic ninety-five-year-old grandmother, who hadn't lived above sea level in fifty years.

Those two had their hands full.

I felt a little guilty about calling my mother that morning and adding something else to her plate, but before I had even finished saying the word "accident," she was walking out the door to come watch my kids.

"I'm calling your dad. He'll meet you at the hospital," she said breathlessly.

"Oh, Mom. Don't make Dad leave work. They said Brad was

fine. I'll feel terrible if Dad has wasted the day," I said, knowing that my dad didn't miss work for anything.

"He's coming." *Click.*

While I waited the twenty agonizing minutes it took my mother to get to my house, I ran upstairs, took the quickest shower in history, and looked over the contents of my closet. What to wear? It was hot outside, but I knew that the temperature in hospitals could vary from muggy and hot to chilly and "I wish I had a sweatshirt" cold. I decided on layers and then packed a bag, thinking that if I was prepared for an overnight stay, it probably wouldn't happen. And in that bag I packed Brad's favorite shorts, T-shirt, and sneakers so that he would have something comfortable to wear on the ride home.

My mother finally arrived, and I barely said hello to her before I threw everything into my minivan and screeched out of the driveway. I started driving south, mentally going through routes in my head to figure out the fastest way. Finally deciding to go through Castle Rock, I thought for sure I had missed rush-hour traffic and would be able to slide right onto the highway. And then I saw the signs and flashing lights just before the on-ramp.

Construction.

"You gotta be kidding me," I muttered. Looking around, trying to figure out if I could take a side street, I sat helplessly in my car, fidgeting in my seat until the traffic finally gave way to the wide-open highway.

When I got down to the hospital in Colorado Springs and entered the trauma area, I was greeted by a woman who looked eerily like my cousin, adding to the surreal feeling of that moment. As I waited for forty-five minutes in the tiny, curtained room in the ER, I kept thinking to myself, "What in the world is JoAnn doing up here from Louisiana, and when did she become a nurse?"

It's weird how the mind works during moments of extreme stress.

After waiting what felt like hours for something to happen, everything seemed to happen at once. My dad walked into the room with a nervous expression on his face that I didn't want to see. And then a skinny little police officer with a mustache that looked like it had been a work in progress for twenty years came stomping in with an accusatory look.

"Do you know what your husband did?" he demanded. "He passed a whole line of cars on his motorcycle on a two-lane road and hit a guy up ahead of him turning left."

All of the moisture left my mouth. My hands began to shake, and I seemed to lose any sort of handle on how to speak.

As if I wasn't shocked enough, he followed that with, "Wait until you see his helmet. You'll wonder how in the hell he survived this."

At that moment, a couple of nurses wheeled Brad in. He was laid out on a gurney, neck stabilized, but looking pretty good for the most part. I mean, you T-bone another car when you're on a motorcycle going sixty miles an hour...I kind of expected him to look worse. Lucky for him, he had been wearing his helmet, with clothing covering every inch of his body. I think the "powers that be" knew that I'd have a hard time trying to nurse someone back to health who looked like something the road had chewed up and spit back out.

Don't judge me...it's not that I'm really into looks. I'm just incredibly squeamish. I'm more of a PG girl, and most motorcycle accidents are on the R-rated side.

"Now, he's got a pretty bad dislocated knee and some broken ribs," the nurse said. "He's going to be taking it easy for a while."

"Brad. *Brad!*" The officer's voice suddenly came out in a staccato, as he tried to peer around the nurse who was untangling an IV. "Do you remember what happened?"

Dazed and immobile, Brad tried to look up at him. "No."

"You hit another car. You passed a whole group of cars going at a high rate of speed and hit a guy and knocked him out. You don't remember that?"

"No?"

Dissatisfied with Brad's inadequate answers, Captain Inappropriate marched out. And my husband's first words to me in the trauma room were, "Shit. We're going to get sued."

I will say that one of my proudest moments as a wife was that I didn't just let him have it while he was lying there, voicing my concern over matters that, in the grand scheme of things, really didn't matter. I could have immediately gone into how our insurance rates will go up, and we'll have to buy someone a new car. How I know I didn't leave enough milk in the refrigerator for the kids, and my parents will have to go to the store now. But like an angel, I stuck to nice, soothing words, telling him the accident was no big deal.

I figured I'd have plenty of time to lay into him later while he was at home and recovering.

However, I did have the presence of mind to say to him, "Remember how you made me watch the Steelers game the entire time I was in labor with Sarah?"

His eyes slanted and he tried to look at me from his immobile position.

"Yeah?"

"I have *Pride and Prejudice* in my bag. Maybe we can watch that tonight."

He rolled his eyes and gave a small, painful sigh of defeat.

About an hour later, the hospital staff decided that Brad was ready to be checked in to a regular room. With his leg injury, they thought he would probably be there for a couple of days while they monitored him and taught him how to walk on crutches. And knowing that we would be there for a while, I told my dad to go home.

"Are you sure?" he said. I could see he was having an internal battle between wanting to be there for me and wanting to get the hell out of that hospital.

"I'm fine," I said. "After he gets settled, I'm going to go grab a sandwich downstairs and read my *People* magazine. We'll be okay. I'll call you and Mom later when I know what's going to happen next."

I gave my dad a hug and gathered up my purse and Brad's belongings, which had been put into one of those white and surprisingly durable plastic bags they have at every hospital. I followed the orderlies and made polite conversation as they wheeled Brad into the elevator and then up to the second floor.

"Brad?" I said, after he'd been settled into his new bed.

"Yeah?"

"I'm starving. I think I'm going to go down and grab something to eat. Do you want me to get you anything?"

"No...I'm so tired I don't think I could eat anything. But... do you think they have Jell-O? I have the weirdest taste in my mouth."

I laughed. "This is a hospital. Their specialty is Jell-O."

I walked down the hall to find the room that hospitals have on every floor that contains the coffee, crackers, juice, and Jell-O for its patients and the people who have the unhappy task of sitting around and waiting for people to heal. I found some cherry Jell-O and a spoon, and made my way back to Brad. I awkwardly tried to spoon a few bites into his mouth, carefully trying not to spill it all over the neck brace he was still wearing, until he sighed a little and said, "That's fine. That's all I need. I just want to go to sleep now."

"Are you going to be okay for a minute?" I asked. "I'm going to run down and get something to eat, and I need to go to the car and grab my overnight bag. It has my book and everything in it.

I'll call your parents while I'm down there because I'm not getting any reception in here."

"Okay."

And that was the last conversation I had with my husband. Believe me, had I known, I would have talked about something more important than a sandwich and inadequate cell service.

I went down the elevator and wound my way through the maze of the hospital until I found the parking lot. The sunlight made my eyes water a bit as I scanned around, trying to find my car because in the mayhem that was that morning, I had no idea where I'd parked it. Round and round the parking lot I walked, hitting my panic button, trying to set off the alarm so that I could find it. I imagined some bored patient looking down at me from their window above, laughing at this crazy woman in mismatched clothing looking for a beat-up minivan.

I hope I at least provided someone with a little entertainment.

Once I'd found the car and gotten my bag, I dialed the number to Brad's parents' house in Pennsylvania.

"Bonnie?"

"Hey! What's going on with you guys?"

"Now...I don't want you to panic. But Brad was in an accident on his way to work."

"*What?*"

At that point, I did my best to calm her down, explaining that while Brad was injured, he wasn't in any real danger. I promised to keep her updated and that I'd have him call her as soon as he felt up to it.

"Well, I just hope this means he's off of riding motorcycles for good," she said before we hung up. "Tell him that we love him and that we'll talk to him soon."

"I will."

I started making my way back up to the room, and by the

time I got there, Brad had fallen into a deep but restless sleep. He wouldn't wake up, even with all of the noise I was making, setting my bag up on the heater next to the window and getting my stuff out. His body kept twitching, something I dismissed, thinking that he had to be so medicated for pain and everything else he had been through. And so I sat there, reading my celebrity gossip and munching on a bag of Doritos, having no idea that that would be the last meal I would eat for the next three days.

"Excuse me?" A male nurse poked his head into the room.

"Yes?"

"I'm Rodney. The doctors sent me down to get Brad. They just want to do a quick ultrasound of his neck and make sure there aren't any clots or anything else they should be worried about."

"Oh. Okay."

Rodney moved the gurney into the room and positioned it next to the bed. And as he started talking…Brad didn't even stir.

"Brad? BRAD? *BRAD?*"

"YEAH!" Brad's response sounded like a three-year-old who was talking way too loud.

"WE'RE GOING TO TAKE YOU IN FOR AN ULTRASOUND. OKAY?"

"K!"

Another male nurse walked into the room to help Rodney move Brad over to the gurney. He stayed asleep as we made our way into the elevator and to what seemed like the basement of the hospital, where he would have his ultrasound.

"This is as far as you can go," Rodney said as we stood outside a set of automatic double doors. "There's a waiting room down the hall to the right. As soon as he's done, someone will come down and get you."

"Okay. Thanks."

I made my way down the blinding white hall to the waiting

room and sat on an overstuffed couch that looked like it was a cast-off from 1984. The only sound in the room was the bubbling aquarium that seemed to take up an entire wall and the quiet typing of a woman working behind a glass window. After what seemed like hours, I began to worry because as the time passed, what sounded like a routine ultrasound began turning into something more sinister in my head. Eventually, the receptionist went home and I was left alone, too scared to do anything but stare at the fish swimming in circles. I kept thinking to myself, "If he's okay, a nurse will come and get me. If he's not, a doctor will."

When I looked up, three doctors were walking toward me, quietly talking to each other.

It was hard to distinguish who was who in their matching white coats. They all seemed to move in unison, like three marshmallows who had somehow managed to graduate from medical school. I watched them walk down the long hall that was too brightly lit with fluorescent lights, and as they made their way closer to me, I knew without a doubt that they were about to tell me news that I didn't want to hear.

They arranged themselves in chairs around where I was sitting on the outdated couch. Perched and looking like they were ready to flee, they all stared at me and didn't say anything for a moment, as if hoping that one of their colleagues would take over.

"Mrs. Tidd?" one of them started, looking serious and like he would rather be anywhere else than in this waiting room with the unnecessary fish.

"Yes?"

"It seems that…" The younger of the three tried to take over.

"Your husband's had a stroke," said the third, the one with graying hair, in a businesslike way. "We don't know why and we don't know how it happened. There is a good chance that the impact to Brad's head and neck has caused this, but we really don't know for sure."

"My husband...Brad's had a...a *what?*"

"A stroke," he said. "He's had a stroke."

"But...no, you don't understand," I said, my mouth feeling like sandpaper. "My husband is thirty-four. Thirty-four-year-old people don't have strokes."

I felt sure that this rationale would cause them to all stand up simultaneously and slap their heads with the palms of their hands and say, "Shoot! You're right! We thought you were married to that eighty-year-old we just brought in. Our bad! Your husband's fine! He's waiting for you in the cafeteria!"

Nope.

"Brad will be paralyzed on his left side," said the youngest, pushing his wire-rimmed glasses up farther onto the bridge of his nose. "There's a good chance that he will be in a wheelchair for the rest of his life."

I couldn't do anything but stare at the Doctors of Doom in stunned silence. Which apparently made them feel uncomfortable, because they started to shift and get to their feet, relieved to have this moment over so that they could go home and eat dinner like normal, unparalyzed people.

"He's being moved to the ICU right now," said the gray-haired doctor. "Just go on up to the fifth floor. You'll be able to see him there in a few minutes."

My stomach started to churn. I grabbed my purse and desperately rummaged around its disorganized contents to try and find my cell phone.

No reception.

"I need to use a phone," I said. "I need to call my parents. Do you have a phone I can use?"

"Of course," said the younger doctor, relieved, as if giving me a usable phone was good enough news to buffer the blow he had just delivered. "Use the one on the receptionist's desk."

I tried calling my parents at their home. No answer. I tried calling my dad's cell phone. Nothing. Finally, in desperation, I called my older sister's cell phone, and on the fourth ring, as I was about to give up, she answered.

"Kristi? Are Mom and Dad there? I need them."

I could hear the joyful noise of her children playing at the park in the background, and she had to yell to be heard over the noise.

"Cath? What's going on? What's wrong?"

"I'm not sure if I heard this right. But I think the doctors just told me that Brad had a stroke. Is that right? Could they have told me that?"

"Oh my God."

"Mom and Dad aren't answering, and I don't know where they are. Can you find someone for me? I need someone else here to listen to what the doctors are saying. I'm scared they'll say something that I won't understand," I said, suddenly feeling more alone than I'd ever felt in my life.

"I'll find Mom and Dad," I heard Kristi say breathlessly as she tried to round up her kids and take them home. "*Brian!* Get over here! Cath? I'll find them. Okay? Someone's coming. Can you hear me? *Someone will be there.*"

I'm betting there's not a person in the world who hasn't felt a weird, inexplicable moment of calm when the news or diagnosis they have feared is actually given to them. It's almost like adrenaline working in reverse. We somehow find temporary inner strength that we didn't know we possessed and later, when we're dealing with the aftermath of whatever fate has handed us, we wish it had stuck around. Because in that moment, I didn't panic. I didn't fall to my knees. I didn't even cry.

My mind immediately rushed through future scenarios,

changing what I'd imagined earlier—rearranging the furniture on the main floor of my house for a man on crutches—to wondering if the ranch-style house around the corner was still for sale for the man in the wheelchair who needed a home without stairs. I reminded myself that Brad was larger than life, and I felt sure that he would bounce back…or at least bounce back enough to maybe work from home somehow. Ever the planner, I started worrying about things that would happen six months from that moment, so that when one of them happened, it would be something that I would expect.

For someone who doesn't like surprises, this was a biggie.

After grabbing my bag from the room that I thought we would be staying in, I moved into my fourth area of the hospital that day and waited for Brad to get settled in his ICU room. When I saw the phone sitting on one of the end tables next to a vacant chair, I knew that I needed to make one more call. And as I slowly dialed the Tidds' Pennsylvania number for the second time that day, I started feeling like I had lied to them. I had told them that he would be okay. This was all my fault.

"Bonnie? It's Catherine."

Suddenly, all of my attempts to "be strong" dissolved into a hiccup-cry into the palm of my hand. I started to fear that if I said the words out loud again, they might actually be true.

"Brad's…he's had a stroke, Bonnie. I don't know how this happened, but he's had a stroke. Oh God. I'm so sorry. I'm so sorry. He's in the ICU now. I'm so sorry."

"Oh no," I heard her breathe on the other end of the line. "Jim! *Jim!*" I heard her say away from the phone to my father-in-law. "Brad's had a stroke."

"We're coming," she said to me into the phone. "Hang in there, sweetie. We're coming. We'd already bought tickets after you called this morning. We thought we'd come up and give him a hard time and just give him a hug. We're leaving first thing tomorrow morning."

After hanging up the phone, I sat there staring blankly at the white walls of the waiting area, ignoring the sounds of CNN from the television mounted on the ceiling. I was vaguely aware of other people sitting around me, some doing their best to make conversation with each other and some looking too despondent to even try. Through the window, the sun started to set on that perfect summer day, and I felt my earlier hope and resolve begin to fade with the light.

"Mrs. Tidd?" said a nurse. "You can come on back now."

I followed her through the doors into the ICU with my eyes focused straight ahead. Because the nurses needed to see anything and everything that was going on, there was no privacy. Each individual space had a glass wall looking into the hall so that you could see the entire room and anyone in it. If I made the mistake of glancing to the side, I would see all of the horrific situations of the other patients surrounding my husband.

As it was, my peripheral vision was picking up enough. Another motorcyclist who hadn't been wearing a helmet and was bandaged from the top of his head down to his toes. The old man with his wife by his side, silently weeping and holding his hand, preparing for a life alone. The beeps. The hissing of ventilators. The hum of machines that were keeping these strangers alive.

I couldn't believe that Brad was now one of them.

When I walked into his room, I stopped for a moment, looking at the man who had always been in perpetual motion, now lying still and quiet and seemingly smaller than he had been when he left for work that morning. Tubes seemed to sprout from every limb, pumping in fluid to keep him going and then draining out what wasn't necessary. There was a small cut on his nose that I had been too distracted to notice before. I swallowed hard, taking in the oxygen tubes coming from his nose and the lump of his right leg under the blanket that had been bandaged to twice its size because of the dislocation.

I desperately wanted to climb into that bed with him, under the blankets that had been washed and sanitized so many times they had softened to the perfect weight. I craved curling up next to him and putting my head in the crook of his shoulder until I felt his arms around me in a silent assurance that everything would be okay.

Instead, too scared that if I started crying I might never stop, I pulled a plastic chair over to his side and quietly took his hand. I ran my fingers over his wedding band and thought about what we had promised each other almost exactly eleven years earlier on our July 20 wedding day.

In sickness and in health. Till death do us part.

About an hour later, my dad finally arrived in the work clothes he had been wearing when he met me earlier that day in the trauma room. He wrapped me in his arms for a second and just said, "It's okay. I'm here. Mom's coming. She's just trying to find someone to watch the kids."

We sat in Brad's ICU room, making the most idiotic conversation as if our normal behavior might make this all go away. The nurses came in and out, changing tubes, checking monitors, and trying to be as upbeat with us as they possibly could. Occasionally, they would ask us to step out while they changed tubes or updated other medical personnel on my husband's condition. We sat in the ICU waiting room, which has to be one of the most miserable places on Earth because you're surrounded by the horrific stories of illnesses, accidents, and life in general gone wrong.

And, worse yet, it's your story, too.

By midnight my mom had finally arrived, having found a family friend to come over and watch the kids so that she could get to the hospital and relieve my dad. She walked into Brad's room, catching her first glimpse of him tethered to every tube imaginable and breathing with the help of whirring machines. The three of us—my mom, my dad, and me—all quietly hugged. And then my dad left, too choked up to say anything else.

"I want to get you out of here for a while," my mom said, giving me a one-armed hug. "Who knows how long Brad will be here. You need to make sure that you get some rest. Otherwise you'll be no use to anyone."

"You should," said a nurse behind her. "You have a long road ahead. You need to get all the rest you can right now so that you'll be ready."

"But we can't just…go, can we?" I asked my mom. "We can't just leave him."

"Catherine, you could be here for weeks. Months even. There is no place for you to sleep here, and you're going to have to rest at some point. We'll be back in a few hours, but you need to get out of here."

We started gathering up my things and moving toward the door. I suddenly heard Brad making noise and I rushed over to his side, hoping that he was about to wake up. I stood there holding his hand and staring at him as if willing him to start talking to me like nothing had happened. And then I realized what the sound really was.

My God. Was he *choking?*

I left my mother in the room and ran to find the nurse. I pulled her in, saying, "*Do something!* He's choking!"

She remained irritatingly calm as she took out her stethoscope and checked his vitals. I could not figure out why she wasn't as alarmed as I was, and the fact that she wasn't running out the door for more medical personnel made me want to hit her over the head with a bedpan. "He's not choking," she finally said. "He's got the hiccups. It's not uncommon."

"Can't you do anything about it? He's got broken ribs. That can't feel good."

As if to confirm what I was saying, Brad jolted upright in bed, the first activity I'd seen from him in hours.

"Feel bad," he said with his eyes still shut, collapsing back onto his pillow.

"Brad? Brad?" I said, taking his hand again and hoping that he would say something else.

"He'll be fine," the nurse said and walked out of the room. I sat next to him for a few more minutes, feeling helpless. My suspicion that he was in pain had finally been confirmed, even though everyone had been assuring me that he wasn't feeling anything. I waited until the painful hiccups subsided and Brad was quiet once again, his breathing slow and measured, his body relaxed.

"Cath?" said my mom from the other side of Brad's bed. "Let's go get some air."

Reluctantly, I let go and let her lead me out of the room. I had no idea that "feel bad" were the last words I would ever hear my husband say. But I left, thinking that everyone was right and that I should prepare myself for the marathon of caregiving we all thought loomed before me.

My mom and I checked into the first roach motel I'd ever been to, complete with one working parking-lot light that made me suddenly feel like we were actors in a bad made-for-TV crime drama. If the situation hadn't been so serious, it would have been comical. As we let ourselves into the room and quickly bolted and chained the door behind us, we took stock of the threadbare blankets and pillows that had the support of good envelopes. I took one look at the shower and decided that it just wasn't worth the risk of infection.

We each lay in our beds, waiting for the other to fall asleep. I knew my mother was watching for movement, and I was doing my best to stay still and stare straight up so that she would go to sleep and get some rest. I tried to make designs with the popcorn on the ceiling that was illuminated by that one dim light in the parking lot, badly wanting to numb my mind from the fear that was circling around, trying to sneak its way in.

But it was stronger than I was.

Silent tears started streaming down the sides of my face, and I heard my mom move from her bed to mine. She wrapped me up like a two-year-old as I hiccuped my way through, "Oh God. What's going to happen to us? What am I going to do? How do we move forward from this? How can I handle a man in a wheelchair and three toddlers?"

"Shhhhh." She rocked me back and forth. "It's okay. You won't be alone. We're here. We're going to figure this out."

"I can't just lie here anymore," I said, wiping my eyes. "I need to be with Brad."

So, my mom and I made our way back to the hospital after spending only hours in that motel room (something I felt sure that the management was used to). At 5:00 a.m., the doctors took Brad in for a CT, and when they were finished, they led us into a windowless room no bigger than a walk-in closet and sat us down.

Dr. Robins, the gray-haired trauma doctor who had been following Brad since his admittance into the ER the day before, cleared his throat several times as if trying to cough up the words he didn't actually want to say.

"Catherine." He looked me straight in the eye. "Brad's brain is swelling. And at the rate it's going, I don't think he's going to live past the next seventy-two hours."

I heard my mother inhale sharply, and she suddenly turned to me, her blue eyes wider than I had ever seen them.

I grabbed her hand and said in disbelief, "Did *I* have the stroke? Is Brad really okay and I'm in a coma, dreaming this whole thing up?"

I watched her mouth working as if she was trying to say something.

But nothing came out.

2

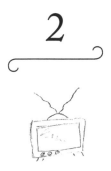

I 've seen TV shows and dramatic movies where once the soon-
to-be widow has been given the tragic news, she falls to her
knees in a theatrical heap, screaming and crying that her life is over.

I didn't do that.

But I knew everyone was watching and waiting to see how
I was going to react. And I felt guilty that I didn't feel like
reacting. After all, if there was ever a time when making a scene
would be forgiven, this would have been it. But my body had
suddenly gone numb.

I walked back into his room and took in the changes that had
been made that morning. The small oxygen tubes that had been
in his nose the night before had been replaced by an ominous-
looking blue hose that was hooked to his mouth and made even
more noise than the machine before. He was bound in blankets,
his bed sitting up at a comfortable angle, but his coloring had
changed. Instead of looking like a man who might be coming
home someday, he had taken on the pallor of someone who
would never open his eyes. Who would never hold his children.
Who would never hold *me*.

It scared me that I didn't feel like crying. To be honest, it made me feel like a cold, heartless bitch, and if *I* felt that way, I couldn't imagine how my attitude was being perceived. And so I walked into Brad's room with many eyes watching me and I somewhat threw myself across his chest.

"Oh, Brad!" I forced a sob. "Oh, sweetie! Don't go!"

And for some reason, I felt like that little display made the other people around me feel a little better.

I'm not saying that I wasn't sad. I was. But I was in complete shock. Anyone who has been given information suddenly like that can't possibly fathom the enormity of it all. Because if the body let all of those emotions in at one time, I feel sure that it would shut down.

"Ah, yes," everyone was probably thinking with relief after my public display of grief. "There she goes. For a second there it looked like she was going to keep everything bottled up. Whew! She's doing this right. That's right, kiddo. Get it out so that you'll be fine in a few weeks."

In reality, this was it. A defining moment for me. This was when my ability to react "properly" grabbed my sense of normalcy by the hand, suddenly did an about-face, and left me for good. From the moment I heard the words "He's not going to make it," my life changed from disgustingly boring to "She's doing *what?*" I went from no one really noticing (or caring about) my responses to feeling like people were counting the number of tears I shed or how many times I probably shouldn't be smiling.

What began to happen then was that time slowed, sped up, and then stopped in an unexplainable pattern. One minute I would think that the clock was broken, and the next it seemed to have jumped ahead two hours. People came in and out. New nurses began their shifts. Kristi arrived, looking scared and pale, and I felt a rush of relief when I saw her.

Although we have always been incredibly close and think a lot alike, I've always thought of my older sister as the more capable of the two of us. A woman with a wicked sense of humor and no time for bullshit, she would get this whole mess straightened out. I was sure of it. But when she saw me standing in the waiting room of the ICU, she took me by the shoulders and looked me straight in the eye.

"Cath," she said, tearing up. "You know how people blow things off by saying, 'Oh…this isn't the worst thing'?"

She took a deep breath.

"This *is* the worst thing."

I stared at her, stunned with disbelief that even Kristi couldn't make this go away. And for some reason, that seemed to confirm without a doubt that this was actually happening.

We all took turns pacing back and forth between Brad's room and a smaller, separate waiting room within the confines of the ICU that we, all at once, seemed to have taken over. I began to feel the need to sit on the floor because I had reached a point where I could no longer sit in chairs, sure that the spinning gravity in the room would knock me down at any moment. In the corner, I would rock with my knees to my chin and my arms trying to hold my legs as close to my body as possible. I needed to feel grounded. I needed for my body to feel stable. I needed to feel the structure of the walls holding me up.

"Mrs. Tidd?" I heard from the doorway of the waiting room. My sister and my parents turned to look at the chubby, gray-haired man wearing suspenders and a cheerful rose color on the apples of his cheeks.

"Yes?" I said from the floor in the corner.

He walked over and sat down in a chair in front of me as if he was used to talking to people who couldn't stand up. One of Brad's nurses followed and shut the door behind her while my family circled around so they could hear what he had to say.

In a daze, I listened to the doctor explain to me that there was an option, a possibility of keeping Brad alive. "We'll remove part of his skull," he explained. "That will give the brain room to swell. There's a good chance that he still won't make it. But I wanted to give you that option."

Needing someone to explain this procedure to me in plain English and knowing that most doctors aren't capable of that, I turned to the nurse and asked her to really tell me what he was talking about. She gave me the statistics—that if they did the surgery there was still only a 5 percent chance that he would make it—and then I asked her, "But what will he be like if he lives through it? Can he make a full recovery?"

She knelt in front of me and forced me to look her straight in the eye.

"Sweetie," she said in a quiet tone. "*If* he survives the surgery, he won't ever know you. He won't ever recognize his children. He won't be able to feed himself. *If* he makes it, you'll have to put him in a nursing home with twenty-four-hour care for the rest of his life."

I looked at her with wide eyes and forced myself to swallow. For the first time, I felt the need to run from this situation as fast as I could. They could carry on without me. There were plenty of people more capable than I was to make this decision. I mean, I wasn't even smart enough to know how to set the clock on my VCR.

Were they *really* going to leave a decision like this to a thirty-one-year-old woman who had almost failed every science class she'd ever taken?

I started thinking about a day just weeks earlier when Brad and I and the kids had visited my grandmother in the nursing home. We walked the halls, looking at people limp in their wheelchairs who were having an "outing" that involved just getting them out of their rooms so that their beds could be changed, and Brad said to me, "I hope something like this never happens to me. Promise me you'll do anything you can to keep from putting me in a nursing home."

"I promise."

As I sat there, rocking on the floor, I glanced up at Kristi, who looked more terrified than I'd ever seen her. My dad looked like he would prefer jumping off the top of the building than watching his youngest daughter make this decision. And my mom watched me with watery eyes, waiting to hear what I thought.

"I don't think I can do that," I said. "I don't think he would like that. Do you? What do you think? I just can't do that to him."

I watched them all exchange silent glances as if telepathically agreeing what should be done. And then my family performed one of the greatest acts of bravery I have encountered before or since.

They backed me up.

"He wouldn't want that."

"Brad would hate to live that way."

"We're with you 100 percent."

I suddenly found myself, the proactive worrier, living in the moment because it was safer than picturing a future that I could no longer imagine. Finances. The house. What health insurance would cover from all of this and what it wouldn't. The kids. College. All of it tried to break its way into my mind.

So, in that moment, I decided to focus on a more immediate problem.

The fact that we were waiting for my in-laws to arrive so that we could give them the news.

3

Brad's family had taken off early that morning to catch a flight from Pittsburgh to Denver and had assured me that they would be at the hospital by noon. Since they left so early, the last thing they knew was the information I had given them on the phone the night before: that Brad had had the stroke. I found out that he wasn't going to make it while they were on the plane, and I really didn't think this was news I should deliver over a cell phone while they were waiting to pick up their rental car.

So we waited. And waited.

After hours of torture, it occurred to me that my in-laws never get anywhere on time. It's hard to even get them all going in the same direction at the grocery store, much less off a plane, into a rental car, and to a final destination in another town. Normally this little idiosyncrasy is just a trait to be chuckled over, but at that point, the waiting was about to drive me completely insane.

I started to worry that even though the doctors had given Brad seventy-two hours, my in-laws might not be able to make what would normally be a two-hour drive from the airport before he died.

I didn't realize it at the time, but I wasn't the only one who was in panic mode over when my in-laws would arrive. Kristi kept running back and forth from Brad's room to the main lobby, trying to intercept her husband, Sean. He'd jumped on a flight home to Denver from Seattle, where he'd been on business, the moment he heard the news. Knowing that he not only thought of Brad as a brother but also a best friend, Kristi realized that Sean would probably be somewhat of a weeping mess and was petrified that he would walk into the hospital at the same time as my in-laws, who didn't know the full extent of what was happening.

But, thankfully, they missed each other's grand entrances. As I sat, holding Brad's hand, I heard the soft voice of the nurse behind me.

"Brad's brother is here."

Looking up and expecting to see Brad's younger brother, Jeremy, I saw Sean in his usual business attire, his face red and tear-stained, so choked up he couldn't say anything as he pulled up a chair and took his place next to his friend.

The room was quiet with just the two of us sitting there. At one point, Sean left and I watched him go into the hall and ask the nurse for the results of Brad's CT, something I knew wouldn't make any sense to him, but it didn't matter. It was something tangible that might explain why all of this was happening. I watched as he nodded and asked the most educated medical questions a business consultant could possibly come up with. But in the end, he never got the answer he was looking for, because no one could ever successfully explain how a perfectly healthy thirty-four-year-old man could suddenly be dying in a hospital bed.

That is something we would never understand, even if the experts had an answer.

Time stretched on, and by three, my in-laws still hadn't arrived. I started worrying that they had gone to the wrong hospital or that, Heaven forbid, something had happened to *them* during all of this madness. I stayed in Brad's room, staring at the clock and clenching my teeth while my parents, my sister, and my pastor, Doug, waited for them outside the doors to the ICU. And that's where, at 3:30 p.m., Bonnie, Jim, Brad's younger brother Jeremy and his wife Bobbie Jo, his sister Brenda, and his two-year-old niece Amanda finally heard that he wasn't going to make it.

It seems cowardly, doesn't it? That I made my family and my pastor perform my dirty work for me? And it was, in a way. Since my in-laws were a very religious family, I was hoping that Doug might have some words that would comfort them as they were told the news, words that completely escaped me. And after losing their oldest son, Jeffrey, when he was only four years old, I couldn't bear to tell them that they were about to lose another one thirty years later. Part of my fear was that I couldn't stand being the person who was about to bring their whole world crashing down around them. But what I was really scared of was that, somehow, they might blame me for the situation we now all found ourselves in.

As many widows do, I had been going over and over what had happened, trying to figure out what I could have done to stop it. This is a complete waste of time, but most of us do it anyway. And as I sat there waiting for them in the hospital, I obsessed about the decisions I had made over the entire course of our marriage, especially in the last thirty-six hours, wondering where my in-laws' blame might land.

When they finally walked into Brad's room, I waited for a moment to see how they were going to react to me and felt immediate relief in the hug that was my answer. And as I pulled away, I saw a reflection of what I knew my own face looked like.

Complete and utter disbelief that this was happening.

Bonnie quietly sat down next to her son and held his hand, while

I took the seat that I had been perched in for hours and grasped the other hand. Like me, she seemed too shocked to cry and just sat there, gently stroking his hand and staring at his face as if willing him to wake up. The rest of our family members drifted in and out of the room, and everything began to blur in the time warp that is the ICU. At one point Brad seemed to be breathing on his own, and I excitedly grabbed a nurse and showed her, only to have her reply, "Sometimes they over-breathe their respirators. It's normal."

Normal?

A little while later, his body began to shake, and once again, I asked Tina, the woman who would become my least favorite ICU nurse, what was going on.

"Oh, he has a fever so he probably has chills. It's his body's way of fighting what's going on," she said as she walked in and adjusted some tubes that didn't need adjusting. "We can give him some Tylenol. That'll make us feel better, but it really won't do anything for him. He's just poopin' out on us."

I'm not kidding. That's what she said.

Pooping out on us? *Pooping out on us?* Lady, my husband is *dying.* He's not taking a nap. He's not even in a restful coma. He's *dying.*

Oh, how I wish I had been better at speaking my mind in that moment. Because at the time I was just so damned stunned at her response that I couldn't think of anything to say. She walked out of the room without ever really looking at me, off to find the unhelpful Tylenol and leaving me feeling more helpless than I've ever felt before or since. That we were all going to be forced to sit there while Brad spiked a fever, knowing that there was nothing we could do to ease whatever discomfort he might be experiencing, was an excruciating feeling.

For the rest of that day, I tried to distract myself by attempting to take care of everyone else, making sure they had enough water, tissues, and food to fortify them for the emotional journey ahead. I, on the other hand, stopped drinking and eating, positive that my dry mouth and growling stomach were the only things that were reminding my brain that this wasn't a dream.

This was really happening.

Eventually, day turned into night. Sean went home to take care of my nephews, while Kristi and my parents stayed and tried to blend into the background so they wouldn't be in the way. As the sun set on that endless day, my mother walked up to me and said, "I think you need to get out of here for a while." I began to protest. "There's nothing that we can do right now, and tomorrow will be another long day," she continued. "One of us will go to a hotel with you, and the other two will go home and be with the kids for a while. Who do you want to stay?"

Although leaving Brad was the last thing I wanted to do, I looked over at my in-laws who were standing around him in a circle. Even though I knew I wouldn't be able to stay away from Brad the entire night, I realized that I had had the night before alone with him and that I wanted my in-laws to have that time, too—time when they wouldn't have to worry about the rest of us so they could say what needed to be said.

I walked over to Bonnie. "My parents think I should leave for a little while. I won't be gone long. Is that okay with you?"

She nodded silently and I turned back to my family.

"Kristi," I said. "I want Kristi to come. You and Dad go home and check on the kids and make sure they're okay."

I'm not sure if Kristi was flattered or terrified that I had chosen her. But being not only my sister but also my best friend, she shouldn't have been surprised that her calming presence was the one I wanted. I hugged my in-laws and my family, and we made our way out of the ICU for what would turn out to be just a few short hours. Kristi and I didn't talk at first as we strapped ourselves into her car and she began to drive to a destination she had already chosen.

"I can't believe this," I broke the silence, "but I need to stop by the store. I don't think I brought any contact solution, and I've got to take my contacts out for a little while."

"That's okay," she said. "I didn't bring anything to spend the night. I need to grab a nightshirt and a toothbrush."

A small smile crept across my face. "We need to go to Walmart."

It was an inside joke between Brad and me that we could never take a road trip—big or small—without needing to go to a Walmart. A month earlier we had been in New Mexico for a friend's graduation from medical school, and I realized that I had forgotten to get him a card to go with his gift.

"Can you even spend one day away from a Walmart?" Brad had asked jokingly as we stepped into the bright fluorescent lights.

"I can't help it," I said. "They have everything. Stop giving me a hard time. I just need a card."

The irony of it was that by the time we left, Brad had also picked up two shirts, a pair of sweatpants, and a package of socks. As we shopped, we laughed about how it didn't matter where you were, the shoppers in any given Walmart across the country were all the same. And we made the comment that it probably didn't matter where we traveled or for how long, we would always have to spend at least forty-five minutes in a Walmart.

So, there I was in a Walmart, getting stuff that I had forgotten because I'm always forgetting something. Only instead of Brad shopping next to me, I had Kristi, who had probably never even been in that store before in her life.

"What about something to make you sleep?" she asked as we wheeled our way through the pharmacy looking for the contact solution.

"Sleep?" I asked as if she had just said a foreign word.

"You need to get a little rest," she said.

"But what if something happens and I'm all doped up?"

"It won't," she assured me. "You still have all day tomorrow to get through. Just get something. Benadryl. Tylenol PM. Anything."

I picked up a package of Unisom, telling myself that I would just take half of one, hoping that would be enough to make my body relax a little and sleep for maybe an hour. We made our way to the checkout, and I looked around at all of the people buying groceries or plants for their gardens. I could not believe that I was standing in line, buying contact solution like a normal person, while my husband lay dying in a hospital only miles away. I had this inexplicable urge to tap the woman in front of me on the shoulder and say, "Did you know my husband is dying? Yup. Never coming home again. But I needed contact solution and a sleep aid, so here we are!"

But I kept quiet as I loaded my purchases onto the counter.

"Have a nice day!" said the clerk cheerfully as we picked up our bags.

And we both just stared at her.

For the second night in a row, I found myself staring at the ceiling of a hotel.

It was a nicer ceiling—Courtyard by Marriott beats a roach motel any day. But I lay there staring straight up, still and quiet, listening to the sounds of Kristi unsuccessfully trying to sleep in the next bed, her soft sniffles giving her away. By that point, I had taken two whole Unisom, which should have been enough to knock me out for at least a few hours.

I thought I had at least another day—probably another night—with Brad in the ICU, and everyone was right: if I went another night with no sleep, I would probably collapse. But despite my best efforts, sleep never came. My body stayed rigid and pulsing as if I were being emotionally electrocuted right there in the bed. I remained there in agony, wanting desperately to get back to the hospital but also wanting my sister to get some rest.

And then my cell phone rang.

"Catherine?" I heard my mother-in-law's voice. "You need to get back here. He's getting close."

I jumped up from the bed and switched on the light. I *knew* I shouldn't have left. Kristi was already pulling on her clothes while I searched for mine in the pile where I'd left them on the floor. Neither one of us said a word as we ran down the hall and out of the hotel, jumping into her car and speeding toward the hospital while calling my parents along the way.

It was 3:00 a.m. And in a few hours my life would change forever.

We walked into Brad's room, where Bonnie was still sitting in the chair I'd left her in. Brenda had moved two-year-old Amanda to the quiet waiting room we had taken over at the end of the hall to hopefully let her get a little sleep. Jim stood in the corner, shifting his feet, a helpless look on his face that seemed to mirror what we were all feeling. Brad looked the same to me, the relentless machines beeping and the ventilator making his chest move up and down in a maddeningly rhythmic way. I sat back down in my chair and leaned toward Brad's ear.

"It's okay to go," I whispered, not believing what was coming out of my mouth. "I'm here now. It's okay to go if you need to. I love you."

"Mrs. Tidd?" said a doctor behind me. "Can we speak to you for a minute?"

I slowly stood up and followed him out of the room. We stood in the hall with several other doctors and I waited for them to begin.

"I know that this is a particularly difficult time for you and your family, and there is really no good time to ask this," he said, "but have you given any thought to organ donation?"

"Organ donation?"

"Yes…well…given your husband's accident, and that he is young and in excellent shape, as far as we can see, he is an ideal candidate. The only thing that isn't functioning properly is his brain. But the rest of his body will probably be able to help a lot of people."

I know that some people struggle with the concept of organ donation, thinking it's gross or insensitive or some combination of the two. But I didn't. As soon as I found out that Brad might be able to help others, I knew immediately that's what he would want to do. He was a registered organ donor, but not only that—my husband was the most generous person I knew: volunteering with the Boy Scouts before we even had kids, changing tires on the side of the road for strangers, and dropping everything to help a friend if they needed it. Of course Brad would want to do this.

And practically speaking, what in the heck was he going to do with all of that stuff anyway?

"What do I need to do?"

"We have a representative here from the Donor Alliance who needs to ask you some questions. Then you'll just need to sign some forms and that will be it."

I asked my mother-in-law to come with me to meet Rita, the Donor Alliance counselor, just in case I was asked some questions about Brad's childhood that I wouldn't know. Rita led us to a private room to fill out the forms, and she asked us questions about his way of life, allergies, previous surgeries, and sexual habits. And suddenly it occurred to me.

God, we were boring.

I mean, Brad had never done anything with a prostitute. We thought about having a joint crack habit but could never seem to find the time. We hadn't even traveled overseas and contracted a good case of mad cow disease.

When I looked at our past written out on that questionnaire, I realized that we had to be one of the dullest couples on the planet.

I didn't know much about the organ donation process, never once thinking that it would actually be something I *would* need to know about. And something that I don't think most people realize is that what makes organ donation possible is the one thing that is hardest on the surviving family members: the doctors have to keep that person alive and everything functioning in order to remove the organs.

Once the family has agreed to the donation, the transplant team has to wait until the person is declared brain dead by a battery of doctors before they can proceed. Once that declaration has been made, they are just waiting around for you to go so that they can get to work. And it's up to you to decide when to leave.

In other words, there is no final moment when you hear some machine flatline and you feel better about taking off and grabbing a latte on your way home.

So, you're in kind of a medical stalemate. You don't want to leave your spouse because all those beeps are telling you that he's still functioning. But the doctors can't do what they need to do until you take off. And, frankly, there's probably someone in that hospital who's waiting for a heart and thinking, "If that thing doesn't come within the hour, I'm sure as hell not tipping 20 percent."

When it comes to dilemmas, this question of when to leave ranks right up there with which child do you love more. It's damn near impossible.

"You know, many of our family members find it helpful to take a little memento of their loved ones, such as a lock of hair," Rita said gently as we waited for the doctors to agree that Brad was officially gone.

And at that point I looked into her innocent, helpful, well-meaning face. And I laughed.

This sound was probably a little startling in the halls of the ICU. Laughter is not something you hear a lot over the beeping and ventilators because, for some reason, people don't find death, near death, or comas very funny. But it was suddenly apparent to me that this woman was prepared to take all of my husband's organs and she had never even laid eyes on him. And the reason I know this is because Brad was bald. Completely. Mr. Clean. Not one hair on his head.

So, with a hysterical note in my voice, I replied to her. "From *where?* His chest?"

Exhausted, mentally depleted, and completely confused about how I had suddenly found myself in this situation, hysteria seemed like a logical progression. I had finally reached the point where I was too tired and too busy leaping from cozy suburban mom to insane young widow to really care what anyone around me thought. Now that I think about it, it was probably the healthiest emotion I'd had during the entire three days at the hospital because it was the most genuine. And it was my first hint that I wasn't in danger of losing my most precious coping mechanism—my sense of humor.

After all of the questions had been answered and the paperwork had been signed, Bonnie and I found ourselves back with Brad, on either side of him, each holding a hand.

"I can't leave. We can't just *leave* him, can we?" I asked tearfully.

"I don't want to go either," she said. "He just looks like he's sleeping. We can't go."

"I'll stay with him," I heard behind me.

I turned around and there was Cindy, my mom's best friend from college, who had just gotten off the plane from Houston to be with us. A nurse who had answered dozens of calls from my mother throughout my childhood about what various rashes might be and what does it mean if I can't bend this or that. Cindy had been outside the room, talking to the ICU nurses and getting updates on what was going on.

"I'll stay with him when you feel like you can go so that he won't be alone. I'll stay through the whole procedure. I won't leave him alone. Just let me know when you're ready."

And she left the room.

Bonnie and I sat there for another twenty minutes. The only sounds in the room were the beep and hiss of the machines. Brad didn't twitch and the only thing that made him move at all was the technology around him keeping him alive.

And then suddenly everything felt different.

I don't know how to explain it, but I knew he was gone. The coloring in his face changed, so maybe that was it, but other than that he looked the same. I just knew he wasn't there. In an instant, an intense loneliness invaded my body and I knew that he wasn't with me anymore.

"I'm ready," I said to Bonnie. "I'm ready to go. That's not Brad anymore."

"I don't think so either," she said.

And with each of us kissing him on the forehead, we let go.

I left the hospital almost exactly as I had entered it three days before, clutching the bag full of the clothes I thought he would be coming home in. That bag would stay packed in my closet for years, as if waiting for the call to come saying I could pick him up. I was wearing the same thing I had left the house in seventy-two hours before, clothes that had been sweated in and then, once damp, had given me chills. The sun was shining, the summer air smelled sweet, and life was buzzing all around me. There was only one major difference.

I was a widow.

Memorializing

if I get the casket without the four-wheel drive, how much will that run me?

4

A fter three days in the ICU that ended in someone handing me my husband's wedding ring as I stumbled out the door, the only thing I wanted to do was get home, find the smallest corner in my house, and sink into it. But, as we all know, the time in our lives when we want to be alone the most is also the time that it's least likely to happen.

As my mother drove me home from the hospital that afternoon, neither one of us spoke. I could feel her glancing nervously at me every once in a while, which was something that I would eventually get used to. I looked out the car window in wonder at people going to work, going to the zoo, and just going about their lives. Kids played at the park; people talked on cell phones; and restaurant parking lots were full for the midday lunch rush. It amazed me that the planet was still turning on its axis and that no one else had felt the earthquake that shook my world the moment Brad died.

I fluctuated between not being able to function and wondering about silly details, like whether anyone had remembered to take my daughter to ballet the day before. When I asked my mom what had been going on with the kids for the last few days, I could tell that she didn't want me to worry about such minute details. But little did she know that those little worries were keeping me from thinking about the big picture. It was a lot easier to wonder in that moment if the kids had been to the park that day rather than think about an enormous life in front of me that I would have to lead as their only parent.

But I should have known that I didn't have any reason to worry about the small stuff because the women in my family have always been great communicators. As soon as my family found out that Brad wasn't going to make it, they made one phone call and immediately my kids had someone watching them who loved them like her own family.

"Candice? Brad's not going to make it. We need you to come."

I've known Candice since I was around eight years old, but I've known *of* her since I was born. Our mothers were both Chi Omegas at McNeese (a little college in Louisiana that, rumor has it, was originally built because the town wanted a new rodeo arena and building a college was the best way they could figure out how to fund it). Carrying on that legacy of friendship, Kristi and Candice had been Chi Omegas at Colorado State University together. Being four years younger, I had always looked up to Candice as another older sister (and, when we were young, was the pesky younger sister she never had). As we all entered adulthood, the differences in our ages ceased to matter and the three of us had a friendship that we knew could be counted on for anything.

"I'm coming."

With just a few phone calls, news of Brad's accident had spread like wildfire, and I was already getting reports of people who were starting out from various parts of the country to be there in time for the funeral. Our local friends in Denver had been coming by the house during the three days I was gone, bringing food and helping with the kids during the day while Candice spent the night. Her husband, Rob, was holding down the fort at their house at night, caring for their girls, who were five and three, and bringing them over during the day to distract mine.

As I walked in the door for the first time in three days, I saw more people in my house than I knew it could hold. It seemed like every friend I had was milling around, trying to figure out a way to simultaneously be helpful and stay out of the way. Nobody really said anything to me, but I could feel them watching as I slowly walked over to the French doors that opened out onto the back porch.

And I watched through the glass in amazement at how my backyard had transformed itself into what looked like Sesame Street on crack.

Three children were up in the middle of our big pine tree (the best tree-climbing tree around with strong branches that start about a foot off the ground and stretch over twenty feet high), and Sarah was wailing as she stood holding on to the lowest branch, bitter that she couldn't keep up with them. Michael, who had the chubbiest cheeks God ever put on a kid, was playing tag with another little boy, who I immediately recognized as one of Steve's, Brad's roommate from the Academy who was stationed in Texas and had driven through the night with his wife and three kids to be there. And Haley was sitting calmly on the porch surrounded by Barbies and two of her closest friends.

Having a tragedy like this happen to children so young is both a blessing and a curse. At five, three, and one year old, they were easily distracted and, surrounded by all of their friends, blissfully unaware of what was going on.

But on the other hand…they had no idea what was going on.

My friend Sheila spied me watching through the glass and slowly made her way from the back porch into the breakfast room where I was watching all of the madness in the backyard. Friends since Haley and her daughter, Hannah, were still in diapers, we had met when we both joined a local moms' group and then had our sons within three weeks of each other.

Sheila opened the door and looked me square in the face. She reached for me, and the shaking in her hands matched the tremor in her voice.

"I don't know what to say to you," she said.

And then she left.

I was in too much of a fog to really digest anything that was going on or any words that were said. But I would later come to realize that that was one of the most honest responses to Brad's death I would ever receive.

It almost seemed like Moses parting the sea as I stepped out onto the back porch. People moved aside to let me reach for my children who, I'm sure, thought I was hugging them so hard because I hadn't seen them in three days, one of the longest stretches we'd ever been separated. Sarah wrapped her little arms around my neck, happily sucking on her pacifier as Haley cried, "Mommy! You're home!"

"Guess what?" Michael said with excitement. "Nathan, Alex, and Annika are here for a visit!"

And it hurt my very core to think about telling them why everyone was here.

So here it was. The moment of truth. But how to say it? How to tell a kindergartner, a toddler, and a baby that Daddy's gone to that big jungle gym in the sky? How to be sensitive, but honest enough so that they really understand that Daddy isn't just working on a project in Virginia for a while?

How to do it without landing them in therapy for the next eighteen years?

I wanted to be very careful with my wording, and I didn't

want to completely fall apart. This was our first big loss, but I knew enough about parenting to know that kids take their cues from us. Even when my children were babies, if I was stressed, they would be cranky. If I was in a bad mood, they would be, too. If I was singing and happy, they would giggle and play along. And if I could take a deep breath and handle things calmly...they would hopefully feed off that energy and do the same.

From the moment I thought about telling the kids what had happened, I knew that I would have to be very cautious about my grief in front of them. I knew that it would be okay to cry and be honest about what I was feeling. But to have a full-blown panic attack would only do one thing.

Make them panic.

So sitting there in front of them, my whole body wanting to run screaming down the street, I had to rein in my own emotions and just hope that I got this right. After all, I didn't want the end result of telling them that Daddy had died from a brain injury to be that every time one of them got a bump on the head they'd scream, "I'm gonna die! I'm gonna die! I just know my brain is swelling!"

I'm always thinking long-term about how to avoid the next potential disaster, but as a mom, even more so. Because in the end, that's just more work for me.

I sat them down in the TV room with my parents and in-laws, hoping that as my children heard the worst news of their short lives, they would look around and see the faces of the people closest to them and be comforted. Somehow, without saying a word, the crowd of friends that had gathered in our home seemed to dissipate and find other places to be. Extra children were brought outside and the house became unnaturally quiet as I sat down on the couch, Sarah squirming in my lap, Michael on one side, and Haley on the other.

I took a deep breath.

"Daddy got hurt," I said, surprised at the calm voice that came out of my mouth. "I know that Nana told you that Daddy was in an accident the other day. And we thought he was going to be okay."

Hard swallow.

"But Daddy's head got bumped really hard. It's not like when you bump it at the playground or when you're running around. It got bumped much, much harder than that. His head got hurt so bad that he died."

Sarah continued to wriggle in my lap, completely oblivious to the news I was delivering. Haley and Michael looked up at me with wide, puzzled eyes like they knew what I was telling them was important but they couldn't figure out why.

"Look around the room," I continued, pointing to the family surrounding us. "There are all of these laps that would love to have you in them. You can ask anyone a question or just get a hug or whatever you need. Everyone here loves you and will help you however they can.

"And Daddy loves you very much. But now he's in Heaven. And he's not coming home."

Now, I'll be honest with you. My own views about religion are somewhat conflicted. Actually, I don't know if that's the right word. Let's just say that I'm the kind of person who likes to study something before I fully believe it. We attended church as a family, and I liked the church we went to because it seemed to fill my need to be educated, with a few peppy hymns to break up the hour. But now that I was faced with how to explain that Daddy was gone and knowing the next question would be "but where?" Heaven was the easiest explanation I could come up with on short notice.

And then I just had to cross my fingers that some Sunday school teacher would be able to fill in the blanks on how the whole system works.

I could hear sniffles around the room from the adults, and even though I was exhausted, I was a little proud of myself, sure that this little mommy moment would land me in the Parental Hall of Fame. My kids nodded, indicating that they understood what I was telling them, and then they began peppering me with the most insightful questions.

"Can we go back outside and play?"

"Can Alex stay the rest of the afternoon?"

"If we go to McDonald's later, can we play in the play place?"

So much for a heartwarming discussion and my Lifetime Original Movie moment.

My kids jumped up from the couch and ran out the back door, determined not to let this pesky death business get in the way of their dream playdate with every kid they had ever known from around the country. Worry about whether they were experiencing the toddler version of denial was trying to ooze its way into my head, but the anxiety I felt about everything else that was going on wouldn't make room for it.

One of the first lessons that I learned during the beginning stages of widowhood was to take every moment (and problem) as it comes, for the simple reason that all of the moments and problems are so enormous that if you let them all in, you will suddenly find yourself with smoke coming out of your ears as you try to think about everything at once.

The fact that my children didn't seem to be digesting that their dad was gone suddenly wasn't my biggest problem. *That* would become my biggest problem years down the line when, say, my daughter wanted him to walk her down the aisle or my son wanted his dad to lead his Boy Scout troop.

By then, the problems of *now* would have dissipated a little and I would be able to focus on the problem at hand.

But that day, I decided to just be grateful for the fact that the kids had twenty little distractions running around my house. And that they were happy. Because in our new situation, I didn't know how long "happy" would last.

"I need to be alone for a minute," I said to the family that was still standing there, seemingly in shock that nothing more monumental had come from the discussion I'd just had with the kids. I excused myself as everyone watched me walk up the stairs with expressions on their faces that I thought were strange then, but which would become very familiar to me in the near future.

They didn't know what to say or what to do with me.

I headed up to my room with a very detailed plan that involved lying on my bed and letting all of the feeling drain out of my body. But I couldn't. The restlessness that would plague me for the next six months seemed to begin in that moment. I lay there on my bedspread with my eyes wide open and every cell in my body so active that they all seemed to be competing to see which one could make me move first.

I finally couldn't stand it anymore and rolled over, reached for the phone, and dialed the number of a friend I'd known since kindergarten. In all of the hubbub that had been going on for the last three days, I had no idea if Christa even knew Brad was gone, if anyone had called her. For some reason, I felt the need to say it out loud, to shock someone else the same way I had been shocked. If something like this had happened to someone else, I would have immediately called her and said, "Did you hear...?" only to listen to her reply, "You're kidding! When did that happen?" And we would have gossiped about it for a healthy length of time.

But this time, the "did you hear" was about me.

And at the moment Christa answered the phone, I'm afraid that I began to wail.

"He's gone! Christa, Brad's *gone*! I don't understand it. He's gone!"

Lying on my stomach, tears streaming down my face and drenching the phone, breathing so fast it seemed like I could pass out at any moment, I said it over and over and over again, trying to make it seem real and hoping that she would convince me that it wasn't. But what I got was the only thing anyone could say at that point.

"I know, sweetie. I know."

5

I would like to say I woke up the next day ready and able to plan Brad's funeral. But there are two things wrong with that sentence: First of all, you can't wake up if you never went to sleep. And second, no one is *ever* ready to plan a funeral. I don't care if the death was sudden, after an illness, when you were twenty, or when you were ninety. Even when you know it's coming, when someone dies, the moment they take their last breath always feels unexpected. And no one can ever really picture what it's like to be carrying out someone's "final wishes."

I find it grossly unfair that one of the first things we have to do as widow rookies is put together a large event that, even when done well, still leaves all of the attendees feeling uncomfortable and like they'd rather be anywhere else. Funerals seem to have almost nothing to do with the widow and, in fact, very little to do with the person who died. A lot like with our weddings, we tend to put together an event to pacify at least one person in the group who not only fancies themselves an amateur event planner, but the resident expert on our lives, as well.

I realized this when, a few years after my husband died, I

went to a funeral, and while speaking to the bleary-eyed spouse and telling him how beautiful everything was, he finally looked at me and said, "My in-laws planned the whole thing. I'm giving a party next month and we're all going to get smashed."

Good plan.

In another, more obvious way, funerals are eerily like planning a wedding because not only do you spend an obscene amount of money to commemorate one day (and create an event that has "compromise" written all over it), but you'll also find that the more funerals you go to after the one you planned, the more you wish you had done things differently.

For example, since Brad and I were the first of our friends to get married, I was the first to make my bridesmaids wear dresses that they would never wear again (despite my assurances to the contrary) in burgundy and the finest fashion the '90s had to offer. I was the first to pick out flowers that, when they arrived, looked nothing like the picture. And the first to plan a reception at a large banquet hall that for some reason had a large papier-mâché-looking tree in the middle of the room.

As we got older and attended more and more weddings, I started feeling a little frustrated with myself that I hadn't picked a bigger ball gown, butterflies instead of bubbles, and a better bar. My sister and I used to joke that we'd do better the second time around, when we were marrying for money. I remember, after Brad and I had been married for about six years, purchasing an amazing wedding guide for my friend Christa as an engagement present. As I showed it to Kristi, I said, "Now why didn't *I* have that to help me plan my wedding? Look! It even has its own calculator!"

To which she replied, "There's always next time!"

Unfortunately, now I know that could be true.

It's the same thing with funerals. After doing the planning

yourself and then going to a few after that, you start thinking, "Now why didn't *I* get the flashier urn and the comforting shaman to preside over the service instead of that big, clunky casket and the geriatric minister?"

And you feel a little guilty, wishing for a do-over.

All widows go about funeral planning differently. Some want all of the control; some don't want any; and some don't even want the funeral. I guess, for the most part, I fell into the middle category. I had some idea of what I thought my husband would like, but as far as the logistics went, I was open to suggestions. I didn't know where to start, and if it had been left up to me, the funeral home would still be charging me a monthly storage fee.

The day after Brad died, I woke up in my room, after finally getting a peaceful hour of sleep, to my mother gently shaking me awake. I don't remember personally feeding my children, bathing them, or putting them to bed the night before, which was a good indication that she had stayed the night (and why I didn't win the 2007 award for Mother of the Year).

"Sweetie? You need to get up. We have an appointment in an hour."

My mother had been hard at work looking for the best funeral home in the area, and she had settled upon the one that Doug, the pastor, recommended. I'll tell you, the funeral business is cutthroat (no pun intended), and it's certainly not an industry where you want bad word-of-mouth. Can you just imagine what must have happened in the past to make someone say, "Call this funeral home, but *do not* under any circumstances call *that* one?"

I mean, how horrible would it be to have a botched *funeral?*

My in-laws followed my parents and me to the funeral home, and when we arrived, I was surprised that it was not only across the street from the preschool I had taken my kids to for years (I had never noticed it), but it was also located at the end of what looked like a strip mall. I had always pictured funeral homes in large, old stately houses, not plopped right next to a chiropractor's office and two doors away from a liquor store (although in the throes of grief, both of those services *could* come in handy).

My parents and I got out of the car and walked through the glass door of the funeral home into its front office, followed by Bonnie, Jim, Brenda, and Jeremy. We were greeted by the owners, Steve and Nanci, who gently shook our hands and spoke to us in hushed tones, which is something that I think must be in the rule book for all funeral directors.

Rule 1. Fill up hearse with gas.

Rule 2. Keep bottle of Lysol in car at all times (just in case).

Rule 3. Talk quietly in case family is still in denial and does not realize yet that the person you have in your care will not be waking up any time soon.

Rule 3½. Keep Tic Tacs in pocket to provide a better quiet talking experience for both parties.

They led us all into the area beyond the office, which was dim and comfortable. The only thing that made it seem slightly awkward was all of the funeral stuff lying around. I took a seat in a leather armchair while my in-laws sat on the couch next to me. My parents paced around a little, as if wanting to be mobile for anyone who might need their assistance. In the soft light of the room, my vision seemed to blur and I looked in disbelief at all of the photo albums and catalogs of products that I would have to choose from.

From what I understood in the hum of quiet conversation going on around me, we needed to come up with a general game plan, starting with the visitation that would take place the next day. My in-laws had already picked up a few catalogs, and not wanting to seem like I wasn't going to participate, I picked one up as well, looking at headstones while again wondering how in the hell I could possibly be here.

"So," Steve began with a sympathetic lean to his head, "have you given any thought to how you would like the service to go? Flowers? Casket? Viewing?"

Wait. Service? You lost me already.

I think my husband and I were, unfortunately, like a lot of people. We really hadn't talked about what we wanted, should one of us decide to make an early exit. Comfortably delusional, thinking that nothing could happen to us at a young age, we assumed that we had plenty of time to get into the "casket vs. cremation" debate and were still sizing each other up to make sure that we wanted to be entombed together.

After all, it says "till death do you part." After that, who knows? What if, once the other person is gone, you meet someone else with a flashier plot?

Even if you *have* had that discussion, that doesn't guarantee that those wishes will be carried out. I know some widows who had to sneak a tablespoon of their husband's ashes out of the urn so they could sprinkle them where he specified, all because his mother felt sure he'd rather be collecting dust while sitting on her mantel next to her collection of porcelain dogs.

Bottom line: Final wishes are never as final as we think they are.

So not only were Brad and I the first people in our circle of friends to get married and the first to have kids, we were first to have to bury the other one. What can I say? We were ahead of our time. And since we had never really talked about our final wishes and I hadn't gone to a lot of funerals myself, I found myself winging it at the most inopportune moment.

As I bumbled my way through the funeral planning, I kept wondering if he was looking down at me thinking, "You knew me for thirteen years, and *this* was the best you could come up with?"

Up until that point, I had only been to a handful of funerals and almost all of them had been in Louisiana, where my family is from. And let's face it, those people do funerals right. I mean, you can't beat the food. Usually there's a band. And most of the time the mourners sit around drinking and telling embarrassing stories about the deceased. Because he can't really do anything about it now and there's nothing we Southerners like better than laughing at the expense of someone else…living or dead.

As had been the case at the hospital, I concentrated on making this whole experience more comfortable for everyone else. After all, it was going to be hell for me and that I couldn't avoid. So I figured I might as well be as accommodating as possible to the rest of the family. Not only that, but I'm not a person who thrives on conflict, even though I secretly admire people who do. And at that point, I was even more scared than usual. Scared of the funeral being an epic failure. Scared of entering territory that was so uncharted for me. Scared of saying something that would make people angry with me because I was afraid of being abandoned at a time when I desperately needed support (however it might come) the most.

So as Steve gently prodded me for answers, I looked to my parents and my in-laws like a lost, helpless kitten.

"I don't know. Mom? What do you think about the flowers? Bonnie, here's the urn catalog so that you can look at what you'd like for your half of the ashes. Dad? Do you have any thoughts about the casket? Sure, I can find his suit somewhere in his closet."

Just as I had been with the kids, I was fairly impressed with how the whole thing was going. Everyone seemed to feel like they had a piece of the action and as if their opinions mattered, and this made all of the parties involved as happy as they possibly could be, given the situation. And working on being the Perfect Widow gave me something else to think about—I could concentrate on my actions instead of why I was really there. I felt sure that if I could keep that up, someday I would be inducted into the Surviving Spouse Hall of Fame with a special award in Grace under Pressure.

I just didn't realize that by trying to be that perfect, I was putting a lot of pressure on myself—pressure that would eventually need to be released.

While we were doing that planning, I had no idea that viewings were optional. I've been to quite a few funerals since Brad died, and most of them have had me thinking, "*Why* did we have a viewing?" I don't like viewings. Never have. I know you're thinking, "Who *does*?" But I'm telling you that every viewing I've been to has left me with a churning stomach and a light head. I don't like to be around things that are supposed to be breathing but aren't. Hell, I didn't even take biology in high school because I couldn't stand to look at a dead frog.

Why would I want to stand around and look at my dead husband?

But as we were putting Brad's funeral together, I didn't have a clear picture of all that was available or optional. I didn't know I had so many choices. And since I didn't have a clear picture of exactly *what* he wanted, thanks to his procrastinating nature and his impatience with paperwork, I was pretty much willing to go with the flow of whatever my parents and in-laws suggested.

I was fortunate that neither my parents nor Brad's had the energy or the attitude to fight about what should and shouldn't be done, even though the two couples had completely different styles. It almost seemed like, in some ways, we were planning two different funerals. Oh sure, I could have voiced my opinion about what I knew Brad would want, what he would find funny, and what was the most "him." But since funeral planning is a group affair, with people expressing their opinions about what is right, what is "proper," and what the other people attending might expect, very little of it had to do with me.

In reality...very little of it had to do with *him*.

Many relationships start changing as we enter the Widowhood, and memorial planning is often the catalyst that begins that evolution. This is because a handful of friends and family members usually start flexing their "I knew him best" muscles, and the widow has to decide whether it's worth the fight to put him in the basketball shorts he loved for the viewing, or give in and let her mother-in-law put him in the uncomfortable suit he hasn't worn in ten years.

Whether the widow is up for an epic battle of "hereafter wardrobe" all depends on her mental state at the time. Some of us are angry and itching for a fight, ready to smack someone over the head with a hymnal because they suggested we sing "Amazing Grace" instead of "How Great Thou Art." Some of us are pleasers and are just trying to get through this whole thing with a minimum of hurt feelings and possible arrests. And then there's the group that is so medicated at this point that they're one step away from drooling on the casket order form and trying to decide which carnival games would be the most fun at the visitation.

I tried my best to go a little "on the cheap" because I knew that's what Brad would have wanted. This was the man who saved every cardboard box we'd ever owned because he couldn't stand to pay for a new one on the off chance we might need to ship something. Who saved Kool-Aid containers to store and recycle every nut, bolt, and nail that came across his path. Who couldn't stand the thought of actually paying twenty-five dollars for an oil change when it would take him a mere four hours on a Saturday to do it himself.

If it would have been at all appropriate, I would have had everyone attending wear sweats, and we would have all sat around in beanbag chairs sipping beer and eating hot wings, while playing the dozens of PlayStations I had brought in for the occasion. But since this didn't seem possible, I decided to try to take control where I could. And not buying things we didn't need was something I knew Brad would have appreciated.

As I looked at catalog after catalog of flowers, urns, and caskets, I could hear him in my head saying, "What are you thinking of, looking at that flower arrangement for five hundred fifty dollars? Don't you know you're just going to throw it away? Don't you know you still have to feed all of these people? Don't you know you're going to have a hefty wine bill for the next couple of years?"

"Catherine?" my mother asked, breaking me out of the silent conversation I was having with Brad. "What would you think if instead of having a big flower arrangement from the family, we just had him holding four roses, one for you and each of the kids?"

"Sounds good to me."

"Jim?" I heard Bonnie ask my father-in-law, as she sat on the couch and flipped through the catalog of large standing arrangements. "Why don't we get this big flower arrangement from the family?"

At this point, Steve pulled my dad aside and spoke to him in his hushed way. My dad nodded in agreement. I would later find out that as our tastes and apparently our floral budgets were different, Steve was suggesting two separate bills—one for us and one for my in-laws. I have a feeling that that little moment saved us what could have been a grand meltdown, and it made me wonder what Steve had witnessed in his years of funeral planning to suggest it.

I'm betting it wasn't pretty.

I had decided to go with cremation and to split Brad's ashes between his parents and me. No one asked me to do it...it just seemed like the right thing to do. Brad loved Colorado, but he considered Pennsylvania home. I also figured that if his family had their *own* ashes, I wouldn't have to worry about getting their approval for what I wanted to do with my half.

Ah, yes. My sneaky widow ways.

Because I was planning on burying my half, I needed an urn, and assuming that his parents were planning on doing the same, they needed one of their own. So I sat there at the ripe old age of thirty-one looking at hideous Japanese urns that would probably cause Brad to haunt me for the rest of my days if I bought one. I put so much pressure on myself to find just the "right thing" that was so "him"...not really thinking about the fact that we were going to bury it and no one would ever really see it. Truly...I could have stuck him in a pickle jar and probably no one would have known.

"Do you have any urns with the Steelers logo on them?" my brother-in-law suddenly asked Steve, as my parents and I looked for the plainest urn we could find for my half of the ashes. "Or something in the shape of a football?"

"Can't you just drink a bottle of Bud Light and put him in that?" I blurted out before I could really think it through.

This comment was met with silence and a wide-eyed stare from everyone in the room.

"This one is pretty," my mother-in-law said, turning back to the catalog in her lap. "This one with the road etched in it. Brad loved to drive on those windy roads back home."

I bit my tongue before I started recounting all of the havoc that he and his buddies had created way back when on those country roads. How he wore holes in the tires of his Trans Am by coming to a dead stop while going eighty miles an hour so he wouldn't miss a turn. How he would dodge the deer in the road like he was playing a life-sized video game.

How we once went "parking" in a field off an old dirt road because he had convinced me that it had the most fireflies.

All of those images flashed through my mind as I nodded to her.

"It's perfect," I said.

It was as we were looking at options for caskets that that surreal "I can't believe I'm here" feeling washed over me once again. Caskets were what old people wore. They were for people who had lived their lives. They weren't for people who were just getting started. They weren't for thirty-four-year-old men who were just on their way to work. They weren't for young fathers or older brothers. They weren't supposed to be for anyone *I* knew.

What in the heck were we doing there?

Brad wouldn't want a casket! Caskets are clunky and made you look fat. And since I'd decided to have him cremated, I really didn't think that he cared at that point how plush the interior lining was or how the shinier chrome would make him look a little more well-to-do for the viewing. If anything, he might have liked something a little more streamlined with a spoiler (this was the man who once wanted to lower my minivan and put sport wheels on it). But unfortunately that wasn't an option.

"You know, we *do* have one other option," said Steve, seeing me struggle and trying his best to be helpful. "You can rent the casket for the viewing instead of purchasing one."

My ears perked up. *Renting a casket?* This was brilliant! We'd use the casket for a few hours and then someone would vacuum it, spray in some Febreze to get rid of that used formaldehyde smell, and prepare it for the next "customer." It was like the Hertz of funeral services!

I was one step away from rifling through my purse to see if I had a coupon.

We finished with all of the decisions and paid the man, my dad graciously putting the bulk of the bill (except the extraneous flowers and my in-law's urn choice) on his credit card. I made a deal with him that I would pay him back later, once my financial situation had been somewhat straightened out, a promise he waved away as if he was used to putting thousands of dollars in funeral services on his MasterCard.

We left the funeral home, my in-laws and my family going our separate ways. Not realizing that when they flew out they would be attending a funeral, my in-laws left to find appropriate dark-washed attire, and my parents and I headed home to pay the babysitter and make sure she hadn't been tied to a tree in the time that we had been gone.

Steve and Nanci sent us out the door with two enormous picture frames, suggesting that we put together collages of Brad's life for guests to look at when they arrived at the viewing the next night and the funeral the day following. Now, I know there are some widows who pored over pictures of their husbands the moment each of them took their last breath. But I was not one of them. I was more than happy to hand over albums and old loose pictures to some creative, scrapbooking family friends and leave them huddled in my dining room while they laughed and cried at pictures of Brad from toddlerhood to fatherhood.

But I couldn't help them. And I felt so guilty about it. What kind of a woman can't look at pictures of the man she loves right after he dies? What kind of woman looks down at the floor as she passes the pictures in the hall of him holding each one of his children? What kind of woman doesn't download the last pictures she's taken of her husband off her camera so that she can look at them on the computer…and then delete them to make more room for the future?

That would be me. Over here.

Unfortunately, memorial planning does not really care how painful these things are for you. Its main job is to kick-start the grieving process. Things need to be done *now* or the food in the fridge will start to smell bad and your extended family will never leave.

And for some reason that evening, as our friends pasted pictures into those frames that were supposed to tell the story of Brad's life but didn't even come close, my mother kept gently asking me over and over again for the most current pictures of him. I had a suspicion that she was keeping something from me because I knew she wouldn't be nagging me about them unless she really needed them. But I was so frustrated that she kept requesting this from me that I finally broke what was, up until then, my Perfect Widow form, and I blew up.

I had been surrounded by people for days, making conversation I didn't want to make, but it would have been frowned upon if I didn't. I had smiled and nodded so much that my cheeks were sore and I felt like the Perfect Widow bobblehead doll. I had just been my most accommodating at the funeral home, agreeing to suggestions I didn't understand, holding my tongue about things I knew would rock the boat, and paying thousands of dollars for a party Brad wouldn't even be able to attend.

I had had *enough*.

"Why? *Why* do you need that *now*? I don't want to look at them. I don't even want to look *near* them. *Why* can't you just leave it alone?"

Her eyes watered. "Because Steve needs them to make sure he makes Brad look like himself for the visitation," she said.

I suddenly realized that if I didn't want my husband to look like Marilyn Manson lying there in his casket, I'd better suck it up and start flipping through some pictures.

Picking up our digital camera, I started viewing the photos that were still stored on it. Brad had given it to me just three weeks before for my birthday, and I had taken tons of pictures of him and the kids as I tried to figure out how to use it, pictures I wouldn't download and delete until months later because I couldn't stand the thought that I would never take another picture of him. There he was. Smiling. Laughing. Holding the kids. Going about his life with no idea of what was about to happen next.

How could we not have known?

Ironically, in the days before he died, I had taken a bunch of pictures of Brad's head. I know that sounds funny but, being completely bald, he was getting ready to try a new shampoo I'd bought him that was supposed to help with hair loss (which at his stage of follicle deprivation would have taken an act of God). We wanted an accurate account of this miraculous hair growth so that he could fulfill his dream of being on a 3:00 a.m. infomercial. So, when I had to supply pictures of him, I was able to provide a series of every angle of his head.

How handy.

I downloaded them onto the Walgreens website so my mom could pick them up and bring them to the funeral home, where Steve would try and somehow make Brad look like the man I loved, which would be impossible. Because the man I loved was full of life, laughter, and the perfect amount of craziness. And there's no way Steve could make an immobile shell look like the guy who could never sit still.

Now that I think about it, since Brad was completely bald at the time of his death, I should have given Steve an earlier picture of him with hair. I would have loved to have seen how he would have worked that one out. And the looks on everyone's faces passing by him at the visitation would have probably kept me entertained for hours.

Oh well.

Again, there's always next time.

6

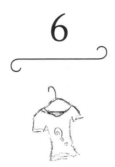

In the days immediately following Brad's death, I got into the really weird habit of going into our closet and talking to his clothes.

I don't really know why, but I would just sit there and tell his clothes everything that was going on and then, every once in a while, I would stop and look to them for some sort of solution.

Unfortunately, when I asked, "*How* could this have happened?" his pants really didn't have a good answer for me.

But it was oddly comforting to sit there on the floor and look up at all of his things just as he'd left them. I remembered all of the times that I made fun of his typical engineering mind that could put together a rocket but couldn't coordinate an outfit ("Just because they're both *green* doesn't mean they *match*") and how I asked him if I needed to put tags on his clothes like blind people do. I looked at the T-shirt that he'd worn as a joke the day he proposed to me, which said, "Sacrifices Must Be Made," and the combat boots he no longer had to wear for work, but that came in handy one night when he had to dress up for an '80s-themed party.

Ah, yes. My husband in a neon tank top, camo shorts, and combat boots. Proud moment.

I could smell his cologne and sweat, mixed with the comforting scent of dryer sheets. I could rub the sleeve of his favorite flannel shirt on my cheek, the one my parents had given him for Christmas one year, and pretend that his shoulder was absorbing my tears. I could hug his favorite sweatshirt, the one I'd tried to find a substitute for in recent years before finally coming to the conclusion that you can't replace something like that.

You know you're missing someone when you start cuddling his shoes.

The visitation and memorial, ironically enough, came at a good time for me when it came to my own wardrobe. Brad and I had gotten into watching TLC's *What Not to Wear*, and in the months before he died, I had actually been trying to beef up my apparel because I'd started noticing that all of the clothes I was wearing had one thing in common.

They were all sweats.

Panicking that, at thirty-one, I was one bad wardrobe choice away from wearing a muumuu, I started hitting the discount stores, trying to find some things that Stacy and Clinton, the hosts of the show, would approve of.

But I guess I'll never really know if I got it right because I've never seen "What Not to Wear: The Funeral Episode."

Brad was very supportive of this change (as I'm sure he was tired of seeing me in clothing that always had an elastic waistband). In fact, for my Mother's Day present, he had gotten me a hefty gift certificate to get fitted for bras, something that I desperately needed.

As I opened the envelope from Nordstrom, he said, "Now, there's a business card in there from a woman I talked to who will get you all fixed up. Every time we watch that show, the first thing they say is that the clothes aren't fitting right because the woman doesn't have the right bra. After nursing three kids, I think it's time."

Surprised at his thoughtfulness, I said, "Wow. Nordstrom! I would have never thought to go there! I would have guessed Victoria's Secret or something. How did you know?"

"I called all of your friends and asked them where they bought their bras."

When I think back on it now, I sure as hell hope he told them all *why* he was asking that question.

I dressed for the visitation in black pants and a flowy, flowered top. I don't know why I bothered to put makeup on since all I had been doing for three days was crying it right back off again. But taking the time to get completely ready made me feel like I was doing something normal.

When what I was getting ready for was so far out of range of "normal" that it didn't even get reception.

As probably anyone who has attended the visitation for their spouse will tell you, the entire night is a complete blur. I don't remember how I got there. I really don't remember how I got home. Feeling like a "viewing" was just too damn complicated to try and explain to three toddlers, I was grateful that the kids were still at the age when they could be easily distracted by an animated talking mouse. They stayed home with a couple of teenage babysitters who showed up looking completely shocked about the whole situation.

The viewing was set up in the lobby of our large Methodist church. The lights were dim and the lobby seemed to be waiting for us in an eerie quiet. As I walked in, the first thing I saw were the enormous collages my friends had labored over, with pictures of Brad from child to adult. The guest book was lying open on a table, sitting in between the frames of photos with a basket for the sympathy cards that I would later cry over in disbelief. And as

I turned to my left, I saw the casket settled in a corner next to a window and near the entrance from the outside, a spot I've never been able to look at the same way since.

I don't know who wanted the open casket...all I know is that it wasn't me. I tried to stay as far away from Brad's body, dressed in his best suit complete with Pittsburgh Steelers tie, as I could. Brad's mother stood vigil near him, waiting for people to come to her, while I circulated and marveled at how, if we weren't here for such a tragic reason, I would really want to catch up with all of these people. Doing what I could to be the best hostess possible, I tried to put everyone at ease...which actually probably made them feel more uncomfortable than if I would have just broken down like they were all expecting.

People kept offering me their seats, which I didn't want because that would mean that I would have to sit still and then it might really sink in why I was there.

"We're so sorry," puffy faces said to me. "How are you holding up?"

"Who, me?" I would say brightly. "I'm fine! Why shouldn't I be? And how was your trip to Denver? I hope the weather was good!"

After a few hours of hanging around with a dead body (never my favorite pastime), I will admit I was relieved to get home. My babysitters for the evening had gotten the kids safely tucked away in their beds, completely unaware of what they were going to have to experience the next day with the first and probably most significant funeral of their lives.

I went upstairs to my room, shed my uncomfortable clothes, and pulled on a trusty pair of sweats. When I made my way back down, my parents were sitting in my family room with Cindy and the rest of her family, who had made their way to Denver from various parts of the country. After putting on a brave face for so long that day and trying to make pleasant conversation while standing in a room with my husband's body, it was comforting to just sit and listen to them talk without feeling like I had to make any contributions of my own. But just as I had gotten settled into Brad's favorite chair, I heard my front door open.

And there were my in-laws.

When we were at the hospital a few days earlier, I had offered to let Bonnie and Jim stay at the house until the funeral was finished and it was time for them to go back home. They'd assured me that they would be comfortable in a hotel so my sister's husband, Sean, had made reservations for everyone nearby. And I thought that was that.

Until 9:30 p.m. the night before Brad's funeral when they showed up at my front door.

Pulling me aside, my sister-in-law, Brenda, quietly said, "The hotel was too expensive. We just couldn't afford to keep staying there."

Well, sure. I could understand that. Which was why I had offered to have them stay at the house three days earlier.

What I couldn't understand was why, since I had just been hanging out with them for the entire evening at the church, they hadn't mentioned that they might be stopping by.

Indefinitely.

When my in-laws made their surprise entrance that night, I will admit I was not prepared. To take a piece from the Bible: the inn was full. I had my mother staying there, as well as myself and my own three kids. Adding more adults, plus my two-year-old niece, was really stretching the square footage of my house. And to be quite honest, I was not about to displace my kids and move them out of their rooms. Even though they seemed to be handling everything really well (and part of me wondered if they understood what was happening *at all*), I was worried that one more little bump might really upset the apple cart.

And frankly...I just couldn't deal with that yet.

So, with my exhaustion accompanying me, I set about trying to find sheets, air mattresses, a playpen, and extra towels so that Brad's family could take over the basement, while my parents and their friends sat in the TV room somewhat shocked about what was going on. We dragged out the extra mattress under Michael's bed so that my mom could move from the guest bedroom and sleep on the floor in his room (and as the week wore on, move from room to room because all of the kids wanted to share Nana).

As I scurried around, trying to figure out how all of this was going to be logistically possible, Brenda followed me and asked, "Can't we just put an air mattress in the dining room?"

Count to ten.

"I'm going to have over a hundred people at my house tomorrow morning after the funeral," I replied as calmly as I could. "I can't have a bedroom set up in the middle of where everyone is going to be."

And so, at around midnight that night, after the in-laws had been fed and tucked away in the basement, I finally retreated to the quiet of my own bedroom. With Cindy's family in tow, my dad had returned to my parents' house to get a little rest before the next day. My mom was uncomfortably situated on the mattress on the floor in Michael's room. Sarah was sleeping peacefully in her crib, while Haley snored softly under a mound of blankets in her room.

And I climbed into my bed.

Alone.

7

In the end, I knew in my heart that the funeral had not been a raging success. My suspicions were confirmed when, years later, I was talking to my babysitter about it. A girl with a heart of gold, Catie had been babysitting for me since before Sarah was even born, and she had been to Brad's funeral.

I don't think I'd ever heard anything negative cross her lips, but when she was home from college and we were talking about times past, I mentioned the service to her, saying that in hindsight I wasn't sure it had gone all that well. Catie looked a little nervous when I started talking about it. "My mother told me I was never to bring up the funeral with you," she said.

Now, that's a bad party.

Before I could even get to the event that I had been dreading for days, I had to tackle something rather important.

Talking to the kids about what they were about to see.

Now, please keep in mind that I'd pretty much been running on no sleep and no food for the week prior, so I wasn't completely with it. But I came up with the best explanation I could think of that three children under six might understand. I sat them down on my bed, all dressed up and ready for church...and looked straight into their little faces.

"Now you guys know that Dad is dead, right?" I started out, watching their little heads bob up and down uncertainly. "Do you know what that means?" Another solemn nod.

"Well, today you're going to be able to see him. But it's not really him. You'll see his body, but he's not in his body anymore."

And then suddenly I had an inspiration.

"Dad is like a turtle. You're going to see his shell, but he's really not living in his shell anymore."

Hey. It was the best I could do on short notice. When you have an accident, death, wake, and funeral all packed into five days, that doesn't leave a whole lot of time to run to Barnes & Noble to pick up a book on how to explain death and dying to your children without scarring them for life. And when I tell most people my little analogy, they find it creative and endearing.

However, when I later told my father how I had explained it, he couldn't stop laughing. "I can't wait until your kids are teenagers and they tell their friends, 'You won't believe the story my mom laid on me when my dad died,'" he said.

But the kids seemed to understand it, and what the heck does he know anyway?

As we all trooped downstairs after our little discussion, I asked them, "Now...what are we going to see?"

"Dad's turtle shell!" they said in unison with misfired enthusiasm.

"And what does that mean?"

"It means that Daddy's shell is there, but he's not living in it anymore," said Haley in her wisest five-year-old voice.

Deep breath.

"Exactly."

The kids and I all piled ourselves into the minivan and, with my mother at the wheel, headed toward the church a little earlier than everyone else. A family friend had suggested that viewing the body might give the kids closure, or so the experts said. That seeing the body of their father might give them a sense of finality and that I might be able to reference that later when their young minds got confused and they asked where he was. And I could see how that might be valuable as they tried to deal with what has happened and move forward.

But I'll tell you this: I'll bet you that in about ten years the "experts" will have changed their minds and decided that nothing scars a young child more than hanging out in a room with a dead parent.

And that will *really* piss me off.

Deciding that Sarah, at eighteen months old, was too young to really understand what she would be looking at, my dad stayed outside with her as she ran around in her Sunday best. As the other two kids and I entered the church, my stomach was in a knot that seemed to be twisted around all of my vital organs. I took both of their little hands in mine and steered them over toward where Steve had placed Brad in the lobby.

Haley took one look at him and decided that she'd rather walk around the church with Nana, away from her dad's "shell." Michael, however, focused his little three-year-old eyes on his dad and then said, "I want to go look at Dad's pictures."

So we walked over to the collages that had been set up on stands near the entrance and he looked at the pictures, trying to find himself in scenes with his dad.

Then he walked back over to the casket and looked at Brad again.

And then took another trip over the collages.

I knew that little boy's mind, even at three. So much like his father, he was literally trying to piece together what was happening, trying to figure out how the man in the pictures could possibly be the man who was lying there lifeless. Seeing himself in the photographs, some of which were taken so recently, and attempting to understand that those arms that were holding him as he blew out the candles on this birthday cake were now crossed over his father's body holding four yellow roses was, I'm sure, confusing.

Hell...I was confused about it, too.

As I watched his wheels turning, the "guests" (is that what you call people at a funeral? The audience? Attendees?) began to arrive. As they trickled in, so did the kids' friends, which seemed to make the event a little more normal to them. Michael's concentration on his dad was broken by a swift almost-tackle from another little boy. Sarah came in with my mom and dad, and Haley started running circles around the lobby with her friends.

Before things got really crazy, I pulled them aside and said, "The church nursery will be open so I'm going to give you a choice. You can either come into the sanctuary with me for the service or go into the nursery with the other kids."

Uh. *That's* a no-brainer.

I watched Haley and Michael race to the play area with Sarah toddling behind them as quickly as she could. They all peered over the half door and waited to be let in with the rest of their friends. Judging by the one scared-looking girl the church had working in the nursery that day, I don't think they were prepared for how many young children would be attending. Actually, I don't think anyone was prepared for that. One of the saddest moments for me during that service was watching all of those toddlers run into the nursery while the adults walked into the sanctuary.

God...we were all so *young*.

Knowing that my kids were in good hands and delightfully distracted, I turned around and made my way back to the lobby. On the way, I was greeted by everyone I knew (and some that I didn't). One of the strangest things about funerals is seeing everyone from your past and present, all gathered together. I wanted to visit. I wanted to go out for a beer. I wanted to do something, anything, with all of these people, other than what we were doing.

Everyone hugged me, kissed me, and tried not to show me their damp eyes. The most memorable people were the people I didn't expect to see there. Women from the young mothers' group that I had belonged to when Haley was a toddler but hadn't had the time to do much with in the last few years. The director of the preschool that Haley and Michael had attended who walked right up to me and said, "Your tuition is free from now on. And any time you need to drop the kids off and take a little time...you don't even have to call."

At a time when I didn't know how I was going to cope financially, she had no idea the burden she lifted from my shoulders that day.

But the group of people who threw me off the most was Brad's coworkers from Lockheed Martin. Because I'd never met them. Not one. As a proposal manager, he traveled all the time, and so did everyone he worked with. When they were out of town working on a proposal, some of them were together nonstop for weeks, and the people who *weren't* with them were working on their own projects in various parts of the world. It was very rare that their schedules overlapped so that happy hour in the middle of the week was possible, and even when they did, most of those guys were gone so much that the last thing they wanted to do when they had time off was to leave the comfort of their homes to spend time with people they saw more than their own families.

Brad had always been fairly quiet about work for a couple of reasons. The first was that he was determined never to "bring work home" with him in a way that would keep him distracted from his family life. That meant that he rarely talked about what went on during his day, a hard adjustment for me because, as a stay-at-home mom, I longed to hear the office gossip and details about his work that he was less than forthcoming with.

Not only that, but most of the time he and his coworkers were all working on classified jobs. In other words…I rarely knew who he was working *with*, much less what he was working *on*. So as people came into the church, every so often some random person would walk up to me and say, "I worked with your husband on Project X," and I didn't have the heart to tell them, "I have no idea who you are or what you're talking about."

The only names I recognized were the guys who had given Brad a hard time at work. Not that I'm judging…believe me he gave as good as he got, and that's what made them all successful. They worked on multimillion-dollar (sometimes billion-dollar) contracts, and when they were in the middle of a project, the work was around the clock and they were under a lot of pressure. Tensions could run high, to say the least.

So as I was standing in the lobby while people made their way into the sanctuary, one gentleman walked up to me and said, "Hi. My name is Greg and I worked with Brad on several projects. I'm so, so sorry for your loss."

I smiled a little as I thought of the handful of times Brad had brought up Greg's name in frustration, and before I could stop myself I blurted out, "Oh, I know exactly who *you* are. Brad told me all about the two of you working on that Virginia project together."

There was an uncomfortable pause as he seemed to ponder what in the heck Brad might have told me about him before he said, "Yes…well…he will really be missed around the office."

And he shuffled as quickly as he could away from me and into the safety of the crowd.

I met Brad's boss, Mary, for the first time and she seemed

as completely shocked as the rest of us. Missing a girls' weekend (and what I'm sure was probably her first vacation in about ten years), she had flown in from the East Coast the night before. As she shook my hand, heartfelt sympathy flowing from her voice, I felt unreasonably annoyed that this was the first time I was meeting her. I mean, we all know that when meeting a spouse's superior, we want to impress a little. That introduction should be at a dinner or an awards ceremony or the Christmas party. Not at a function where the only person we have in common is dead, we each have an oozy, wadded-up tissue in our hand, and only one of our eyes has managed to keep its makeup on.

Needless to say, I was not at my best.

As everyone made their way into the sanctuary, I was told by Steve and Nanci to stay behind and make my Grand Widow Entrance just before the guest of honor—the casket—and a few of Brad's closest friends from Pennsylvania and the Air Force Academy who had stayed behind to accompany Brad into the room. I watched as all of the boys who were now men, the ones who had stood next to Brad at our wedding, took their places next to his casket to bring him into the church.

And then things got interesting.

When we'd met with one of the pastors from my church, a woman named Teri, during the planning process the day before, there were several people present: my parents, my in-laws, and my husband's childhood minister, Gerald, who had flown in from his small hometown in Pennsylvania. I was amazed and grateful that this man took the time to be present and preside over the funeral because, even though we had been members of our church in Colorado for many years, it was a large congregation and we didn't know our pastor very well. I was relieved to have someone who knew my husband well enough to speak for him and run things.

Boy, was I in for a jolt.

Now, to me, a funeral should not have *too* much of a religious overtone, unless it's a small, private ceremony. To some, I know it's a comfort to hear that your loved one has moved on to a better place and all that, but I knew that a lot of people attending probably didn't belong to any sort of organized religion, and if they did, it might not be the same one. And it was important to me that the attendees felt comfortable.

I guess I should have put that into a memo and sent it to all parties involved.

Gerald strode to the podium and began his sermon, talking about what a remarkable person Brad was and I sat there thinking, "So far, so good."

But then things started to turn a little more religious. And then a little more. And then he jumped off the spiritual high-dive when he boomed in his best fire-and-brimstone preacher voice, "If anyone here chooses not to attend church regularly and is not bathed in the blood of Christ, know that you will *not* see Brad in the Kingdom of Heaven.

"Amen!"

This declaration was then followed by a peaceful rendition of "Amazing Grace."

I was sitting in the front of the church, which meant that I couldn't see the faces of the other people around me. I gave a little sideways glance toward my parents and, judging by my mother's white knuckles as her hands tensely clutched the tissue in her lap, this pronouncement was as unexpected as I thought. Everyone in that room was reeling from Brad's death at such a young age, and clearly, my hope that they would be made comfortable by a nonreligious, peaceful service was not to be fulfilled.

Then the eulogies began. People came forward and spoke about Brad's friendship, what a great coworker he was, and what a difference he had made to so many. It's weird how you never seem to know what an impact someone has had until they're gone. Things that should have been said and moments that should have been appreciated seem to come to the surface when you know you'll never have them again.

"Brad Tidd was one of the most valued employees I had under me," said his boss, Mary, her short frame allowing her to barely see over the podium. "His sense of humor got us through many a project, and he had a 100 percent win rate on the proposals that he managed. This not only helped the company, but more importantly, it provided thousands of jobs across the country, something that we will always be grateful for."

I started tearing up. I didn't know that Brad had done that. I felt a swell of pride and wished that I could be sitting with him, proudly holding his hand at some event where he was receiving a plaque that would get dusty on his office wall, instead of listening to her say that next to his casket. I knew that to him, the money he brought to the company wouldn't have mattered. But the fact that he would be remembered as someone who helped provide jobs…that would have meant the world to him.

Then Jason, one of Brad's friends from the Academy, strode to the podium with military precision. Now the husband of Cheryl, my roommate from college, he took a long, deep breath before he began to speak.

"Brad and I have been friends for years," he began, "and he was one of the biggest patriots I've ever known. We've seen each other through just about everything—school, the military, marriage, fatherhood. One of his favorite sayings was, 'To be old and wise, you must first be young and stupid.' Through the years, we've had plenty of young and stupid."

He paused for a minute and then said, "I just wish we would have had more 'old and wise' together."

I sat there grasping wadded-up tissues and blinking back

tears, thinking that I had never pictured myself in this situation. Not in my wildest nightmares. The lights seemed too bright and the lump in my throat was so big I couldn't swallow. I suddenly had the feeling that if I started crying, I would never stop.

And that terrified me.

It then came time to sing a hymn that Gerald the minister had suggested during the planning process, one that I had never heard of, but I assumed was popular back in good, ol' Pennsylvania. Hoping to make the folks who had traveled from the East more comfortable, I had agreed to add it to the program. After that whopper of a sermon, I did feel a little trepidation when the organist began the introduction and everyone opened their programs and stood to sing.

Not one person in the audience knew that song. Not one. Everyone, and I mean *everyone*, spent five painful minutes stumbling through this really complicated—and *long*—hymn that really didn't have anything to do with the deceased.

I don't even think my in-laws knew it.

The only clear thing we all heard was the loud baritone of the Pennsylvania preacher who I guess missed his chance on *American Idol* and decided to make up for it at my husband's funeral. And when it was done and we had all taken our seats again, I spent the rest of the service hunched over in a position that I'm sure everyone thought of as "doubled over in grief"…when in reality I was laughing so hard into the wadded-up tissue in my hand that I just about couldn't breathe.

God, I'm sorry that Brad missed that.

8

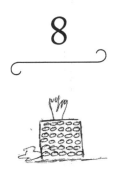

O nce the performance was over, I breathed a sigh of relief. The crowd watched as Brad's casket was wheeled out the sanctuary doors, through the lobby, and out to the hearse that was waiting for him. And they all stood to follow.

I walked behind Brad to where cadets in Air Force uniforms were waiting to remove the flag that had been laid across his casket. They stood completely still, saluting him as he was wheeled out toward the hearse. With the slow, excruciating meticulousness that only the military can carry out, they picked up the flag, folded it into a neat triangle, and began to make their way toward me.

"They're not coming over here," I thought in horror. "They're not going to give *me* that flag. That's not *mine*."

The cadet handed me the flag and slowly saluted me. And I finally broke down, burying my face in the lapel of my dad's best suit.

"He's gone," I mumbled into his shoulder, not able to catch my breath. "They're taking him. He's really gone. Oh my God. He's really gone."

"It's okay, it's okay," my dad whispered in my ear, hugging me to him.

But that was just the thing. It *wasn't*.

Since Brad was going to be cremated, a trip to the cemetery wasn't necessary. People began to murmur around us and quietly make their way back to their cars so that they could join us at our house—*my* house now—for a reception. I picked my head up, blinked at the bright summer sun, and took a deep breath, knowing that I still had a long day ahead of me. Flag in hand, I made my way back toward the church to help gather up whatever had been left behind.

I walked in the doors as friends and family were picking up the collages and the guest book. My mother had the basket of cards that everyone had left and was leading the kids to her car. And I fully intended to leave right then with everyone else.

But then I saw her.

The church pastor, Teri, who had sat patiently near the altar while Brad's minister conducted what I felt sure would go down as one of the most uncomfortable memorial ceremonies in history, was standing in the lobby waiting for us to clear out.

I walked up to her and said, "Teri…can I talk to you for a minute?"

She looked at me, surprised. "Of course."

I don't know why I went to her. I didn't really know her. I didn't even know what I wanted to talk about. But the second we walked into one of the Sunday school rooms, I'm very much afraid that I exploded on this woman who, up until that point, had been almost a complete stranger to me.

"Why? *Why?*" I screamed. "Why did this happen? We did everything right! I don't know a better person than Brad. Why did this happen? What am I going to *do*? How am I going to live? Why would God do this to us? You have to tell me! *Why?*"

Teri led me to one of the hard plastic chairs that surrounded the school tables. She sat down with me as the tears flowed down my face and took my hand in hers. Her face was so full of concern, watching someone suffer…someone who was desperate to find an answer that she knew may never come.

"I don't know, sweetie. I couldn't explain it when my husband died of cancer when my daughter was ten, and I can't explain it to you now. All I can do is pray with you now. And if you're not ready to do that, I'll pray *for* you."

For the first time, I really started to digest how I was not in control of anything in life. None of us are. I looked at this woman who seemed to be so disciplined and who appeared to have all of the answers every Sunday at church and realized that none of us are running the show here.

It was as I was looking at Teri's face, filled with pain and sympathy, that I began to discover that the question of "why" may be vitally important…but it would never be answered. Men and women have been going through what I was about to face since the beginning of time and have never been able to answer the question, "How could this have happened?"

And even if they could, it wouldn't ease the pain.

I could ask, "Why was my husband taken away from his children when they were just babies?" and even if I got an answer, it would still be incomprehensible.

I could ask, "Why did my husband have to leave me to deal with this all on my own?" and even if I got an answer, I would still be angry.

I could ask, "How could this happen to a man who was just so damn *good*?"

And even if I got an answer, it wouldn't stop what I was about to feel.

He would still be gone.

Death makes *no sense*. Brad had survived his dangerous teenage years, driving too fast and constantly testing fate, only to die on his commute to work. I've had family friends who have spent years with someone who was the picture of health, only to be shocked by their sudden heart attack. I know people whose husbands have been diagnosed with very "curable" forms of cancer and have followed the doctor's instructions down to the letter... only to lose them two years later after countless rounds of treatment and false hope.

Our husbands are dead and Keith Richards is still alive?

Um...hello? Is this thing on?

Everything that I thought was a "sure thing" in my life had suddenly been ripped out from under me. I'd always thought that if Brad and I worked hard, loved each other, and were just generally good people, we would be rewarded by a long, happy, boring life together. Bad things were what happened to other people. Bad things lived in the abstract in my life and were never within reaching distance. And even if bad things were to happen to us, the one thing, the *one thing* I was sure of in life was that Brad and I would get through it together.

But then "together" was the one thing that had been taken away.

And although I didn't completely understand it as I was sitting in the Sunday school room of my church, tears streaming down my face, looking at a woman who was a virtual stranger, but one I was sure up until that moment had all of the answers...the question of "why" would become something that I would struggle with for years.

And then it would become something that I would eventually have to let go of.

I finally dried my eyes and blew my nose with the clump of tissues that my clothes seemed to be growing. My dad, who had been patiently waiting outside the church while I had my breakdown with Teri, watched me walk out of the room, puffy faced and hiccuping, and we made our way to the car.

We stayed completely silent until, while sitting at a stoplight, I had a sudden realization.

"I'm going to have to go back to work," I said, the magnitude of the shift in our lives starting to sink in. "I'm going to have to sell my house. I'm going to have to figure all of this out alone. What...what am I going to *do?*"

"Not today," my father replied quietly, one hand taking mine while he kept steering with the other one. "You don't have to figure that out today. And when you do...we're going to figure it out together. Okay?"

Brimming with self-pity, I nodded and we drove the rest of the way in silence.

As we got closer, more and more cars dotted the side of the road until we got in front of my house, where we could barely squeeze through to park in the driveway. The party was in full swing. Many people were seeing our home for the first time, and for one wild moment, I thought, "Oh, I wish I had gotten the house painted before everyone came over!"

The crowd was so thick that I was sure that if the fire marshal caught wind of what was going on, he'd shut down this shindig for sure. I longed for the quiet of my bedroom and the camouflage of my covers. But I pasted a smile on my face and hugged and hugged...and hugged.

Seeing all of the people from the funeral gathered in my house was surreal. Brad's friends from Pennsylvania mingled with his coworkers from Lockheed. People who hadn't seen each other in years cried out as they recognized one other and then bent their heads together and spoke in whispers. Everyone bonded over the platters of Chick-fil-A chicken nuggets and HoneyBaked Ham that had been set out in the breakfast room with more food than I'd ever seen before.

Kids found cracks in the crowd so that they could run figure eights through the house and then out the back door, only to run right back in again. Neighbors who I had never met before walked up the street and brought flowers and cards, and I shook their hands uncomfortably as I said hello to them for the first time at the reception for my husband's funeral.

Talk about awkward.

I took off the shoes that had been threatening blisters all day (I'm always grateful for the first girl at any event who takes off her shoes, thereby giving us all permission) and continued to circulate. As anyone in this position will tell you, I have no idea what people talked to me about and I have no idea what I said.

All I remember is laughing and crying. Mostly at the same time.

When I finally made my way to my dining room, my dad was standing there talking to his best friend from college. He put his arm around me, hugged me close, and quietly said the words I thought I'd been wanting to hear all day.

"Is it okay if we open the bar now?"

I nodded as he reached for the bottle of Jack Daniels. Knowing that my dad rarely drank anything harder than wine was yet another reminder of the gravity of the situation. And while I longed for the numbness of a good, stiff drink, I was suddenly worried that if I had one, it would soften me to the point where I might break down in front of everyone. So I excused myself and walked over to some of Brad's friends from high school who had flown in for the service. All of these people Brad would have loved to welcome to his home for the first time were standing in a corner, trying to make normal conversation.

"Craig wanted to come, but he…he just couldn't," said Brad's friend Chris.

"I think this has all been too much for him," his wife concurred.

Well, I could certainly understand *that*.

A moment later, I heard a burst of laughter coming from the other side of the house. I moved away from the Pennsylvania crew and made my way through the kitchen and into my family room. And there they were, Brad's buddies from the Academy, ties loosened, laughing with each other and their wives.

The ones who had helped Brad create some of his most memorable moments—Matt, Jason, and Steve—hadn't all been together in the same room for years, and they sat talking and joking like they hadn't missed a beat. Their conversations were like a secret language that the rest of us didn't understand, as they began sentences with, "Do you remember the time…" and before it was finished, they were all laughing in unison.

I couldn't believe that he was missing this.

We all sat on my oversized family-room furniture and flipped through my old photo albums of our college years together, marveling at Brad's ability to drink three beers at one time and remembering his first love, his Trans Am. Formals, football games, and then weddings and kids…their passage into adulthood seemed to be bound tightly together.

And I couldn't help but wonder (and fear) that, now that Brad was gone, this might be where my story with them would end.

After the last piece of ham had been eaten that day and most of the guests had gone, I sat on the edge of my bed feeling physically exhausted while my brain worked in overdrive, thinking of everything and nothing at the same time. I tried to process all that had been said—the memories, the tears, and the laughter—almost wishing that I could have recorded the whole day so that I could replay it and remind myself of how important Brad had been to so many. But I couldn't. Even though I could hear people moving around downstairs, I felt like I no longer had the mental capacity to tell my legs to get down there and help them clean up. And so I sat, blankly staring at the wall, having no idea that would become my favorite pastime for the next year.

The sound of the phone ringing startled me out of my stupor, and when I looked at the caller ID, I saw a phone number I didn't recognize. I hesitated to answer it, but I had learned that lesson before, hadn't I?

"Hello?"

"Mrs. Tidd?" said a quiet voice.

"Yes?"

"My name is Cindy. I...I was the witness to your husband's accident."

There was a sudden roaring in my ears, and my heart started pounding a mile a minute. I clutched the phone so hard I thought it would break. Part of me wanted to slam it down because I wasn't sure if I wanted to hear what she had to say.

And part of me needed to know.

"I hope you don't mind me calling you like this," she continued, "but your husband gave me your phone number while we waited for help. He was unconscious for a while, but when he woke up, I asked him if there was anyone I could call for him and he gave me your phone number. Right when I was going to call, the police arrived so I didn't have a chance."

My mouth was completely dry at this point.

"What...what *happened?*" I managed to get out, even though my throat felt like it was starting to swell shut.

"I'm a courier for the hospital," she started to explain. "I deliver blood. I was on my way down to Colorado Springs, and the driver in front of me slowed down and was turning left. Brad couldn't see around my van and tried to pass me and hit him."

"How many cars were in front of you?" I asked. "The police said that he passed a whole line."

"Oh no, no," she said quickly. "It was just me. He was just trying to pass me."

In that moment I realized how angry I had been for the last couple of days. I didn't necessarily blame Brad for what I knew was just an accident, but I was so bitter that he would have done something so reckless like pass a line of cars on a two-lane highway. My anger at him was immediately transferred to the police officer who had barged into the trauma room, accusing my husband of doing something he obviously didn't do and giving me that extra burden when, needless to say, I really didn't need it.

And making Brad worry about something as trivial as getting sued during what he didn't know would be the last hours of his life.

"Anyway," she went on, "I hope you don't mind me calling you like this. I just wanted to let you know that I was with him and that he wasn't alone. I've been calling the hospital and a friend of mine had given me an update a few days ago that he was okay. I just found out this morning that he didn't make it."

And then she said something that I will never forget.

"While he was lying on the road, you and the kids were the only thing on his mind. You were all he talked about. He sure did love you."

I don't remember how the conversation ended. At that point I was so flooded with every emotion…even some I didn't know were possible to have at the same time. Grief. Anger. Disbelief.

And love.

Coping

an all-inclusive trip to the island of crazy

9

B ecause the funeral had taken place on a Saturday, it wasn't possible to have Brad cremated until Monday. And since I had been told by my mother-in-law that they were planning on staying until they had their share of the ashes (or up to sixty days if I needed them to because they had open-ended tickets), I was in a panic to have him cremated as soon as possible.

While I appreciated their offer to stay and help out, I needed my house back. I needed quiet. I needed to feel like I didn't have to be "on" all of the time.

I needed those ashes.

Which was why at the crack of 8:00 a.m. on Monday, Steve, the funeral director, found me waiting in his office with a wild look in my eye, begging him to get the job done.

I've often wondered if he's ever had a widow plead with him, "*Please* cremate my husband, the sooner the better."

I stayed on top of Steve all day. I must have called him every hour on the hour, and every time he assured me that he was doing everything he could to get it done. I was a complete wreck until I got the call at 5:00 p.m. informing me that the deed had been accomplished.

I then called my mother and told her, "I have great news. Brad was just cremated."

I never thought I would say that.

In a flurry of bag packing and tearful embraces, my in-laws prepared to leave with their share of Brad's ashes, along with a certificate that would allow them to carry the urn on the plane. (Wouldn't that have been an awkward thing to get stopped with by the TSA?)

"You'll always be our daughter-in-law," Bonnie said, hugging me hard before she climbed into the rental car. And with that one sentence, a seed of uncertainty was planted. As I waved good-bye and watched the car round the corner of my street, one question flashed in my brain.

Was I still their daughter-in-law?

Any hope of giving that further consideration was quashed as I walked back into my house and was greeted by my three antsy toddlers and my mother, whose expectant look told me that she was there to listen if I was ready to talk. But I wasn't. It was too much. Too much happening all at once that I couldn't even begin to verbalize yet. I couldn't worry about where my relationship with my in-laws was going to go or how everything would shake out. Not yet. That was an issue that, for better or for worse, would somehow take care of itself. The more pressing problem I had in that moment was broader in scale and seemed to be completely out of my control.

Figuring out how life was supposed to go on and how I would be able to do everything alone.

I took a seat in my living room with my mother, and as if reading my mind, she said, "Your father and I have decided that I'm going to move in here for the next couple of months. After that, I'll just come every weekend for a while."

"Okay," I replied, a little uncertain. After all, I was thirty-one years old and hadn't lived with my parents since I was nineteen. But in the haze of grief, I was somewhat grateful that someone was just willing to take over. And I knew that if she left, she would be worried that she shouldn't have. Although by staying she would worry that she was overstaying her welcome.

My mom was in a position of support where she just couldn't win.

She was running on fumes at that point, just doing her best to keep the show on the road. And ever since that moment at the hospital when I was told that Brad was not going to live, I had been operating in such a fog that I was positive everyone else around me knew what needed to be done better than I did. In that moment, I was looking at my parents through the eyes of a child—*their* child—and was immediately accepting of their advice and suggestions.

I should have realized then that they were in uncharted territory, just as I was. They had never been widowed. Single parenting was something they'd only read about or seen in the abstract. They had never been suddenly forced to look at the road ahead without seeing the person that they trusted the most no longer in the driver's seat.

In other words, I didn't know what the hell was going on or what to do. But then again, neither did they.

I was sure that I was crying at the wrong time, not crying when I should have, sleeping when I should have been functioning, and running around in manic circles when I should have been sleeping. I just knew that I was doing everything wrong and my poor, loving husband was looking down on the most mediocre widow in history. I didn't know yet that coping doesn't come naturally to *anyone*. It's not something that we're born knowing how to do. You can't practice it, and it's not something you can study. Unfortunately, it's like the most horrible on-the-job training you can possibly imagine. You have to figure out what in the hell you're doing while you're actually doing it. It involves a lot of trial and error, and giving up on learning how to do it is *not* an option.

In other words, you can't tell grief to "shove it" and walk out the door when coping with it gets too hard.

Learning how to manage grief is a very individual process and has a lot of elements involved. What works for one person may not work for another. So, you can't necessarily talk to someone who has been through something similar and know for sure that the path they found through it will also be yours.

It's hard to explain to other people how, when you're starting out on your journey as a new widow, you don't have a clue about who to turn to for help. Everything about life is so overwhelming that it becomes impossible to make *any* decisions, even ones you know might help get you out of this hole. I knew that some people found comfort in prayer, but things were so bad that I didn't know what to pray *for*. I knew that counseling would be something I would need to look into (for myself and the kids), but that required research and an attention span I just didn't possess anymore. I knew I could call friends and talk to them, but what was I going to say?

"I'm really depressed because Brad's dead."

Well...*that's* not new information.

Even though I craved my mother's help and comfort, a part of me needed to be alone. I felt like I was constantly being watched and silently evaluated by everyone. While other people were around, even the people closest to me, I was trying so hard to act normal and take care of things that needed to be taken care of so that they wouldn't worry that I felt like I could never let loose with my grief. I needed the freedom to sob while I was doing the dishes or sit on my bed and scream into a pillow for five minutes while the kids were watching cartoons downstairs. And

I needed to do this without feeling like I was making someone else uncomfortable.

Having never gone through a tragedy even close to this magnitude, I had been thrown into the deep end of the emotional pool and there was no lifeguard on duty to fish me out. That rescuer had died. Oh, sure. I had had my share of minor upsets and worries, some that I'd shared with Brad and some that I'd dealt with on my own. But I'd never been a person who allowed sobbing to catch her by surprise or who suddenly felt like the world was closing in so fast she couldn't catch her breath. And now, I was not only liable to cry at the drop of a hat or laugh at inappropriate times, but my ability to control these outbursts had died with my husband.

So at that point, part of me was just happy to have someone at least attempt to take the reins of my runaway life, even though I really should have had more confidence in myself and what I was capable of. And if I had been able to think like a normal, rational person at that point, I probably would have realized it.

After all, Brad had been out of town for a good portion of the kids' lives, leaving me to keep things running. I knew more about being on my own and keeping things going than I gave myself credit for. But my sudden insecurity about every inch of my new life was overwhelming and I needed ways to channel the nervous energy that I had.

I had a constant feeling that I was coming out of my skin, which was one of the worst sensations I have had before or since. It was like every cell I had was bouncing inside the confines of my shell. I felt like my grief and nervous energy were on the verge of rocketing out of my body and going into orbit. I couldn't move fast enough or do enough stuff.

And even though I wasn't alone to have the breakdown I probably needed, I wouldn't have allowed myself to do it anyway.

There was no way I was going to slow down and feel what was going on. So, in that regard, it was a huge comfort to know that, with my mother around, I would have the babysitting backup I needed to be the manic person I had become—walking endless miles and running meaningless errands—during the course of those first few weeks.

It was also handy to have my mother on hand to watch the kids while my sister, Kristi, who was a Certified Financial Planner, forced me to deal with one of the more concrete issues immediately—my financial future. I was already thankful to her for any financial security I was about to have because years earlier, when Brad had gotten out of the Air Force, Kristi had hounded us about retirement funds and life insurance since we were no longer under the military umbrella.

"You will max out your 401(k)," she had said in a voice that left no room for discussion. "And I want you to make sure you have enough life insurance to at least pay off your house if something should happen."

Now, she was helping me settle Brad's estate so I could see how long that money would last and when I would need to go back to work.

Brad had had no will, something I was initially worried about, but she assured me that under Colorado law, it shouldn't be a problem. She started talking about things like "rolling over" funds, health benefits, Social Security, workers' compensation… all things I had no idea about and was relieved to just hand over to her. Kristi scheduled meetings, made phone calls, and handled a bunch of stuff I generally had no attention span for at the time, making me eternally grateful that I had someone I could trust in my corner.

After all, she knew that if she somehow screwed up my investments, there was a distinct possibility that she would find me on her doorstep with three kids, suitcases in hand, looking for a permanent place to stay.

That would get any financial planner motivated.

Kristi was the one who was with me the day that I spoke with Social Security and we figured out that, thanks to her insistence on having enough life insurance to pay off the house, I would be receiving enough every month to cover most of our living expenses. She worked through finding me the best deal on health insurance. And she was with me the day I called a company I had never heard of before to find out why they had sent me a check in the mail. As I dialed the number, I was positive that someone would tell me that it was a mistake and that I needed to send it back.

But once again, I was in for a surprise. Thankfully (and *finally*), a good one.

In the days following Brad's death, my dad had asked me, "Catherine, do you know if Brad was on the job during the accident?"

"What do you mean?"

"I mean was he on the clock?"

I thought about it for a minute and said, "You know what? I think he was. He was on the clock any time he had to travel more than fifty miles away for a job. And that proposal he was working on was fifty-five miles away from the house."

My dad nodded silently, and in my grief-induced stupor, I was too out of it to ask why he wanted to know.

Then, at the reception at the house after the funeral, Brad's boss made a comment about how she would make sure that I received as much financial compensation as I could, a remark that mystified me at the time because I didn't know how that could possibly be in her hands. At that point, I figured that what we had invested was what I had to work with and that, for better or for worse, any way my finances ended up would be because of the decisions we had made in the past.

So, I was shocked when I heard the woman from the company in charge of Lockheed's workers' comp benefits tell me that, yes, I was supposed to receive that check. And that I would be receiving checks every month because he had technically been working when he died.

I cried when I hung up the phone that day. I wasn't wealthy, but I was going to be okay, at least for a little while—hopefully long enough to figure out my future without putting too much pressure on myself to get out of the house and start working immediately.

By the time Brad died, I had been out of the workforce for five years, something that we had both agreed was the best solution when we started having children. When Haley was born, Brad had just started working for Lockheed, and even though he wasn't a proposal manager yet, his job as an engineer had him traveling back and forth to Florida for weeks at a time. And before she was born, I had been traveling quite a bit for my own job with a large company in Denver.

After graduating from college with a degree in English, it had taken me years to move up from being an administrative assistant for various helpless executives to working as a marketing manager and then finally landing my dream job as an event planner, planning corporate events around the world. And even though I didn't travel constantly, when I did, the trips would usually be back to back for weeks. The job was time-consuming and stressful, perfect for a woman with no children.

But not ideal for a mother whose husband traveled as well.

I didn't plan on not returning to work when I left for maternity leave. Actually, I didn't really have a plan at all. We hadn't checked into daycare, and we hadn't looked at our finances to see if it was even possible for me to stay home. We were winging it at a time in our lives when, really, a firm plan would have been handy.

I spent the first six of my twelve weeks of maternity leave getting to know this new little person who kept us up, made us smell bad, and was generally unaccommodating. And when crunch time came and we really needed to make a decision, I walked out of the first daycare provider we interviewed—a sweet woman with a lovely home, a dream for any working mom—looked at Brad, and said, "I can't leave her. I can't leave her with someone else."

Brad took this news in stride, and I think was a little relieved. We had both been raised by stay-at-home moms who had gone back to work when we were old enough to get into the house on our own. Even though we hadn't really talked about it, I don't think we realized until we had Haley how important it was to us both that I stay home.

Brad and I fell into our roles seamlessly. I did everything to take care of the house while he was the primary breadwinner. I cooked, cleaned, paid the bills, took care of the kids, and did what was necessary to keep everything going. Brad worked hard and was always gone, his goal to rise quickly within Lockheed.

"I want to be a vice president by the time I'm forty," he said to me often. "I know I'm working a lot now, but don't worry. It will all be worth it someday."

But that someday never came.

It's somewhat ironic to me how our lives turned out. I was the first of my friends to have a kid, but everyone soon followed. And as each one of my friends had a baby, they all went back to work when their maternity leave was over.

"How can you stand being at home with a newborn?" I was asked more than once. "It's so…isolating. You don't have anyone to talk to!"

"You have to be creative," I would say. "You have to find ways to occupy yourself. There are groups for moms and all kinds of stuff out there. You just have to be proactive."

But the one question that I was asked that still haunts me was, "Aren't you afraid of quitting your job? I mean, what happens if something happens to Brad? Doesn't that make you nervous?"

And with the naivety that comes with youth, I confidently replied, "What in the world could happen to Brad? Do you know what the chances of that are?"

Well. Now we know.

It seems cruel to me now, the work that Brad put in and the time he spent away from us. On the day that Michael was born, he started his new job as a proposal manager and then the traveling really began. Oh, he loved it and thrived on the long hours and hard work. If he was home for two weeks straight, in between jobs, eventually his foot would start bouncing and he would get antsy, ready to go after the next big fish.

But he was torn. In his heart he was a family man and loved his children. And I think he had dreams of working hard, being rewarded by promotions and raises, and then eventually leading a more settled life by the time his son was ready to throw a baseball and his girls were old enough for father-daughter dances at school.

And I didn't think my stay-at-home status was permanent. I really thought that once our kids were at an age when they had their own lives and interests, I would have mine as well. I had hoped that by the time Sarah was in preschool, I would be able to find some sort of part-time job or even volunteer for a worthy cause. My mind was constantly thinking about what I would do when the kids were older.

One of the many fears rattling around in my head right after Brad died was, of course, money and the idea of going back to work. What was I going to do? I knew enough about the plummeting job market at the time to know that I really wasn't marketable. Just weeks after his death, as Kristi and I worked to put my new financial puzzle together, I scrambled around, researching and tracking down old employers, telling them what had happened and asking for updated letters of recommendation.

I had nightmares about going into a job interview and blurting out, "As you can see from my résumé, I haven't worked in years and I'm probably not up on all of the latest technology. What it *doesn't* say on paper is that I'm widowed. So if you hire me and one of my kids gets sick, there's a good chance I'll be out of the office for two weeks while I take care of them."

I wasn't the only one with money on the brain. Even though they were so young at the time of Brad's death, Haley and Michael still had questions about it. Because up until that point, the question, "Where's Daddy?" was always answered with, "Daddy's out of town. He works very hard so that we can have all of these nice things."

So, once he was gone, one of the first things they thought of was, "Well, if *he's* not here to work for all of these 'nice things,' where's the money going to come from?"

It was hard to try and explain to the kids how investments, 401(k)s, Social Security, and life insurance work. The best that I could come up with was, "Daddy and I saved money. We saved just in case something bad happened. We'll be okay."

That explanation seemed to alleviate some of their worry.

So, as I hung up the phone that day after being informed that Brad was actually on the job at the time of his death, I somehow felt like he was still doing his best to take care of his family, even though he could no longer physically be there to do it. Like he was saying, "Stay home with the kids a little longer. I'm going to give you enough to take care of you immediately and allow you some time to figure everything out."

"I feel so lucky," I said to Kristi tearfully, a comment she quickly dismissed.

"You're not *lucky*," she said. "Your husband died. You invested and you planned. Brad had a good job with good benefits. That's a far cry from just being lucky."

In the months after that, I completely understood what she meant and would take great offense when people would imply that I was "lucky," mainly because it usually meant they were asking about my finances—something they really had no business inquiring about. I would usually answer them honestly when they asked because I wanted them to know that the kids and I would be okay, that Brad and I had taken measures to ensure that we would be, and, in a way, hinting to them that they would be wise to do the same.

But I also knew that I *was* lucky in many ways. Because until that moment I didn't have a clear picture of how fortunate I was to have the people I'd had around me all of my life—my parents who were still my safety net and who I knew would never allow us to be left out in the cold. My sister who had helped us plan for a future we had no idea would be so hard.

And Brad who made sure he'd keep taking care of us all, even after his death.

As my financial picture began to develop, I was also made aware of a family fund that had been started on our behalf—a fund that, through the extreme generosity of our friends and family, had grown to a healthy amount. At one point, I found out that strangers had even contributed to the fund. And I'll never forget that moment.

I was walking in to meet Kristi, my mom, and a few other friends for lunch about a month after the accident. I was late, as usual, and slid into the booth in the middle of their conversation.

"Guess what?" Kristi said to me.

"What?"

"I just heard from a massage therapist about Brad."

My stomach plummeted and I could feel the color drain out of my face. For some reason, in the back of my mind, I had been wondering if I would find out something about my husband after his death—something I didn't want to know. Even though Brad had never given me any reason to suspect unfaithfulness, I feared that some other woman would show up at my door with two kids and tell me that he had had a second family across town.

I know. The weird widow mind.

When Kristi said that, I thought, "This is it. This is when I'm going to find out he's been having it off with some *massage therapist* and I can't believe Kristi is telling me this over Cobb salad and iced tea in front of our mother."

"What...what did she say?" I said slowly.

"She said that she wants to donate a day of massages to the family fund. Isn't that amazing?"

I'm sure my sigh of relief could be heard around the world.

The generosity of others amazed me. And since I had been brought up by a Southern mother who drummed into me that it doesn't matter if someone gives you a diamond or a dandelion, thank-you notes are a *must*, I needed to find out who had contributed. I went to my bank, certain that they would have some sort of record of who had deposited money into that account. But my request was met with a confused look by the clerk and: "Uh. We don't keep track of that sort of thing."

Great.

Trying to figure out who had added to the family fund became a huge source of stress for me. My mom was trying to ask her friends, most of whom were too humble to take credit for anything, and for weeks we tried to piece it together. As I think back on it, I find it completely ridiculous that immediately following my husband's death, *thank-you notes* were something that I was really worried about. I could understand how that acknowledgment was a must for any birthday, Christmas, wedding, or graduation present. But a *death*?

Don't we mourners have other things to do?

As with all things, there was a lesson to be learned. Since then, if I've found myself in the position of giving money or a gift to someone during a difficult time, I specifically write in the card, "And don't send me a thank-you note. I know you appreciate it." I take it upon myself to make sure the gift was received by checking my bank account to verify that the check was cashed. I'll ask other friends or family members if they saw a plant or bouquet being delivered. Never once do I think the person who is going through such a difficult time should need to muster the presence of mind to sit down and write a thank-you note.

Now, *that's* a gift.

With my mother looking after my kids and my finances being dealt with by my sister, I started looking for something that would just make me feel good in the moment. And what I stumbled upon as my immediate self-help cure made absolutely no sense to anyone else but me.

And that would be the almighty pedicure.

Before Brad died, I had had one pedicure in my entire life. But, with my mom at my house with the kids during those first weeks, if you listened closely, you could hear my tires screech to a halt at the sight of that one magical word.

Nails.

Now, I realize that not many people may understand my brand of coping. And that's okay; we all have to do what works for us. When I look back at how I dealt with the beginning stages of widowhood, I'm surprised that my toenails didn't just surrender and fall off. Because if I had a spare forty-five minutes without an appointment to go to or something pressing that needed to be done for the kids, you would find me in a chair, feet soaking, contemplating if I just wanted to vibrate or if the day was bad enough that I needed the back roller.

Initially, getting my feet "did" was about making a decision—nail color—and feeling like I'd accomplished something. And if I didn't like my choice, I could go back the next day and change it.

Very few decisions in life can be changed with a cotton ball and some alcohol. So that was a big comfort.

But, it was deeper than that. In most nail salons, they don't talk to you. They don't even ask you how you're doing, and if they do, they don't really expect you to answer. Any place else you go—the grocery store, the mall, even the hair salon—they'll ask you how you're doing and expect the perfunctory "I'm fine," because they don't want to hear, "Well, my dog pooped all over my house, the school bus never showed up this morning, and I spent the better part of my day talking to the phone company trying to get my dead husband's name off my caller ID so I don't make people immediately start crying every time I call."

I could sit there and have someone touch me in a nonsexual, noninvasive way—but touch me all the same. Contact with another human being was something that I wasn't getting enough of and something I craved. Just having someone rub my feet and then work their way up my calves relaxed me, and I could feel the pressure of widowed life being scrubbed away with the exfoliating salt.

Getting my nails done wasn't the only activity I turned to for instant gratification. In the weeks following Brad's death, when I wasn't sitting in a vibrating chair getting my toenails painted "Hooker in a Red Dress," my parents and I started working in home-improvement mode. Even though Kristi and I had figured out that I would probably be able to stay in my house, I wasn't sure if I *wanted* to.

I fluctuated between feeling like I could never leave all of the memories we had made there and wanting to get away from remembering things all the time, which could be agonizing in its own way. Not only that, but I itched with a nervous energy that couldn't be scratched. So working on the house not only provided me with mindless activity I desperately needed, but meeting with patient Realtors to look at houses also gave me something else to do. Both activities had me looking toward the future and trying to picture an environment I could live in with my new life.

So it was somewhat of a gift that Brad left me in a house that had been built in 1979, that we had half remodeled, and that still needed plenty of work.

Home improvement isn't such an abnormal thing at the beginning stages of widowhood. Of course, I didn't know that at the time since I didn't really know any other widows. But I've since learned that most of us go through what I like to call the "remodeling phase" of grief at some point or another.

I recognized this unofficial stage one night about two years after Brad died when I was having dinner with a widower who had lost his partner a month earlier. I asked him, "So are you going to stay in your loft?"

He replied, "Oh, yeah. And I'm going to repaint the entire interior, rip out the bathtub so I can have a huge shower, and put in new kitchen countertops."

I saw that crazed gleam in his eye, checked my watch, and thought, "Yup. Right on time."

I'm telling you, there's probably a newly widowed woman in Africa who is re-thatching her roof and rearranging her cot as I write this.

My first unintentional foray into widowed home renovation was about two weeks after Brad died. The funeral was over; everyone was prepared to go back to their normal lives; and I had no normal life to go back to. Thinking about the big picture was too overwhelming, so I was trying to just focus on what was right in front of me.

Literally.

I was sitting on my bed, blankly staring at the 1980s flower pattern that covered my bedroom walls. Now, it wasn't obnoxious paper, but it certainly wasn't my style. And although we had updated most of the house from its 1979 glory, our bedroom had been the last thing on our list.

I looked over and saw a little corner of the wallpaper coming up, and without even really thinking about it, I leaned over and pulled.

Rip.

There is no better therapy in the world than ripping paper off the wall. It's somewhat destructive and messy, and it offers instant satisfaction. If your spouse is currently suffering from a long, drawn-out illness, I highly recommend wallpapering a room now in a hideous pattern so you have something to do the week after the funeral.

After that initial wallpaper tear, I ran downstairs to get the stripping chemicals, old towels, my scraper, and the pressure washer I had used to drench the walls when I stripped the miles of wallpaper (three layers thick) on the main floor of the house a couple of years earlier. When my mother walked into my room, she found me completely focused on the disaster area I had created, surrounded by misplaced furniture and shards of ripped paper.

"*What* are you doing?" she asked.

And although I had started this project on a whim, it suddenly became clear to me why I was doing this.

Visions of long Colorado winters entered my mind, when the days are short and sunlight is at a premium. Knowing that I'd be stuck in the house with three small children, I needed to make this room my cave. My sanctuary. I wanted something bright and cheerful, comfortable and almost spa-like. I needed a place I could go where, when the kids had turned the rest of the house into something that should be featured on *Supernanny*, I could shut myself away in this one room.

I needed a space that was entirely "me," because the rest of the house was so completely "us."

"Making my room my own," I said, taking the scraper and concentrating on the edge of a seam. "I want to feel good when I walk in here."

She leaned against the doorframe, crossed her arms, and said thoughtfully, "Huh. I remember when Miss Kate lost her husband. The first thing she did was redecorate her bedroom."

And, for some reason, knowing that this might be a "widow thing" made me feel a little better.

As I moved forward with my bedroom project, my parents decided to step in and try to get the garage organized. As with most married couples, I had "allowed" my husband to have control over two areas of the house: the basement and the garage. The basement was completely decorated in Pittsburgh Steelers paraphernalia and housed a pool table that he was never in town to play on. And the garage showcased his pack-rat nature, evident in the hundreds of cardboard boxes that he kept around (and had never broken down, therefore taking up the most garage space), old tools, and used car parts that he had "just in case."

The garage drove me crazy. But I had learned my lesson about seven years into our marriage that I should never touch the man-land he had created. He was out of town on business, and I finally got frustrated enough to get in there and get rid of some stuff. I found a box that was still taped shut, a box we had actually moved twice and he had never opened. I was positive that if he hadn't looked at it in five years, he really didn't need the contents.

So I threw it away.

Two days later, he walked into the kitchen and said, "Sweetie? Have you seen that box in the garage that was labeled 'Dishes'? It had some spare cables in it that I need."

So I did what any wife would do.

I lied.

"Haven't seen it," I said, suddenly intent on scraping a carrot to the size of a toothpick.

"Huh," he said, puzzled, as he walked back out to the garage.

The other reason Brad liked to keep everything was that he grew up without a lot of money, which I think explains all of the boxes. As he used to tell me, "When you grow up with nothing, you save everything. Anything can be used for a project at school or church."

Let's be honest, Brad was a potential hoarder. In addition to holding on to odds and ends that may be needed for a project, he was a tinkerer and loved tasks of any kind. He was endlessly ripping apart radios, computers, and cars just so he could put them back together again and watch them work. Sometimes it was like living with a guy from *Mythbusters*. Our lawnmower had been a garage-sale find that had stopped working for its original owner, who had gotten frustrated and immediately bought a new one. Using a salvaged part and a little bit of elbow grease, Brad had that lawnmower working in about fifteen minutes.

So because he was what I call a handy hoarder, our garage was filled with not only piles of boxes, parts, and the standard tools everyone else has, but also a buffer, table saw, pipe bender, and large air compressor, none of which I knew how to use.

My parents spent hours breaking down boxes to throw them

away and organizing the tool bench until, when I walked into the garage, I didn't recognize it.

"There's a floor in here!" I exclaimed. "And...surfaces! I had no idea!"

Little did I know that in a few days, those discarded boxes would completely change how my mother and I interacted with each other.

We were sitting down at the kitchen table and watching the kids through the French doors as they played in the backyard because they were still seemingly oblivious to the fact that our world had completely fallen apart. I was exhausted for many reasons, one of which was the wallpaper project I had started in my bedroom that still had to be finished.

"I think I'm going to call a painter," I said, my eyelids at half-mast, my chin resting in my hands. "I just don't think I can take on painting that entire room by myself."

"Did you finish with the wallpaper?" my mom asked.

"Almost," I said. "I need to do the bathroom, but I have to box up the stuff that's on the counter in there."

And then I said something that I would come to regret, even years later.

"Isn't it funny," I said, "how I need a box to put all of my bathroom stuff in, and now I don't have any?"

Meaning it as a joke, and actually thinking that Brad was probably laughing at me from the Great Beyond for getting rid of all of his precious boxes, my mother completely missed the irony in my voice (or maybe I was too tired to have any) and thought I was bitching about the fact that they had "overstepped."

"You *told* us to get rid of those boxes!" she cried, standing up from her chair, her eyes blazing behind her wire-rimmed glasses. "I asked you, and you told us to do it!"

How upset she had suddenly gotten threw me for a loop.

Since my mother is not one to pounce on me for any reason, I initially thought she was kidding. And since I was just joking around, I could not figure out why she was reacting this way. But one thing I knew for sure: I was in no mood to deal with it.

"I *did* ask you to get rid of the boxes," I said, immediately shifting from exhausted to completely irritated. "What's the problem? I was just making a joke!"

"No you weren't! You think we did the wrong thing! You think that we did something you didn't want us to do. I can't do anything right with you!"

"I can't do anything right with you, either!" I fired back. "I can't say anything right to anyone! I have to watch everything I say now. Don't you understand? I've *lost* the person I can be the most honest with! He's gone and I have no one else. *He* was the one I could tell everything to. *He* was the one I could fight with and still know that everything would be okay. *He* was the one I could be completely honest with because he was the one who knew me...the *real* me!"

I don't know why all of that occurred to me in that moment. In fact, I don't even remember thinking it before I said it. But the second those words were out of my mouth, I crumpled back into my breakfast-room chair in a big lump.

And then I said something that inflicted instant hurt on my mother.

"It's time for you to move back to your own house. I need to be alone."

She gave me one hard, weepy look and left the room. I could hear the sounds of packing going on in the basement guest room as she threw all of her stuff together. I watched as she walked up the stairs with her bags, walked down the hall, and walked right out the front door without saying a word to me.

It's hard to realize this when you're in the heat of battle, but we tend to lash out at the people closest to us when life hands us something we can't handle. To everyone on the outside, I looked like I was behaving normally and progressing with life because that's what I let them see. I couldn't afford to show my emotional hand to just anyone because then I ran the risk of them saying, "That woman is crazy and I'm better off without her."

That fight over nothing important had allowed me to let go, get angry, and finally yell at someone, someone safe, because deep down I knew that I would never lose my mother. I knew that her love would force her to come back and never abandon me. And I think there was a part of her that felt the same way. She was scared and confused and didn't know her place in my life anymore, just as I didn't know my place in my own life. I was irritated that she got mad over something so trivial when, in those weeks right after Brad's death, I felt like I had earned a pass on anyone getting upset with me. It didn't occur to me that I might have been *her* someone safe. That she was letting her emotions go because she knew that in the end we would be okay.

But in that moment, I was scared. Everything had changed, and the life and everything else I had counted on were no longer a sure thing. And that day, when my mother walked out the door, I was terrified that by finally letting go and showing someone my true self, I had just had my first relationship casualty.

Thanks to a heaping serving of grief, with a side of cardboard.

10

In hindsight, I really should have seen it coming. I mean, you put even the closest of relationships together physically and combine that with an extremely emotional situation, and someone is bound to erupt.

One just has to hope that the eruption is the size of a small science project, and not Mount Vesuvius.

I've learned so many things since then about why the cardboard incident happened. Years later, we tried talking about it, attempting to figure out what exactly went wrong.

"We were...we were..." my mom tried to verbalize.

"We were both nuts," I said succinctly and she instantly agreed.

For me, it was the simple fact that I didn't know what to do with myself. Everything was so raw and right at the surface. There was no buffer from the outside influences that seemed determined to bring me to my knees.

In my mom's case, it was the simple fact that she was dealing with what I call "the triple whammy."

My mother was tired. Emotionally and physically, she had been worn down until there was almost nothing left. Not only was she dealing with the fact that she had lost a son-in-law that she loved, but she was also watching her own child reel from the loss and worrying about how her grandchildren would fare, as well. And I could understand that since I was working on my own personal double whammy of missing my husband and worrying about my children. Working to do her best to take care of all of us, while trying to sort through her own grief and confusion about why this had happened, had my mother feeling like the rest of us—at the edge of jumping off an emotional cliff.

"Where's Nana?" Haley asked as she breezed in through the back door on the way to her room the day that my mom left.

"She had to go home," I said, worried that Haley would feel suddenly abandoned by the one sane adult she had living in the house.

"Oh. Okay!" And off she went.

Nana had to go home? I looked around at my empty breakfast room until my eyes settled on the scene in the backyard of Sarah and Michael trying to get their chubby little legs to cooperate and climb the huge pine tree next to the porch.

Oh God. They're all my responsibility.

The house suddenly seemed huge and made me feel lost. My bedroom was a wreck. The whole house was a wreck. I looked at the pile of bills on the counter and knew that someone would have to take care of them. Me. The lawn outside looked like it was growing right before my eyes, and I realized that I didn't know how to mow. The stove seemed to mock me from the corner as if it were saying, "You idiot. Now that you've kicked her out, you're going to have to learn how to use me again."

What in the hell have I done?

I was all alone, which, for some reason, reminded me of when each of the kids was born. At the time, my parents were still living in Louisiana and my mother would always fly in a few days before the due date of each one of the kids and stay for a few weeks after. She would get up with me in the middle of the night, allow me to take some breaks to go on walks, and generally just be there when I needed a shoulder for a good hormonal cry.

But then it would be time for her to go back home, and every time that day came, I felt afraid and unsure if I had it in me to deal with everything on my own. And it usually took a little while, but eventually the routine would come and everything would seem like it had always been that way. And, I had Brad then.

When she left that day, I finally had to take the deep breath that had been catching in my throat for weeks. It was all up to me now. Toddlers won't leave you alone just because your world has come to an end. Dirty diapers still happen; bedtimes need to be recognized; and eventually they all want to eat. So I needed to go to the grocery store or at least look up the phone number for a Pizza Hut.

And life would have to go on.

I've often wondered how Brad would have handled it all if I was the one who died and he was left to take care of things. To begin with, he would have had a heck of a time finding any sort of paperwork upon my demise because I did all of the filing. When I think back, I could have totally taken him to the cleaners and had a very healthy online poker problem, and he would have been none the wiser until I was six feet under.

I know for a fact that he didn't know where the life-insurance paperwork was (because I wasn't sure *I* even knew and I'm the one who filed it). Unfortunately, if he couldn't find that paperwork, he wouldn't have been able to locate his passport (which was filed with it) so he wouldn't have even had the option of skipping the country once things got hard.

I'm not saying I would ever have done that. But at least I knew the option was there.

To be honest, I don't even know if he knew how to get into our bank account. He could have been out there panhandling with a sign that said, "I have money in an account but I can't get to it because my wife took the password to the grave. God bless."

The sign could have been made from the cardboard that my parents hadn't gotten rid of because he wouldn't have let them clean out the garage.

As with most things, time and distance allowed my mother and me to heal, and although we were cautious around each other for a while, the bond between us eventually returned. We swept it under the emotional rug, which is not something I always recommend, but at a time when everyone was in such distress and it was hard to have a constructive conversation about *anything*, it just seemed like the right thing to do.

Eventually our relationship clicked back into place. I would call when I needed a break, and my parents would graciously help me out. I would take the kids over for family dinners, hoping that if I tried hard enough, we would turn back into a family. My life started getting into a routine because with the kids, I really didn't have a choice.

And I finally found a box to pack up my bathroom so that I could finish redecorating my bedroom.

But before the painters could come, I knew I had to do a little housekeeping. A little widow housekeeping. The furniture needed to be rearranged so that I could make the bedroom into the room I had envisioned for myself.

And that meant moving an armoire into my closet.

And *that* meant cleaning some things out.

And that meant going through something I wasn't sure I was ready for.

⁊⁊

Brad was the most generous person I knew, and I could almost hear him saying, "There is a man out there who might have a job interview or something, but can't afford to buy new clothes. Give this stuff to someone who needs it." So, instead of holding on to his things indefinitely, I decided that I should just get it done.

At that point, when I knew I was going to have a bad day, I would try and compact everything horrible on my to-do list into one twelve-hour period. In other words, if I was going to have a shitty day, I was going to have a *really* shitty day. And when those days would happen, I would do other shitty things that I had been putting off so that if by chance I came across a good day or at least a day I could successfully get through, I wouldn't have big, shitty things looming over my head. I would have already finished them on another shitty day.

I'll give you an example.

On a day two months after Brad died, I had to go down to the Air Force Academy for a memorial service for graduates who had died in 2007, so I stopped on the way at the impound lot that held Brad's motorcycle. Brad's smashed, broken motorcycle that, even though I knew was not at fault—that Brad was the one who was driving and in control—I secretly blamed for the accident. The motorcycle had been brought to the lot in Castle Rock, just south of my house, after the police and our insurance company were finished with their investigation of the accident.

And I had received a letter that said I needed to go to the lot and sign paperwork to release it for demolition.

I walked into the impound office all dressed up for the memorial service that was about to take place in Colorado Springs and was greeted by two cheerful women in their thirties. I handed them my paperwork and said, "I'm here to pay this bill and release this motorcycle for demolition."

"Okay!" said the brunette, as the blond peered over her shoulder and looked at the sheet I'd just handed her. "Let me take a look at this."

"That'll be $250 for the demolition and the time we've stored it," she said. "Do you want to go out there and make sure that everything you need is out of it?"

The blond nudged the brunette hard. They made eye contact and the blond ever-so-slightly shook her head.

And I knew that she knew what had happened.

I cleared my throat and tried to ignore the familiar prickling behind my eyes that meant a meltdown was imminent.

"No, thank you. Here's my credit card."

I cried all the way to the Springs, but I knew that I had done the right thing. Thank God I hadn't saved that task for a day that had the potential to be good. Getting closure on the motorcycle was hard, and I had been dreading the Academy memorial service since the day I had received the invitation, so it made sense to just get them both over with on the same day. So, I let myself cry and fixed the makeup on my face with my emergency "cry it all out" kit after I pulled up to the Academy. I took a deep breath, stepped out of my car, and made my way to the clear glass doors of the building.

"Want me to go with you?" my mother had asked me before I left.

"No, that's okay. I'm sure it's just a little reception. I think I'd rather go alone," I said with false confidence.

My mother gave me a doubtful look, but she didn't argue. When I think back on it, I kind of wish she had. Because what I was about to witness was the most beautiful and horrific thing I had ever seen.

And I wish someone else had been there to experience it with me.

The Air Force Academy had always been one of my favorite places to visit because I had so many fun memories of it—meeting Brad, going to dances, attending his graduation, and going to football games. After the rigorous training he had been through, Brad was less of a fan and it took him a few years before he truly enjoyed going back. I think that on every road and in every field he could envision his eighteen-year-old self running, doing push-ups, and generally getting berated by upperclassmen.

I get it. I mean, if my college experience had been comprised of a bunch of guys yelling in my face and poking at me with weaponry, I probably wouldn't have been all that excited to go back, either.

But on that beautiful fall day two months after Brad's death, I walked into the building, which had been set up with formal-looking tables decorated in blue and white and a banquet table along one wall with coffee and snacks. People were milling around, some in uniform and some not, and after I checked in, I immediately made my way over to the table to which I had been assigned. I was in no mood to mingle as everyone else was and I stared down at my plate, hoping no one would talk to me.

"Ma'am?" I heard a female voice next to me. "I'm Cadet Gray. Welcome."

"Thank you," I said.

She sat down and I realized that she had actually been assigned to keep me company—that each table had at least two or three cadets making conversation with the other attendees. While this was incredibly thoughtful of the Academy, I couldn't help but wonder if the cadets there were being punished for something.

I mean, who would actually *volunteer* to go keep a bunch of grievers company?

Cadet Gray was as sweet as she could be, talking to me about current Academy life and telling me her plans for the future. For a few minutes, she did a great job of distracting me from the real reason I was there.

That was, until she said, "I'm an astronautical engineering major."

I swallowed hard. "You're kidding. So was my husband. Our first station was Cape Canaveral. He worked on the Titan."

Her face lit up. "Oh, I would love to go there! That's my first choice."

It was bittersweet, talking to her about life at the Cape, a life that both seemed like yesterday and a lifetime ago. Her hope for the future was written all over her face—kind of like another cadet I had met when I was just eighteen years old.

The crowd suddenly started to move and, to my surprise, people began getting up from their tables and making their way outside to awaiting buses. "Where are we going?" I asked Cadet Gray.

"To the memorial service," she said.

"I thought this *was* the memorial service."

"Oh no. That's over near the chapel."

Like a sheep to the slaughter, I followed the rest of the herd and got on the bus. It drove us from the building just outside the school grounds and dropped us off at the impressive USAFA Cadet Chapel. I followed everyone down a set of outside stairs to bleachers that had been set up just below. Another cadet handed me a program and, bewildered, I sat down next to an older couple. The woman gave me a friendly smile and said, "Who are you here for?"

"My husband."

And then that look of pity. "Oh, honey. You're so young. We're here for my daddy, but it was his time."

Suddenly all of the current cadets began pouring onto the grounds, rigid in their lines, keeping in time with their squadrons. They all stopped at the same moment, each group standing in a perfect square. At first, I didn't understand what was going on and I could hear someone up front announcing a name and then one cadet from out in the field shouting something back.

It took me at least ten names and a look at the program to figure out that they were announcing each cadet that had died that year in order of age and that one person from the squadron they had once belonged to was yelling back, "Absent, *sir!*"

I looked wildly around at the people surrounding me. Not only were there family members of those who had been lost, but tourists had actually lined the wall above us near the chapel so that they could watch the show. I began to panic and felt my breathing grow shallow. They weren't really going to *do* this, were they? Announce my husband's name and then the fact that he was permanently absent? I wanted to run screaming away from that field, away from this public display of pain, into my car and, frankly, to the closest bar I could find.

But having taken the bus there, I was kind of stuck.

I opened the program to see where Brad fell in the lineup, hoping it would be sooner rather than later and that once I heard his name, I would no longer feel the anxiety I knew was written all over my face. Page after page, I flipped through the book, until I found Brad's name and the picture he'd had taken as a senior just before he graduated. His smile. The light in his eyes. The look that was positive that an amazing life was just beginning. The picture that was on the last page of the program, which meant he was one of the youngest cadets to die that year.

And that's when I began to cry.

I cried through the rest of the names. I cried when they announced his. I cried when a group of cadets on the far side of the field stood under the American flag and raised their guns and fired, saluting the officers who had died. I cried at the beauty and ugliness of life shown in this ceremony that I wish I had brought my mother to. Because I knew that when I got home, I wouldn't have words to describe it.

"How could you not have warned me?" I ranted at Brad's roommate, Steve, that night on the phone.

"I thought you knew!" he said defensively. "They do that every homecoming weekend!"

"How in the world would I have known that?" I said. "I didn't meet Brad until after homecoming!"

"Well, I didn't know," he said.

I took a deep breath. "Tell you what. If you know of any other little surprises the military might have in store for me, you have to warn me, okay?"

"Deal."

Later I realized that even if Steve had cautioned me, nothing would have eased the pain of that moment. At that point in time, I was still trying to plan my grief and save myself from unexpected moments of hurt, something that, really, no one has the power to do. I didn't know that grief would sneak up on me without warning six months, a year, three years out. I didn't know that loss would become my constant companion and something that I would just have to make peace with. That hurt would sometimes be the only reason I knew I was still in the land of the living.

And that time would be the only thing that would ease it at all.

So there I was, a few weeks later, facing another shitty day.

I knew that burying his ashes wouldn't be easy. And I knew that cleaning out Brad's closet wouldn't be, either. So like the day I demolished his motorcycle and attended the memorial service from hell, I decided to get them both over within one twelve-hour period.

After the urn that I had ordered came in, Brad's ashes were finally ready to be buried. And even though I had been unclear about a lot of my husband's final wishes, when I knew he wasn't going to make it, there was only one place that came to mind as his final resting place.

I remember turning to my mom at the funeral home while the chaos of planning was going on around me and saying, "I know that it would be more convenient to bury him close to home. But there is a place I just can't get out of my mind."

My mom looked me straight in the eye and said, "Buffalo Creek."

Buffalo Creek, Colorado, is a town so small that it's what my grandmother would call "a wide spot in the road." Settled in the 1870s, Buffalo Creek has the Platte River winding through it, and the area has some of the prettiest properties in Colorado. One of the most vivid memories I have of the beginning of our relationship is of Brad and I taking a drive up there with my mother in her convertible during the summer of 1995, before my parents were transferred back down south. My mother had befriended an old, widowed innkeeper in town and wanted to go up and check on her. So we went along for the ride.

I have a picture of the two of us, smiling from ear to ear and so much in love, that was taken that day on the wide front porch of the Blue Jay Inn just before we got engaged. I'm sitting on the enormous porch swing, and he's standing behind me with his hands protectively on my shoulders as if to say, "She's mine now." That picture was blown up, matted, and signed by everyone who attended our wedding in 1996.

Buffalo Creek still has an actual general store (where you can buy anything from cake mix to tires) and a church so old that it looks like it was made from a Lincoln Log set. The church's only source of heat is from an enormous stone fireplace, and it had just gotten plumbing about two years before Brad died. The town is rural, clearly, and can get some serious winter weather, so many of the residents don't stay year-round and the church only has services during the summer.

The cemetery there overlooks the river, a valley, and a winding mountain road that is popular with motorcyclists.

Since Brad was such a country boy at heart and loved the mountains, I couldn't bear the idea of putting him in a plot in the middle of the city. I used to joke with him that if he didn't behave, someday I would put him in a cemetery I had seen about twenty minutes north of our house that was located in the middle of the parking lot of a Chick-fil-A.

I'm not kidding.

Now that I think about it, considering how old the kids were when he died, they probably would have been just as happy to get chicken nuggets and a toy as we waved to him on our way through the drive-through.

My mother pulled some strings because, even though you were technically not supposed to be buried in that old cemetery unless you were a member of the church, many people in Buffalo Creek knew her from when she had helped take care of the innkeeper before she died several years earlier. So, after talking to the church elders and getting their approval (and paying the one-time two-hundred-fifty-dollar fee for a plot. Seriously, what a steal), we found ourselves heading up to Buffalo Creek to bury Brad's ashes in the urn that had taken me fifty catalogs to find.

The only problem had been that we weren't really sure how to get this done.

I mean, this place was in the middle of nowhere and pretty "old school." At a church without a full-time cleric or central heat, what are the chances that they would have official gravediggers?

As a joke, I asked my mom, "So, are we supposed to just bring a shovel and bury him ourselves like a pet parakeet?"

The answer to that question turned out to be a "yes." It was also suggested that we bring a pick-ax just in case we hit some granite.

I guess I'm lucky.

With that new bathroom, the church elders could have just told us to flush him.

So, on that day, I organized my parents, my kids, my sister, and her family to trek up to the mountains and lay Brad to rest. Everything felt so surreal. I mean, nobody thinks "burial" when they think "family outing." We looked like we were heading up to the mountains for a picnic. And there's something a little odd about carrying your husband to his final resting place while your father and brother-in-law trail behind carrying shovels and picks.

I could faintly hear the sound of banjos and someone blowing in a jug.

Having told the kids that we were going up to bury Dad's turtle shell, I got an enthusiastic "K!" from Haley, a puzzled look from Michael who I'm sure was trying to figure out how Dad's turtle shell got into that tiny box (ever try explaining cremation to a three-year-old?), and a demand for Goldfish from eighteen-month-old Sarah, who seemed to have no idea what was going on.

They ran around playing tag in the woods of the cemetery, distracted by my nephews, Brian and John, who were four and

two at the time, while my dad and Sean did their best to dig into the side of the mountain in order to bury Brad low enough that some woodland creature wouldn't come along and dig him back up again. Then we all pushed the dirt on top of him and stood there in awkward silence, wondering if someone should say something profound and who that someone might be.

Because whoever he was, apparently we forgot to invite him.

"Hey, kids!" I yelled. "Get over here! Let's squish Daddy's turtle shell!"

When Brad stretched out on the floor, it was always a game to my children to come over and sit on him as hard as they could. Usually some tickling would follow, but that day I was working with what I had.

Haley, Michael, and Sarah came running over with my nephews behind them, giggling as they sat on the mound of dirt that covered Brad's final resting place. They mashed that dirt down with their little behinds, and just for a second, I felt like I had done the right thing.

We parted ways at the church, with Kristi and Sean taking their boys to their home downtown and my parents driving the kids and me back to our house at the southernmost tip of Denver. The hour-and-a-half drive seemed endless with the lump in my throat so massive the saliva almost couldn't get around it. My whole body radiated anger at the situation that I still couldn't believe we were in, and that translated into more nervous energy that didn't like sitting in a car that long.

So, when we finally pulled into the driveway of my house, I ran up the stairs with a box of Hefty bags, straight into my bedroom, and flung open my closet door.

"If this day is going to suck anyway," I thought, looking at Brad's clothes with tears rolling down my face, "I might as well get this over with."

I know how I am. I know how I operate. And I knew then that if I didn't at least make an attempt to get rid of some of Brad's things, it would reach the point of becoming too damn hard. And I would never be able to part with any of it.

I tore through that closet with impossible energy, filling bag after bag. Doing my best to separate a few pieces that I would either like to keep for myself, pass on to friends, or pass on to family members. I dripped sweat and tears as I worked away in the August heat. Piles of T-shirts that he wore with his BDUs during his Air Force years, detailing the Titan projects he had worked on. *One for me, one for his parents, one for storage, donate.* The concert T-shirt from one of my aunt's gigs as a blues pianist that Brad thought was hysterical because the cartoon they had drawn of her made her boobs enormous. *Give to Sean.* Steelers T-shirts, sweatshirts, fleece pullovers...divided between my family and his so that they could wear them during games and think of him.

I kept saying to myself, "The clothes aren't him, the clothes aren't him," but every shirt had a memory and every pair of shoes looked like he had just stepped out of them. I loaded it all into the back of Brad's Chevy truck and took off for Goodwill, ignoring the offers of help from my parents and feeling like this was something I needed to do alone.

And as I handed over all thirteen black plastic bags to the attendant, I felt a mixture of relief that I had gotten that excruciating task completed and a pain that I can't explain because between burying Brad's ashes and getting rid of his clothes, I had just given away a part of myself.

Three weeks later, when the bedroom project was finally finished,

I had a room with buttercream walls and brown and turquoise bedding. I had installed shelves on the wall opposite my bed that held some of my favorite pictures of Brad and the kids so that they would be the first things I would see when I woke up. I bought new lamps on consignment, and the lampshades had the faintest leopard print on them, something that Brad would have hated and a sure sign that I was starting to embrace my new independence a little.

And on one wall, I had two antique flashcards framed that, when put together, displayed a phrase I tried to remind myself to do every day.

"Play Again."

I sat on my bed and listened to the kids scream and run around on the main floor of my house and smiled, knowing that all I had to do was shut my door. On the days that we were snowed in, I could set them up with crafts and a cartoon downstairs while I buried myself under my down comforter and turned on a mindless, black-and-white movie in my room. Thick towels without stains were waiting for me in my bathroom for the nights when I would stand in the shower and let the tears mix with the water streaming down my face. For a moment, it felt good to know that I had made the space mine, all mine.

Then I looked over at the other side of the bed, the one that had been empty since July.

It's mine, I thought silently, reality settling in.

Just mine.

"I'm so glad you got your bedroom finished!" my mom said, as she admired my handiwork a few days later. "Now you can relax a little."

Relax? Why in the world would I do *that?*

After a few days of sitting still in my new bedroom and deciding that sitting still wasn't something I could do anymore, it occurred to me that the best time to remodel the kids' bathroom was *right now.* Every time I went in there and saw the chipped countertops and flooring that was the original, yellowed linoleum installed in 1979, it drove me crazy.

And let's face it: all of this remodeling made me feel like I was taking control of *something* in my life.

I learned a very valuable lesson while working on their bathroom. If what you're looking for is control, don't hire a contractor. Because nothing will make you feel more like your life is spiraling into the abyss than babysitting someone who said it would only take three days to finish a project, and then three weeks later, you're still tripping over the contents of that bathroom that are spilling out into your hallway.

When the bathroom was finally finished, I took a good, hard look at my family room. Brad had a sixty-inch big-screen TV that took up an entire wall of that room. And I'm not talking about one of those fancy-schmancy flat screens. I'm talking about the monster rear-projector that sits about three feet away from the wall. It was like having an IMAX screen in the comfort of my own home. When my mom came to visit, she had to take off her trifocals because she would get motion sickness just watching HGTV. But this TV had been great for family movie nights, and I'll never forget watching the breast-pump instruction video with Brad on that thing right after we'd had Haley.

I'm telling you, nothing makes you feel more inferior as a woman than a sixty-inch boob producing what looks like ten gallons of milk in one sitting.

The day Brad bought that TV, we were young and still childless, and I had just been awarded a promotion at work. It was a

Friday afternoon and I couldn't wait to get the weekend started, celebrating with our neighbors over a few beers. I struggled through rush-hour traffic, and when I turned the corner onto our street, there was an enormous delivery truck in our driveway.

"What the—?"

I walked in the front door of the house and down the stairs to the basement. There was Brad, instructing two delivery men on where to center this monstrosity that looked expensive and—not to sound like the bitchy wife—that I hadn't given my consent to buy.

"Congratulations on your promotion!" Brad exclaimed as he gestured to the TV.

I stared at him. "You've got to be kidding me."

"Well, I know how much you love movies. So I thought this would be fun!"

As you can imagine, I had a hard time finding words to thank Brad in that moment for spending my raise before I'd even earned it. I later found out, years after he died, that he and his buddy from across the street, who also happened to have the day off from work that Friday, had gone to look at electronics that morning just for the heck of it when this beautiful sixty-inch TV caught his eye.

"I told him not to buy it," Rod said, laughing at the memory. "I told him you'd be pissed. Then we went out to lunch and had a few beers. Next thing I knew, we were standing at the checkout counter arranging when the damn thing should be delivered."

This story made sense to me for a couple of reasons: Brad's motto in life—through childhood, the military, and marriage—had been "it's better to ask forgiveness than permission." And I never knew what that man would come up with after a pitcher of beer.

Those two things together were a dangerous combination.

Anyway, I just knew that it would make me feel better and grieve less if I got a new TV. I mean, nothing says "healthy grieving" like an expensive trip to Best Buy. The problem with this little project was that I didn't have Brad around to research all of the options for me and I am electronically impaired. So I enlisted the help of Candice's husband, Rob, who, as it turned out, was my kind of shopper.

He researched televisions for a few days, and then we took a little field trip to make my purchase. And as we stood in front of an entire wall of flat-screen TVs, Rob turned to me and said, "Now, I could tell you all of the data I have come up with, but I know the way Candice shops, so I'm just going to ask you a few questions. What size do you want?"

"Forty-seven inch."

"Do you want a flat black frame around it or glossy black?"

"Flat."

He pointed up to the wall and said, "There's your TV."

Done.

As I'd learned with remodeling the bedroom, you can't buy new without getting rid of the old. So I called the church and donated Brad's old TV the day the new one was to arrive. I never thought I'd be sad to see that old eyesore go, that giant black box that I could never seem to effectively arrange furniture around and that was, I thought, a constant source of overstimulation for the kids when they were little and made them cranky. The young wife in me wanted to give it a healthy kick as the men struggled to get it out the door and into an awaiting truck. But the new widow wanted to cling to all of the old things, anything that Brad had bought and loved, even if she had hated it.

On the day they hauled Brad's pride and joy away, I walked back into the house and stared up at the new TV that had been mounted on the wall. It was sleek, modern, and took up much less room. For a moment I wondered what Brad would think of it, and then I suddenly felt like I wasn't alone. It was almost as if I could hear Brad's voice whispering in my ear.

"That new TV is way too small."

11

I n addition to trying to take control of something, *anything* in my life when I felt so helpless, I was really diving into home-improvement mode because I was suffering from what I like to think of as manic confusion. I wanted things done, and I wanted them done *now*. The problem was that I wasn't really sure what *needed* to be done, so I focused on the things I could see.

I had always wondered, how I would react to extreme stress. Up until Brad's death, I'd led a pretty low-key existence, and I had always wondered, if something completely life-altering should happen, would I stay in bed for years or would I feel a sudden urge to find a career that would land me on Barbara Walters' *Ten Most Fascinating People* list? Would I hire a nanny or would I be the most devoted mother in the entire world? Would I balloon up to five hundred pounds or shrink down to nothing?

Well, I didn't get down to nothing. But I came pretty darn close.

Being the impatient person that I am, I didn't want to buy into that whole theory that only time will heal. I'd show those stinkin' experts! I'd find a new career, remodel my entire house, sell it, move someplace new, and find the perfect man to settle down with—and I'd do it *now*. And concerned during the weeks immediately following Brad's death with the fact that I felt I wasn't grieving right, in my widow mind the solution to that problem was simple.

I would try my best to not grieve at all.

The denial that I was in, which surfaced in the form of manic confusion, made me want to do everything I could to make the people around me feel comfortable so they wouldn't drop me like a hot potato. That meant nailing a smile on my face, answering with a chipper "Fine!" when asked how I was doing, and generally pushing everything I had bubbling inside me way below the surface until I was alone and could let it go.

And I thought for sure that if I started emotionally running as fast as I could, the grief wouldn't be able to catch me. I'd get this show back on the road! People will invent an action figure in my honor: Wonder Widow, complete with black catsuit and Kleenex in one hand, paintbrush in the other.

So, in another attempt to channel some of this energy, I started exercising.

Now, this isn't a bad thing. It's a healthy way to de-stress. But the way I went about it was a little excessive. After walking or jogging for an hour, I'd then head to my local gym and work out endlessly. I think I went through two pairs of tennis shoes in three months. Now, in my defense, I *was* training to be Wonder Widow, and a three-baby bulge does not look good in a catsuit. But even I knew I was going a little overboard.

"Uh, I think you need to slow down on the gym a little bit," my personal trainer said to me at one point. "Haven't you been here twice today?"

For the first time, I could understand what anorexics went through. I had lost complete control of most things in my life, but I *could* control how I was eating and what I was eating. Proud of myself for whittling down my food consumption to about one meal a day (and spending at least an hour a day, every day, working out), I proudly watched the pounds fall off. I would feed the kids their meals and sit and pick at my plate (about the same portion as theirs). Since they were so young, they didn't think about how I wasn't really eating anything. And if I knew that I would be meeting up with friends or family during the day, I saved my meal so that I ate it in front of them.

"You look amazing!" I heard constantly, fueling my unhealthy habits. "How are you losing all of this weight?"

"Oh, you know, just eating healthier," I lied. "And walking a little."

It's interesting to me that, during the worst time in my life, I received so many compliments about how I'd never looked better. Thoughts about dating were on my mind, and I felt sure that by doing what I was doing, I would find someone who would make all of this "alone" business go away.

"*This* will make me attractive to someone," I thought. "Who needs grief? I'll be thin and pretty and desirable, and *someone* will want me."

It wasn't just the stress of everything that was going on, although that did leave very little room in my stomach for food. It was more than that. It was almost like that gnawing feeling in my stomach was keeping me awake and functioning. Everything in my life suddenly felt so dreamlike (or nightmare-like) that I had a hard time believing it was actually happening to me. But that constant feeling of hunger was like my stomach giving me a wake-up pinch and confirming what I still didn't believe.

Of course, eventually the pounds came back. Months later, as I started coping better, I started eating more until I was right back where I started. And years later, frustrated by my weight gain, I told my sister that I should go back on the "diet" I was on after Brad died.

"Catherine," Kristi said to me in a firm, mom-like tone. "You were *sick*. Don't you remember how upset your stomach was all the time and how you couldn't digest anything right? You can't do that again."

Losing weight wasn't the only thing I used as a distraction in those first few blurry months of widowhood. In the middle of what I thought of as self-improvement mode, dropping four sizes in about three months and trying to make my imperfect house and life as perfect as I possibly could, I embarked on yet another very common phase of widowhood.

Retail therapy.

Now, some overachieving widows can also combine this with the remodeling phase. I chose to spread the two out a little.

But that's really a personal decision.

Retail therapy is an interesting phenomenon. How does it make any sense to be thinking one minute about how much you miss your husband and then have a realization that you'd be a much happier person if you could find the perfect red purse? For me it was almost like busywork, because I didn't actually keep a lot of the stuff that I purchased. I would buy tons of junk, decide to keep one thing, and then return the rest the next day.

I know for a fact that salespeople in certain stores *hated* to see me walk through the door because they knew I carried with me the false hope of a good sale. They'd see me come in with a crazed gleam in my eye, receipt and merchandise in hand, the day after I'd blessed them with a three-hundred-dollar purchase, and they knew this would require them to go through a very complicated return procedure because I'd used a coupon.

A couple of years after Brad died, I was having dinner with

two new, young widows, and we looked each other in amazement when we realized that we had all done the same thing.

"I realized at one point that I'd spent five hundred dollars at Banana Republic in about an hour," Krista said.

"That's okay," said Leslie. "I bought some Steve Madden boots yesterday, and I just figured out I don't have the right jeans to go with them. I'm taking care of that tomorrow."

"I've got you both beat," I said. "I bought a sports car that none of my children can fit in and it's rear-wheel drive. Perfect for a mother of three in Colorado."

Months earlier, in the throes of retail therapy, I had found myself casually researching new cars—not something to replace the trusty old minivan, just something fun that I could drive around when I didn't have the kids with me. I had thought about buying a used (*very* used) BMW that would make me feel like a young woman in her thirties, not a widow with three kids. For weeks I searched on Craigslist, trying to find something cute within my meager price range, and then one day as I was searching under BMW, I stopped my scrolling and fixated on a car.

A Mazda RX8.

"I would love to get an RX8," Brad had said to me two years earlier when he was shopping for a new car.

"You've got to be kidding me," I snorted. "It's rear-wheel drive. What are you going to do in the winter? Walk to work?"

"My Trans Am in college was rear-wheel drive and I did just fine," he argued.

"It doesn't even have a backseat!" I countered. "And the trunk looks too small for all three of the kids to fit in."

The fact that, four months after his death, I was looking for a new car online and my search did not involve the words "Mazda" or "RX8" in it and that *that* was the car that popped up—the irony of this was not lost on me.

Brad wanted me to have that car.

I brought Kristi with me, and we drove up to the Ford dealership that had listed it, about thirty minutes north of Denver. The moment we sat in those bucket seats, I knew I wanted it. It was so low to the ground that we sat beneath even the sedans we passed on the road. I shifted through the gears and whipped around corners, and I felt like I was in a life-sized video game. I felt a sense of freedom I hadn't experienced in years as I looked around the car and realized that there was no room for a sippy cup. No space for plush toys. It could be a place—a mobile place—that was mine. All mine.

I don't know if Kristi sensed my temporary euphoria while we were taking that test drive. She must have. Because, even though I consider my immediate family some of the most money-conscious people on the planet, when we parked the car back at the dealership, she looked at me and said, "Get it. Just get it."

Then she followed up with, "But as soon as you write that check, I'm taking all that life-insurance money and putting it away for you."

Good plan.

For a while, that car was the best therapy I could have had. It was where I could go and just pretend for a minute that my life was not actually happening. I could drive around and forget for seconds at a time that I had three kids at home who were in the throes of toddlerhood. I felt empowered that I had bought that car completely on my own. I would listen to music I liked, turning it up so loud that it would almost drown out the thoughts in my head. And the tinted windows would show nothing at a stoplight if I just needed to sit there and cry for a minute.

I do think that sometimes my retail-therapy phase alarmed Kristi a little bit, but she handled it really well. Even though she had been in the financial industry for years, for the first time she really had a ringside seat to what happens when life catapults you to a place you've never been before. And this wasn't something that could be easily explained, like downsizing or losing a job. Her compassion for me gave her insight that most financial professionals may not understand: that yes, I did need to be practical and plan, invest and save. But I also needed to live my life and find joy where I could. And sometimes joy costs money.

But I know that, being my advisor, she cringed every time she heard the sound of metal against metal, as I flipped through a clothing rack at the mall while talking to her on my cell phone. I know that deep down inside, the financial planner within her had to be screaming, "Step away from the life-insurance money and nobody gets hurt!"

But being the smart woman that she is, she never said anything. She knew that if she did, I would be offended and stop coming to her for help and advice. Kristi was a master at planting a seed of uncertainty when I needed it so that I would come to the right conclusions on my own.

"Are you sure you want to move right now? Remember that your house is paid off and moving will mean you'll have another mortgage."

"I like all of your furniture. I don't think you have to replace everything at once. Remember that looking for it is half the fun!"

"You could buy that tennis bracelet with the matching earrings, but don't you think you'll get tired of them after a while?"

She never judged and she never verbalized what would take me months to figure out: that all of the purses, TVs, new bedrooms, and sports cars were good for a temporary fix. That, while feeling good in the moment has its perks, it's usually only good for that moment.

And that there isn't a credit limit high enough to fill the void of a dead spouse.

Changes

helping others cope with your loss

12

When I became a widow, I had to raise my parents all over again.

Poor things. There they were, just moved back to Colorado from Louisiana to be closer to their grandchildren. (Kristi and I never really pretended that they made that move to be closer to *us*.) We were all so happy they were here, and my sister and I were relieved that we would finally be able to help them with my ninety-five-year-old grandmother who had moved with them. Mom and Dad had the long-term vision of growing old here, not in their favorite climate, but they knew it would be easier for us to take care of them, should something happen.

Then something did happen. And they ended up taking care of me all over again.

I don't know what I would have done without them. My mom was the one who would get the 3:00 a.m. phone calls when I'd had an anxiety attack. My dad would come help me when I was panicking about which new tires to buy. They would both drive through the snow to my house to pick up my kids so that I could have one night to either sleep (if I could manage it) or cry until my body was dry.

That was during the preteen years of my widowhood. When I needed them and they didn't mind being needed. But then I hit adolescent widowhood. And everything changed.

After pulling them to me for months, I was ready to spread my widowed wings and fly. I wanted to start creating a new life. I wanted to assert my new and complete independence. I wanted to know I had it in me to exist without always calling my parents for help.

As with a lot of changes that come during widowhood, this need for independence seemed to happen overnight and caused frustration for all of us. They couldn't understand why I wasn't depending on them as much as I had been, and I couldn't understand *why* they couldn't understand it. I didn't realize that the changes I was going through were happening at such a rapid pace that even I could barely keep up with them.

So how could I expect anyone else to?

"I want to start my own business."

"No! I'm going to go back to school!"

"Maybe I should just work retail for a while."

"Hey! That guy is cute!"

"Argh. I'm not ready to date."

"Why isn't anyone calling me? Am I *that* unlovable?"

You can see where it might have been hard for them to connect the dots some days.

It became necessary, after a while, to get into a pattern. I would come up with some off-the-wall idea, and then I would give them at least twenty-four hours to digest it before I came up with the next one. I started realizing that since one major thing in my life had changed so drastically, everything else was going to have to follow like a line of dominoes. Of course it was hard for me to keep up with what was going on, but I was living in my head and had some idea of my stream of consciousness.

They were living in their house and getting phone calls every time that stream decided to take a turn. Unnerving to say the least.

And it wasn't just *my* life that had changed with Brad's death. Suddenly my parents were also forced to think about the fact that I might not be the stay-at-home mom we all thought I would be. I might have to—or want to—go back to work. They had to come to grips with the fact that I didn't want to be alone for the rest of my life, and that meant dating and taking their grandchildren along with me for the ride. It meant *my* life, the life of their daughter whom they loved deeply, would never be the same and would have to start down a new path.

And they were forced into trying to keep up.

I realized that while I was expecting everyone else to be patient with me as I worked through where my life was going to go, it was equally important that I be patient with them. We all needed support through this loss and this transition, and I couldn't let myself become so immersed in my own life and story that I wouldn't have the compassion to help them through theirs as well.

I discovered that being self-aware and paying attention to my journey was very different from being self-absorbed and not paying attention to anyone else's. That while Brad was my husband, the loss had happened to us *all* and I didn't want to be the person who didn't recognize that. Sure, my life had been turned upside down in the most obvious way, but theirs had as well. And just as it would be wrong for someone else to not support me through the changes I was going through, it would be wrong for me to ignore that they were going through some fairly significant changes as well.

Being self-aware, I knew that being self-absorbed was not what I wanted to become.

Of course, in considering my relationship with family members, I had to think about more than just my parents when I started out on this journey. In many ways, the relationships that I had with my family and my in-laws after Brad died had to start all over again. I know that on paper, I should have still been Catherine, just without the "& Brad" attached. But I wasn't. And that transformation made me nervous and probably caught them all completely by surprise.

When it comes to widowhood and in-laws, no matter what the situation, there is one question I think all widows ask ourselves at some point.

Now what?

I think I can count on one hand the number of friends I have who truly enjoy their spouse's family. I remember Kristi telling me that one night she and her book club friends got on the subject of in-laws, and by the end of it, the one single girl in the group asked, "Does *anyone* have normal in-laws?"

To which Kristi replied, "Yes. Our husbands do."

And since someone else in the group had just described how her father-in-law owned a Crocodile Dundee–style hat in which he had placed all of his own teeth around the band, that group would know.

Brad and I were no different than most people when it came to families. In fact, we were pretty much the poster children for opposites attracting. He was math; I was reading. He loved science; I was all about the arts. He was smart. I stood next to him. Our upbringings were completely different, something that our hormones ignored when we first met, but after a few years of marriage, the differences became glaringly obvious.

Brad loved his childhood in the rolling hills of the Pennsylvania countryside. Growing up, he rode four-wheelers and dirt bikes, went to the local racetrack, and caused as much trouble as he could possibly get away with…and still get commissioned as an Air Force officer. I have pictures in a little photo box of him covered in mud and grinning, sitting on his family's ATV; standing over a bloody deer that he'd just shot with his own little preteen hands; and holding hands with his high-school girlfriend at his prom, proud of his '80s hairdo and shiny blue bow tie. He played hard, worked hard, and loved hard, and one of the things he was the most grateful for was how close he was with his family growing up.

As far as families go, the close bond we each shared with our families was about all we had in common. My grandmother taught ballet and was a child-prodigy pianist. My side of the family was filled with dancers, painters, and performers. When I sat down to dinner at night, my mother would shoot me a dirty look if my elbows were on the table, and I was taught from an early age to cross my legs whether I was wearing a skirt or pants. Bodily noises were frowned upon; nights downtown at the theater usually happened at least twice a year; and all adults were addressed with a "Miss" or "Mr." before their first name.

You can see where we might have had some differences.

I've often thought that there should be a class taught in every high school introducing the concept to the young female population that once you marry him, you marry his family.

Lesson One: If he takes you home to a double-wide and his dad looks a lot like Dog the Bounty Hunter, think twice about jumping into the backseat of that 1982 Camaro.

Lesson Two: If he said that his parents couldn't pay for his college education because they're still trying to pay off the tattoo artist in town, just walk away.

Lesson Three: If you've seen his sister on an episode of *Bridezillas* planning her wedding, give it some more thought.

This should then be followed by a slide show that fast-forwards about twenty years and shows the unfortunate girl saddled with four kids, sitting around a Christmas tree that blinks and spins to the tune of "Grandma Got Run Over by a Reindeer" with the people she is now forced to call family. I can guarantee that if this course could be offered early enough, teenage pregnancy statistics would take a dive and some girls may even start batting for the other team.

Like many people, when Brad and I got married, we repeated the phrase "till death do you part." But during our counseling with the minister before the ceremony, he failed to tell us what happens after that. Does that mean everyone parts?

I can only speak from my own experience, but no. It doesn't.

I can't deny the love that Brad's family had for him. His mother, Bonnie, cried every time he left home after a visit, and I don't think she ever got over the fact that he abandoned his hometown to attend college at the Air Force Academy. Oh, I know it was something she was incredibly proud of, but since I also have pictures in my photo box of every plane he took off in, the planes that he took on his way back to Colorado after spending a Christmas at home in Pennsylvania…I knew she had mixed feelings about it. And those feelings ran deep.

But it seemed like things changed after we got married. I think that secretly his family always thought Brad would come back home after he finished his commitment to the Air Force. And I think that there was a part of Brad that wanted to as well, but there was also a part of him that wanted something else. And as the years wore on, he talked to his family less and less, and we only made it back to Pennsylvania for a visit about once a year. He didn't make much effort and, to be honest, neither did they. I've sometimes wondered what their relationship would have been like if I hadn't been around because, when he was alive, I would ask him about once a month, "Have you called your mother?"

This question was usually met with a yawn and "Okay. I'll call her tomorrow."

When he died, I alternated between wanting to include them in all of the plans I was making and feeling territorial about my new life. I offered to have them take half of Brad's ashes and consulted them on just about everything that had to do with the memorial because I felt it would have been wrong to take everything over myself. After all, he was their son.

But I had my limits. Just after the funeral, I was in our basement rec room with his brother, Jeremy, when he suddenly pointed to a large frame on the wall and said, "If you want, I could take that Jerome Bettis jersey off your hands."

To which I snapped back, "I'm keeping that."

I'd like to think that Jeremy was kidding, but there was probably a part of him that wasn't. Brad was gone, and we were left with all of his "stuff," and the big question was "who had the right to take it and who didn't?" We all wanted things to remember him by and to keep the things that were special to us. I wanted to save some of his childhood things because I wanted my kids to have them some day. And I'm sure that his family wanted to keep his childhood things because they were actually around when he used them and therefore had the memories to go with them. The things he had acquired during adulthood were displayed around our house and I didn't want them removed.

But was it all up to me to decide what stayed and what didn't?

I really think that this is where divorcées have a leg up on us widowed. In most cases, the relationship has been severed and it's up to the respective spouses to determine who takes what and when the two different sets of grandparents see the grandchildren. When talking about the in-laws, it's okay to say "my former in-laws." And

I think (I don't *know* because I've never been divorced) that it's okay to back away entirely from the relationship.

Not so cut and dried in the widow department.

I wasn't quite sure *what* do with that relationship when Brad was gone. I felt guilty if I didn't keep in touch with them enough and then angry that I was left to deal with it. I felt sorry for what they had to deal with and then even sorrier for myself that I was dealing with it, too. It seemed like the only things we had in common anymore were the kids and Brad's death.

"How are the kids doing?"

"They're doing well. How are you guys doing?"

"Well…some days are better than others…"

And then we would dive into a conversation about our grief, our suffering, and how we never realized it could be possible to miss someone so much. Especially in the beginning, I knew when I saw their phone number come across my caller ID that I would probably be completely dehydrated the next day from crying so hard. I both loathed and craved those conversations because part of me hated to stick my toes in the abyss, but part of me needed to feel connected with people who were so connected to Brad.

And as time went on, we fell back into the routine we had been in before he died. Sometimes we would hear from them; sometimes we wouldn't. And without Brad around for me to ask "Have you called your mother?" I didn't know if I was supposed to take on his role of calling once a month…or just let it slide.

"What am I supposed to do?" I asked a counselor midway through my second year. "Sometimes they send presents to the kids. Sometimes they don't. Sometimes they call, and then sometimes I don't hear from them for months. Am I supposed to be keeping this relationship going? Or do I just let it all go?"

And on that day, she gave me the most helpful advice I've ever gotten.

"Put in as much effort as they do."

This completely changed how I thought about the relationship, but it actually didn't change the relationship that much. I would still talk to them about the same amount, but I was less stressed out about it. When they sent gifts, I would reciprocate, but I wouldn't rush to the post office in the middle of the holidays so that I could get them there on time, knowing that their presents would be coming about two months late, if at all. That one phrase absolved me of all the guilt and anger I had bottled up inside me for years, and I was able to just take the relationship one day at a time.

Genius.

13

During the first year of widowhood, all of the experts say that you're really not supposed to answer any deep questions about life and where you're going. Sure, there are some things you have to decide and that you may not have a choice about—like moving, getting a new job, or selling your kids to the highest bidder. But as far as digging deeper into life and where you're going, it's pretty much a waste of time to try and answer that within the first twelve months of losing a spouse.

At that stage you're still trying to put the pieces of your life back together again. You haven't realized that since the pieces aren't the same, they just won't fit the way you want them to.

Yet.

As the fog started to lift a little and I began to question everything, I found it hard to wrestle with the new issues I was facing at a time when I felt so utterly alone. I remember desperately trying to find the answers to the puzzle that was my new life. I wanted to know why, what came next, was I really alone, and what the future held ten years down the line. And I started looking everywhere to find those answers.

I was constantly watching for signs from Brad, wondering what he thought about what I was doing and always somewhat worried that he hated the decisions I was making. I felt sure that he was looking down at me, angry that I had given away that sixty-inch TV or disappointed every time I told my daughter I didn't understand her first-grade math problems and, therefore, couldn't help her.

And knowing that the fear of his disappointment in me from the Great Beyond was something that most people probably wouldn't understand, I kept it to myself.

I've always believed in signs and have been somewhat superstitious. I've always thought that certain pj's, when worn the night before, will give me luck the following day. I've always made a wish when the clock says 4:44, crossed my fingers for luck, and wished on shooting stars. But right after Brad died, my superstitious nature went into hyper-drive and I started looking for signs from him everywhere. I was fairly quiet about my convictions, afraid that if I told people that Brad's spirit had stopped up my toilet as a joke, Social Services would be at my door, removing my children from the crazy lady who believed that her dead husband spoke to her through her plumbing.

Now, I think most widows believe in some sort of spiritual afterlife, and I'm betting that a lot of them really didn't feel either way about it before their husbands died. And you just can't explain it until it's happened to you.

Actually, it can be pretty hard to explain even then.

One of my first experiences from the Great Beyond came about six months after Brad died. I was with my friend, Tiffany, attending a fundraiser with a Mardi Gras theme in February 2008 at an art gallery in downtown Denver. The weather was horrible that night, icy and cold, and I remember thinking as we slid down the highway that we should have just stayed home.

When we walked into the brightly lit gallery we, of course, immediately made our way to one of the bars that had been set up. The bartender handed us our drinks and a couple of cheap, feathered Mardi Gras masks, which we immediately snapped on, and we made our way through the rooms, looking at art and picking up the rich appetizers being passed around by waiters in white shirts and black ties. And when I looked up at the second-floor balcony, I noticed people mingling around booths and card tables.

"What's going on up there?" I asked Tiffany, pointing to a blond woman who was sitting alone at a table, apparently waiting for a customer of some sort.

"They've provided complimentary tarot-card readings for the night," she said.

"*Really?*" I said, my ears perking up. "I've always wanted to do that! Let's go check it out."

Once we made it up the modern-looking glass and metal staircase (that I looked down at in terror, wondering how I would make it back to the first floor in the heels I was wearing), we approached the blond woman and suddenly...we seemed to turn into two thirteen-year-olds.

"You go first," I said to Tiffany, pushing her forward.

"No, you go first," she said, pushing me in front of her.

"No, you."

"For crying out loud, Catherine," Tiffany said, mock exasperation in her voice. "Just sit down."

I sat down with a thump and shyly looked at the woman sitting across from me. She looked incredibly ordinary for a "reader." No tattoos of Zeus across her forehead. No piercings in places they shouldn't be. Just a sweater, nice pants, and an open smile that made me think she should be teaching preschoolers how to perfect their uppercase letters.

"So...how does this work?" I asked.

"I'm going to shuffle these cards, and as I'm shuffling, I want you to think of a question you want to ask," she said.

"Okay," I said, trying to decide what I wanted to inquire about. Widowhood seemed too complicated for a complimentary cocktail party tarot-card reading, and my mental state wouldn't be able to handle anything bad about the kids.

"What about my job?" I said. "I'm thinking about going back to work someday and I'd like to know about that."

"Okay," she said, as she started laying the cards out in front of me while Tiffany peered over my shoulder.

"Your professional life will go where you want it to go," she started. "I can see you doing something creative. You have goals in front of you that are perfectly within your power to achieve…"

And on and on. Rather benign answers that could be taken any way and could have probably been given to any person.

"Thanks," I said to her, as I started to get up so that Tiffany could have her turn.

"Wait," the tarot-card reader said suddenly. "There's something else you want to ask me."

I lowered myself back into the metal folding chair.

"Well, I'm widowed," I said. "I always have questions about that."

"I know you are," she said. "He's standing right behind you."

I looked over at Tiffany, whose eyes had suddenly gotten as big as dinner plates.

"He's…right behind her?" she asked.

"Yes," said the reader. "He wants you to know that he's okay. He wants you to know that he's with you all of the time. He says that he wishes he could have done more financially, but that he knows you'll be okay."

And then she said something that I will never forget.

"He says that you have three children. He says that your youngest can see him, but your two older children cannot. They don't want to see him. But that he and your youngest daughter speak all of the time."

Now, no one else could have known that because I had been quiet about the strange encounters I had been having. But in the months since he had been gone, Sarah, who had started out as a lurching eighteen-month-old at the time of his death and had developed into a racing two-year-old at the time of the reading, would talk to him and about him all the time. It always struck me as odd that the youngest of my children, the one who really knew him the least and would have the fewest memories of him, would talk about him constantly as if he was still a fixture in her life.

I remember right after Brad died, I had been sitting with her completely relaxed in my lap, as she held her blanket and sucked on her pacifier, fighting sleep and not winning. Suddenly she bolted upright and looked straight at the wall.

"Hi, Daddy!" she said brightly.

Gulp. *What?*

Shortly after that, I was strapping her into her car seat in the minivan after church when she gazed at the ceiling of the car and started giggling uncontrollably.

"Daddy's on the ceiling!" she exclaimed.

And then a few weeks later, I was battling tears as she and I were driving home from running errands. Sarah was sitting directly behind me and couldn't see my face, and I was doing my best to keep my sadness a secret from her...when she suddenly started laughing.

"Daddy's *kissing you!*" she said.

"He is?" I answered, trying to make my voice overly bright so that she wouldn't hear it shaking. "Where? On the cheek?"

"No!" she exclaimed. "Right on the *lips!*"

The night that the tarot-card reader told me all of this, I

knew it was true. I hadn't solicited her services. I hadn't offered any answers. The truth was…I was so shocked that I could hardly speak at all. I had always wondered how I would feel if I knew Brad was always with me. Would I feel self-conscious? Would I feel scared? Would the whole idea of it just creep me out?

But that night, when she told me he was always with me, a wave of comfort washed over me. And for the rest of the evening I almost felt like he was my date.

When I got home that night and told my teenage babysitter what had happened, she breathed a sigh of relief.

"Thank God. I've been a little freaked out about babysitting over here, in case something weird should happen, like your house is haunted or something."

"Well, not to worry," I replied cheerfully. "Sounds like he's always with *me.*"

I wondered for years after that if it was real. If it had really happened. And I have come to the conclusion that, yes, it was real. It did happen. That woman saw him that night and knew things she couldn't have known unless he was with me. And the reason I know this is because since then I have been to some really *bad* mediums.

Here is a tip: Don't ever go to a medium because you got a 50 percent off coupon. That should answer your question about authenticity right there.

I went in to see my counselor not long after the experience at the fundraiser, and when I sat down, I said, "You're going to think I'm crazy, but…"

And then I told her what had happened with the medium.

Now, first of all, you should never start a conversation with your therapist by saying, "You're going to think I'm crazy."

You're in her office. Crazy is a given.

And if your therapist responds with, "Yup. Crazy all right. Let me get my prescription pad and set you up with enough meds that will have you not only thinking that you see your husband…you'll think you're living with the entire cast from *Eight is Enough*"… then it may be time to find someone else who gets it.

That day, I was surprised when my counselor didn't look at me like I was nuts. She said in her matter-of-fact way, "Of course they're here. Where else are they going to go?"

I thought for sure that my dad and my brother-in-law would fall into the nonbeliever category. I hadn't really told them much about all these little things, reserving my stories for my mother who might not have believed me but had the good sense not to say so. But one night right around Brad's birthday, years after he died, I was sitting with my entire family at my parents' house and explaining to them some strange things that had been going on.

"I know this is going to sound weird," I told them, "but in the middle of the night last night I heard all the cabinet doors slam, one right after the other in the kids' bathroom. It was really loud and I heard three really big slams before it stopped."

I expected the story to be met with some eye-rolling from the men in my family.

Instead, I got something I didn't expect.

"Cath…do you have access to Brad's Yahoo account?" Sean asked suddenly.

"No," I said. "I didn't even know that he had one."

"Huh," he said, looking a little embarrassed about what he was getting ready to say. "I've always meant to ask you that. Because he and I used to chat on that all the time during the day while we were at work. And a couple of months after he died, I saw his chat icon go live, like he was logged in. I just assumed it was you."

"Nope," I said, relieved that someone else had experienced the Brad phenomenon. "Wasn't me."

"Well, shoot," he said. "Kind of makes me wish I had typed something in…to see what happened."

"Well, did Dad ever tell you what happened to him right after Brad died?" my mom interjected.

"No. What?"

My dad looked at me and said, "I had just gone back to work and I had to call on a customer. When I got to the reception desk, the secretary asked me to sign in on their guest logbook."

He cleared his throat.

"The person who had just signed in before me was 'Brad Tidd.'"

Now, that would make a believer out of just about anyone.

The truth is…I didn't really need a medium or a Ouija board to answer any of these questions for me. It didn't matter if anyone else believed me when I said that I could walk down the hall and suddenly know I wasn't alone. Or that sometimes flickering lights would follow me from room to room. Or that I could be driving in my car and get a whiff of his cologne. It didn't really matter if anyone else believed it was real or not.

If *I* believe that it's real and it gave me a sense of comfort, then that's all that mattered.

Dreaming about Brad doesn't happen often, but it does happen. For me, there are good and bad things about dreaming about him. I *love* those dreams. Absolutely love them. No matter what they are, it's just amazing to have that feeling of being with him again. The bad thing is then I wake up, rub my eyes, and focus on the room. And realize he's gone all over again.

Usually the days after I have a dream about Brad are the days that I miss him the most. I spend the day with an ache in my soul that just won't go away. Even years later, when I have a dream about him, the way I feel when I wake up is like the loss is as raw and new as it was in the summer of 2007.

Most of those dreams involve us just talking. I'm telling him about the kids and what we've been up to. My favorite was one where we were lying in our bed, the bedroom looking like it did before I went through my remodeling phase, and we're just talking about the kids.

The morning I woke up from *that* one, I just about couldn't get out of bed.

But the dream that made me know that it was real, that he really was with me, was the first one I had about him.

It was in October, just a few months after he died. I vividly remember that it was October because the World Series was coming up, and even though I didn't follow baseball at all (and neither had Brad), it would have been impossible to live in Denver and not know that the Colorado Rockies had a shot at getting there. Even though at that point I didn't have the attention span to watch the news, the city was in baseball mode. We just didn't know who we'd be playing against.

I dreamed that we were having a party at our house and all of our friends were there. Brad was wearing khaki shorts and a fleece plaid pullover that was one of his favorites. Everyone was mingling, drinking beer, and having a good time, which I thought was strange.

Because in my dream, we all knew that Brad was about to die.

He had had the stroke, and I remember dreaming that I was watching him like you would be watching a pregnant woman whose water had just broken. He was standing outside in our backyard with a few of his friends, on the other side of a huge window so that he could still see the TV, watching the baseball game with extreme interest, something he had never really done before when he was alive.

"Does your head hurt?" I kept asking him in the dream. "Is it time for us to go to the hospital?"

"Not yet," Brad would say with a trace of annoyance. "I want to watch the end of this game."

I looked at the TV through the window and saw it was the Rockies playing the Red Sox.

"Since when have you become such a Red Sox fan?" I asked him, turning to go back into the house. I flopped down onto the couch in the TV room next to a friend of mine.

"This really sucks," I said, alluding to Brad's impending death, which didn't seem to be bothering anyone else in the room.

"Yeah, it really does," he replied and went back to watching the game.

I really didn't think anything of that dream. Honestly, I was just so excited that I'd finally had one of Brad. I filed it back in the corner of my mind and went on, trying to live day to day, moment to moment, without giving the significance of that dream any thought.

Until, weeks later, my parents happened to have the news on when the anchor announced who would be playing in the World Series.

The Colorado Rockies and the Boston Red Sox.

Now, if I had known that Brad was going to be giving me sports tips, I would have contacted my local bookie. And since then, I've been waiting for him to just pop in and give me the winning lottery numbers.

No such luck.

But I have no doubt that he was there, and I have no doubt that he's visited my subconscious since then. Many times, he's just a bystander, and in every dream, I know that he's dead. But it's still just nice to see him every once in a while and catch up. (Remind me that I said that when I'm eighty years old and he still looks thirty-four in my dream. I don't think my subconscious is smart enough to age him along with me.)

But the thing that happens to me most often is a meaningful song being played on the radio when I really need to hear it. The Christmas before Brad died, he was stuck in Washington, DC, desperately trying to get home. Colorado had had three major snowstorms back to back, which had delayed and canceled hundreds of flights. So, on December 22, Brad called me at nine at night and said, "I'm not waiting on the airline anymore. I still have my rental car, and I'm leaving right now and driving home. If I drive straight through, I'll make it home by Christmas Eve."

He drove through the night, racing west to spend Christmas with his family. The next morning, worried that I hadn't heard from him, I tried calling his cell phone to see where he was.

And I didn't get an answer.

Knowing how exhausted he must be and not crazy about the idea of him making that long trip by himself, I began to worry about him. I had no idea how far he had driven the night before and where he could possibly be in his trek across the country. I sat down at the kitchen table, wondering what in the heck to do next.

And then the phone rang.

"I'm sorry I missed your call!" Brad chirped from the middle of Ohio. "I had the windows down and the radio cranked up and I was singing that Rascal Flatts song 'Life is a Highway' at the top of my lungs. I didn't even hear it ring!"

Months later, after he died, I still had that image in my head. Of Brad sailing down the highway, coming home to us and gleefully singing as loud as he could. A song that talks about how life is short and how you should live every minute of it. A song that talks about survival.

A song that tells us that life is a journey.

And so, when I'm feeling down or like I can't take this whole widow thing anymore or that if I have to make one more decision, my head is going to explode…and suddenly that song comes on, you bet your ass I believe it's him telling me to hang in there. And that I can do it.

Because I can.

14

Picture it. Colorado, 2007. A new widow goes to pick her dog up at the kennel where she (the dog, not the widow) had been boarded to be out of the way for the funeral. The sun is shining. The air is crisp and clean. And the widow is in such a fog that she probably shouldn't have been behind the wheel of a moving vehicle.

As she waits for her dog to be brought to the counter, one of the groomers strikes up a conversation.

"I heard that the dog had to be boarded because of a family emergency. Did everything turn out okay?"

"Uh. No, actually. My husband died in a motorcycle accident three days ago."

The groomer then proceeds, to the horror of the young widow and the people surrounding her in the waiting room, to tell a detailed, gruesome story of how one of her friends was decapitated in a motorcycle accident years earlier. And as another groomer hands the widow her dog's leash, the woman behind the counter ends with, "So if you need anyone to talk to, give us a call. 'Cause we all know what you're going through."

And although the young widow may have been relieved to know she could always call her local kennel for sympathy and support, she was rendered speechless by the story and could only manage a "thank you" as she stumbled out the door.

That young widow was me. And that kennel is no longer in business.

I think about that story quite a bit...mainly because now, years later, I find it hilariously funny. But I used to wonder why. Why didn't I tell that woman off? Why didn't I tell her that what she was saying was completely thoughtless? Why didn't I bill her for the therapy I later had to go through after listening to her motorcycle decapitation story, right after burying my own husband (who still, thankfully, had a head)?

And now I can tell you why.

Because she meant well.

I think it took me a little longer than most people to notice that good intentions often come in the form of stupid comments. That's probably because I'm a pleaser and would rather walk on my hands through burning hot coals than make someone else feel uncomfortable in my presence. And my widowness was usually enough to make anyone feel uncomfortable, but responding "What the hell did you just say?" after they'd made a comment they thought was comforting would really seal the deal.

It was *exhausting*, the effort I put into making other people think that they'd said the right thing. My body tensed up, my jaw got tight, and I suppressed the urge to scream while all of my mental energy was concentrating on saying, "Thank you for your words of comfort. You have no idea what they mean to me."

When what I really wanted to do was yell, "You *idiot!*" And then run away and submerge myself in a bubble bath like the widow's version of a Calgon commercial.

I've had friends say to me, "You're so strong. You're like

Superwoman!" And I know what they're thinking. They're thinking that they're paying me a huge compliment by telling me that
I've gotten my life back on track so well.

But what it really feels like is, "You're so strong. So don't
break that facade now because then everything will completely
fall apart."

Or the people who would tell me, "This is part of God's plan."

Well, peachy. But it wasn't part of mine. And since God isn't
here to help me put these kids through college, I really wish He
had consulted me first.

Or how about "everything happens for a reason."

Now, what I do when I hear *that* is smile and nod. But what
I'd *really* like to do is say, "You know, you're right. Everything *does*
happen for a reason. I'm a little unclear about what the reason
might be right now, but if you could explain to me why my husband is dead at thirty-four and I'm now raising three children on
my own, I would love to hear your theory."

And then there's my favorite: *I'll never forget how hard it was
when my dog died. I thought I'd never get over it!*

Now, good intention or not, that person should really
be smacked.

I've even fallen into this trap myself. The question of "How
are you" has become such a natural greeting that we don't expect
a real answer. We expect a "good" or "I'm fine." But I can pretty
much guarantee that about 98 percent of the people we ask are
really not "good" or "fine." They're worried about money or kids or
who they're dating. But we never really expect them to give us an
in-depth answer. And when they do, it ups our discomfort level.

I was visiting a friend whose infant daughter had just had
open-heart surgery and was in the ICU at Children's Hospital.
I walked into her room and saw Becky bending over her baby,
who was covered from head to tiny foot in tubes and bandages.

And before I could stop myself I asked brightly, "Hey! How are you doing?"

The second it came out of my mouth, I thought, "You moron. How do you *think* she's doing?"

But at least I knew enough to immediately backtrack and say, "I can't believe I just said that. But really. How *are* you?"

Even a simple question like "how are you" can easily send me over the edge, depending on the day I'm having. On certain days, I can have an automatic response to your automatic question. And then on others, the bitter, sad, irritated little widow within me really wants to let you have it.

"Well, my husband died six months ago. I can't figure out how to use my snowblower; my kids have decided they'd rather camp in the backyard than live with me; and I have a rash right here and I can't tell if it's contagious or not. What do you think?"

I used to fluctuate between not wanting anyone to know what had happened so that I could dodge those awkward moments and resisting the urge to tell complete strangers every detail of my story. Sometimes I would correct them when they assumed that I still had a husband (or an ex-husband), and some days I would go along with pretending that he was still around, giving myself one blissful second of feeling like life was normal.

About a year after Brad died, I was walking into Walmart, wearing my most comfortable oversized Air Force Academy sweatshirt, when the sweet, little old man who was greeting shoppers as they entered the store struck up a conversation.

"Good morning! Nice sweatshirt! Did you go to the Academy?"

"No, my husband did, though."

"Oh! Is he a pilot?"

"No, he was an engineer."

"Well, that's good! At least he gets to come home every night!"

And with that, the greeter sent me on my miserable, widowed

way into the store so that I could stock up on maxi pads and peanut butter.

There were days when I would completely avoid eye contact and only respond to a stranger's friendly "hello" with a small smile and a nod of the head. And then there were other days when I wanted to spill the entire contents of my life on some random person walking down the condiment aisle at the grocery store.

"Do you *see* this jar of Miracle Whip?" I wanted to grab a stranger by the shirt and yell into his face. "I don't have to buy this anymore because my husband died. Do you know how much I hated buying Miracle Whip a year ago and how much I would give for someone at home to want it right now?"

One of the most painful moments I have ever gone through with someone who meant well but whose comment was about to send me over the edge was with my own mother. Now, she is usually the first person I call for comfort and understanding. But right after Brad died, she would often say to me, "Oh, Catherine. This is awful. Awful, awful, awful, awful, *awful*."

And I knew that she meant well. She was trying to commiserate with me. She was trying to tell me that she knew that my life had been turned upside down.

Dammit. She was just trying to *help*.

But it didn't help. It made me feel terrible. It made me feel like I was sinking into a hole I would never be able to get out of. And finally, I couldn't take it anymore.

"Mom. You have to stop saying that," I said to her one day over the phone.

There was a silence and then a little sniffle. And then her voice, shaking with hurt, said, "I'm sorry. What would you like me to say?"

I thought about it for a minute and then said miserably, "I don't know."

I didn't. I didn't know. I didn't know what someone could say to comfort me because there were times I just couldn't be comforted. Jollying me along seemed insensitive, and commiserating with me depressed me. "I'm sorry" seemed shallow and even silence with a look of pity was too much for me to bear. I didn't realize until years after Brad died that in most cases, we widows don't want people to say anything.

We just want you to listen.

That became clear to me when I was attending a reception for a neighbor who had died suddenly. I walked next door and felt like the pressure was on. After all, I had been through this so I should know what to say, right? But at that point I had already learned that what was comforting to me might make my neighbor want to throw herself under a fast-moving Geo in the parking lot of the mall. So, as I walked through the grass between our houses that summer night and let myself in through the gate to their backyard, I was kind of at a loss as to what to say.

"I'm so sorry," I began, knowing that those words were futile. "He was such a great guy. I can't believe that he's gone."

She gave me that little half smile we widows acquire that says, "Thank you for your thoughts but you're really not helping."

I sat at her kitchen table with her mother and her sister, listening to them all talk about her husband's death while she remained silent, and I could see by her face that she was sinking lower and lower.

"You know," I said. "I've never heard how you guys met."

She started talking. And talking. Her face brightened a little as she told me how they met in college and about their wedding. I sat, my eyes fixated on her face, actively listening, nodding my head, and laughing at the crazy things they did when they were younger.

"Hey!" she said. "There's a slide show set up in the other room of us. You want to watch it with me?"

I grabbed my glass of wine and she led me to the family room where there were pictures looping on the TV, and she sat there for about forty-five minutes, explaining every slide to me and telling me what they were doing. There were others in the room, family members and friends, who had either already heard the stories or had been there to witness them. Every once in a while, one of them would chime in with what they remembered. But they all seemed to benefit from having a fresh pair of ears who had never heard any of it laughing along and enjoying the history.

"That's it," I thought. "That's what we all want. To tell our stories to someone who cares to hear them. I don't have to say a word. Just let *her* talk."

I love telling stories about Brad. If you get me started, I'll talk your ear off. Usually, I don't want to talk about his death. I don't even want to necessarily talk about how hard it's been since he's been gone. But when someone I've known for a long time says, "Remember when?" and I can help fill in the blank with some outrageous memory from our life together, I could talk for hours. Or if someone I don't know well says, "Tell me about your husband," I could tell a lifetime of stories. Sure, I'll feel that pang of loss and grief in my heart. But it's no match for the joy I feel remembering the man I love.

And telling those stories reminds me over and over again that even though he's gone, the memories are mine forever.

It wasn't just the remarks of strangers that took me by surprise. My kids developed a knack for making comments that alarmed me on a regular basis and could often stop any conversation midsentence. Remember that old Bill Cosby show *Kids Say the Darndest Things*? Well, those kids had nothing on my own who had many thoughts and questions when it came to their dad and his death—and had no problem sharing them at any given time.

Sarah, in the beginning, had no filter. I'll never forget swimming with her at the local indoor pool when she was a toddler and watching her play with another little girl. I don't know what prompted this, but I suddenly heard the echo of Sarah's voice from across the water: "Oh *yeah*? Well, my daddy's *dead*. DEAD!"

And then I watched the other child quickly swim away from her.

While Sarah seemed to come up with these little comments for shock value, Michael just wanted information. His questions, while difficult for me to answer, were part of his process and as time went on, I began to practice age-appropriate honesty: answering those questions as truthfully as I could at a level I thought he could understand.

"Mom?" he asked me when he was about four. "What does 'extinct' mean?"

And I told him, "It means something isn't around anymore. Like the dinosaurs are extinct."

There was a silence as he pondered that one. Then he asked, "So is Dad extinct?"

Pause. "Yes. I guess he is."

It was a question that really made sense when you think about it…especially to a four-year-old boy. But, of course, as he got older, the questions got harder. And once we had had some space and time away from Brad's death, they were also more jarring when he asked them because I wasn't expecting them.

"Was there a lot of blood on the road when Daddy had his accident?" he asked me about three years into our new life.

"Uh…no…" I said, trying to catch a glimpse of him in the rearview mirror so that I could see his face. "Why do you ask?"

"I was just wondering," he said, as if he had just asked me what was for dinner.

For some reason these questions always seemed to arise when we were in the car. It could have been that just being on the road reminded him that his dad was in accident and that he still needed more information to complete the puzzle that had become the life we were living. It could have been that there was something about the quiet rocking of the car that made him think deeply about things he was normally too busy to contemplate. Or he could have just been testing my skills as a driver, wondering what it would take to throw me off enough to crash through the door of the local Dairy Queen so that he could get a Blizzard.

With kids, it's always hard to pinpoint their motivation.

Of course, my children weren't the only ones who could stop any conversation in its tracks. After a few months, I realized that I, too, had that superpower. I recognized that by merely uttering one phrase—*my husband died*—I had the ability to make just about anyone run from me as if what I had was contagious.

The first time it happened was a few months after Brad died, when I was at a bar in downtown Denver. I'd just been to a Colorado Rockies baseball game with a girlfriend who had somehow scored an extra seat, and even though I wasn't a huge baseball fan, it seemed like a good excuse to get out and have some adult interaction.

I sat at the game with Stephanee, and for the first time in months, I felt normal. No one seated around me knew that my husband had died. No one knew how hard it had been to even think about going out and doing something so normal. No one knew how complicated my life had become and how worried I was that it would never be simple again.

To the people sitting around me, I was just a thirty-one-year-old woman out enjoying an evening with a friend.

After the game, Stephanee and I ran across the street from the Stadium to a restaurant so we could grab a beer. We made our way to the rooftop bar and I watched everyone around me in wonder, disbelieving once again that life had still gone on for all of these strangers while mine seemed to have completely stopped for the last few months. I got so caught up in the "normalness" of the evening that I started talking to a guy standing next to me at the bar.

"So...are you a Broncos fan?" he asked me.

"No, actually I'm a Steelers fan."

"A *Steelers* fan? How did that happen?"

"Well, my late husband was from Pennsylvania. So I guess that would make me a Steelers fan by marriage."

I'm not kidding you, the second I said "late husband," that guy turned around midsentence and walked away, leaving my widowed ass alone sipping my pathetic little beer.

Wow. I had no idea I had it in me.

I've since experienced many moments of extreme discomfort thanks to my dead husband. Those conversations (or lack of) have left me feeling alone and hurt and unlikeable, and it took me a while to figure out that those uncomfortable moments really had nothing to do with me.

They had to do with the idiots that I was talking to.

Eventually, once I had a better handle on this amazing power, I could control it and use it to my advantage. As time went on, I learned not to start every conversation with, "Well, my late husband and I..." but save it so that I could spring it on people when they were least expecting it.

This can also be commonly known as "pulling the widow card."

Of course, it's hard to pull the widow card on people who

know you really well. After a while, they build up an immunity so that when you say, "I can't come to your party tonight because I'm widowed," it's met with a "Yeah, yeah, yeah. Get your ass over here and buy some overpriced cookware."

And in an effort to keep my friendships intact, I would. I have the skillets to prove it.

I learned fairly early on that if I wanted to keep the friendships in my life that I'd had for years, it would be up to me to make a lot of the effort. Oh, I had some amazing friends who would call as if "Call Catherine" was marked on their calendars every week, and I knew that if for some reason I didn't feel like calling them for a few days, they would understand.

But many friendships started disappearing not long after Brad died. And it was as much my fault as it was theirs. I didn't put in the effort I had before he was gone, and since none of my friends had gone through anything even remotely as life-altering as I had, they just didn't know what to do with me. It didn't really offend me that much. I know it probably should have, but since they had no idea where I was coming from or deep down what I was going through, it would have been pretty unfair of me to expect them to suddenly acquire a mind-reading ability the moment Brad took his last breath.

They didn't know what to say, what not to say, what to invite me to, or what I wanted to avoid. And it didn't help that an activity or get-together that sounded good to me one minute would change into something I would rather shave my head than do the next.

At one point, I actually called Kristi about going on a wine tour downtown, and in the time it took me to come up with this plan, pick up the phone, and dial her number, I had completely changed my mind.

"Kristi, I just called you to do something. And now I don't want to. So never mind."

Yes. It's just as crazy as it sounds.

So, if I couldn't keep up with what sounded good and what I wanted to do, how in the world could I expect it of my friends and family? I mean, after a while, dealing with someone who doesn't have the attention span to make a plan and keep it all within the same hour can get a little irritating. I know because *I* was irritated. And I was the one who was doing it.

Being social again became like forming a new habit. Whether I wanted to or not, at any given moment, didn't matter. Because if I listened to myself, someone who obviously didn't know what was best for me, a year later I would have ended up as "the old widda woman" on the block who never turns on her lights and hands out pennies for Halloween.

Oh…you know what I mean.

What compounded the problem were my friends' husbands. Brad and I were constantly throwing parties and having people over. In fact, on the day of his funeral, we were supposed to have our huge summer party and we had invited a bunch of his coworkers and all of our local friends. I had been working for weeks on the menu and decorations, and figuring out how in the world we would have enough chairs to accommodate everyone. And the night before his funeral I remember thinking, "God, I hope the word got out to everyone that we're having a funeral instead of a party."

I mean, how awkward would it have been if some couple had shown up in Hawaiian shirts and flip-flops ready for burgers and beer…and we greeted them at the door wearing black and handing them a plate of HoneyBaked ham?

Anyway, as soon as Brad was gone, so were most of his friends. It actually took me a few weeks to figure out that they weren't there. But after a couple of months had passed and I hadn't seen any of them, I realized that they weren't just busy at work. They were avoiding me. And that scared me.

It was around that two-month mark that Brad's boss from his Air Force days in Florida, Ron, called me to see how I was doing. I was so shocked that he did that, given the fact that I hadn't seen or heard from a male friend in so long, that I actually emailed his wife after he called.

Dear Peggy,

I just wanted you to know that you should be extremely proud of Ron. I was so touched that he called last night to check on how I was doing and I've come to realize that, for a man, that takes more courage than going into battle.

Sincerely,
Catherine

I could never understand why the men avoided me so much. I guess they were worried that I could have a complete emotional breakdown in front of them at any moment. Like the top could blow on Mount Widow without warning and they were terrified of it happening in their presence. I should have explained to them from the beginning that the mountain would stay dormant unless it was fed copious amounts of chardonnay. Then eruption was imminent.

Now that I was alone, I needed to do things like trouble-shoot my plumbing and find out where to get the best deal on tires. Being the mom and the dad meant that I had to broaden my interests past what was in *People* magazine and into deeper subjects…like what was in *Consumer Reports*. I had no idea how to fix my garbage disposal, what fertilizer to use on my grass, and what the optimum temperature was to grill a steak. And even though my female friends were great at a lot of things, I needed those friendships with the men in their lives.

Because I had no man in mine.

It got to the point where I thought enough was *enough*. If *I* wanted my friendships to survive (because, after all, I had been friends with their husbands, too), *I* had to prove to them that they could.

It was obvious that I couldn't wait for everyone else to make this okay. It would be up to me. And that made sense. I mean, for all they knew, it could be really painful for me to be around other couples when I no longer had my better half. And it was. It was incredibly painful. But my instinct told me that I needed to get used to it and the longer I waited to get out there socially, the more painful it would be to try.

The first dinner party I put together was with my old college roommates and their husbands. I needed to have a group that would completely understand and not judge if, in the middle of the conversation, I had to excuse myself to go to my room and be alone for a moment—and they were the perfect choice. I set my dining-room table with five places instead of the usual six. I made gumbo, bought wine, and put together an appetizer. And do you know what happened?

It was weird.

Of course it was! It wasn't normal! And it wasn't anyone's fault...that was just the phase we were all in. They were still trying to figure out what I wanted to talk about and what I didn't. I was still trying to test out conversation starters that wouldn't make everything come to a crashing halt. But in the middle of that weird was a little bit of fun. Enough to encourage me to keep trying.

Night after night, I would have people over until setting a table for five instead of six became more normal. I would still bring Brad up in conversation as if it was completely natural to start sentences with "before Brad died," and after a while my friends stopped fidgeting uncomfortably in their seats when I mentioned his name. As time went on, we all seemed to start working together to fill in what was missing the best we could.

I didn't wait for them to come around. I didn't wait for them to invite me over. I took control. In a way, I forced my new situation on them until it became their new situation as well.

And dammit, it worked. And no one was more surprised than I was.

The husbands started looking me in the eye again. They felt comfortable laughing and starting stories with, "Remember when Brad…?" What was even more amazing was that, as the years passed, we all seemed to genuinely be friends again. I would occasionally hear from friends of his—guys he grew up with in Pennsylvania or buddies from the Air Force Academy—who would call to see how the kids and I were doing and if we needed anything. And eventually, those compassion calls developed into our own friendships, separate from Brad's death. Our conversations became more about what we were doing now, instead of completely consumed with what we had done in the past. Sure, some Brad stories were thrown in there. And yes, our relationships had changed.

But why shouldn't they? Everything else had.

15

I didn't realize that Brad was gone until about two months after he died.

Oh, I knew that he'd died. But for some reason, there was a huge disconnect in my brain that didn't allow me to comprehend that he was actually *gone*.

I was walking out of Walmart when I had this little realization. You see, a few months before his accident, Brad and I had made a couple attempts to go see the movie *Wild Hogs*, and both times we didn't make it. We started both date nights having dinner, and then by the time we were supposed to leave for the movie, we decided that we were having too much fun where we were to interrupt ourselves in order to go sit quietly in a movie theater.

So we never saw it.

Anyway, about two months after he died, I had finished my grocery shopping and was making my way out of the store when I saw the huge sign that said "Coming Soon: *Wild Hogs* on DVD."

My whole body lit up as I prepared to rush out the door so that I could call Brad and tell him that we'd finally get to see the movie. And then my euphoria literally came to a standstill as I stared at the sign and realized that he wasn't there to call.

When Brad was still in the Air Force in Florida, we had seen several space shuttle launches and I remember my whole body feeling the sonic boom as the shuttle made its way into space. Realizing that he was gone—that I wouldn't be able to call him or tell him even the most trivial, everyday things—felt just like that. It was like the sudden change in the atmosphere started in my body cavity and worked its way out through a roaring in my ears. My entire body vibrated with the sudden knowledge that not only was he dead...he was gone.

There is a big difference between being lonely and being alone. Alone is something you choose to be. Lonely is not. Everyone has been lonely at some point in their lives. We've all had a Saturday night when it feels like everyone else is out doing something but us. We've all been to events where it seems like we're the only person in the room who doesn't know everyone else. And we've all sat down to a lonely Whopper at Burger King thinking, "Well, if I have to do this alone, I might as well supersize this bad boy. Who's here to judge?"

Well. Maybe that last one is just me.

The difference between being "regular lonely" and being "widow lonely" is that loneliness as a widow makes you feel hollow. The best way I can describe it is like the worst kind of homesickness you can possibly imagine because you can't exactly pinpoint what it is you're missing. It's more than just losing a person—it's yearning for a way of life you had and know you will never have again. And the difference between being widowed and experiencing other types of loss is that, in most cases, we've lost the person we could lean on and talk to about the despair that we're feeling. We've lost the person we can be the most honest with. We've lost the person who would hand us a box of tissues and a glass of wine, hoping that our nervous breakdown would stop before halftime was over.

Most of us have lost the person we would have turned to when the worst thing we could have possibly imagine happening happened. We want to be able to roll over in bed and say in utter disbelief to our spouses, "Did you hear that you *died?* And you were so young!"

This would be followed by a hug from them, a pat on the back, and the murmuring of some comforting words while we cried on their shoulder.

But when we roll over...well...our spouses already know that they died. It kind of spoils it a little.

And when we roll over, the bed is empty.

Once we come to the realization that we are alone, most of us try to do our best to fix it. And since we can't replace our spouses and we eventually realize that we have a smaller credit limit, making retail therapy a little more difficult, what's left?

Finding people who are going through the same thing we are.

Two months after Brad died, I found myself sitting on a large beanbag chair, looking at another woman around my age who had brought her children to the same group therapy that I had. I could only bring Haley and Michael because Sarah, at twenty months old, was still too young to participate. Once a week, we would make our way downtown after the kids got home from school so that they could play with dolls, color, and go into what was brilliantly called the Volcano Room: a padded room where they could throw soft balls, roll around with large stuffed animals, and generally get out some anger that they might be too young to know they had.

I just couldn't figure out why only the children had access to this room.

After a few weeks, I realized that taking the kids to group

therapy was fulfilling one of my own needs: finding other people who had been through what I had. It makes sense, right? I mean, when you participate in any other activity—golf, tennis, or Texas Hold 'em at the local bar—you're bound to meet people with similar interests. The same holds true for therapy. Just by showing up, we had something in common: we all had kids, all of the kids were young (and so we were all relatively young), and all of us had gone through unimaginable loss.

"So…when did he die?" Sally asked me at the first meeting.

"Two months ago. You?"

"A little over a year ago."

What began was a friendship born of necessity. As our children drew, played with sand, and acted out "therapeutic puppet shows" with the volunteers in the room next to us, Sally and I sat covered in tears and stuffed animals in the room where the kids would eventually join us when their session was done, blatantly talking about our situations and how our lives pretty much sucked more than anyone else we knew.

There is something invaluable about finding a friend who, when you tell them the horrific details of your story, can respond with, "Holy shit! Me, too!" Someone who understands when you tell them that the only cleaning you've done to your stove lately is dusting it off. Someone who doesn't think you look weird when you show up at a restaurant with cheeks so chapped from crying that you look like a Siberian farmer.

That magical person who won't judge you for drinking too much wine at the Christmas party…they'll just offer you a ride home.

"Hey, you want to come to dinner with me and some of my friends next week?" Sally asked at the end of one session. "There are about twelve of us going, and everyone has lost their spouse. You'll fit right in."

"You're kidding!" I said. "There are groups like that? I thought

all of the groups were for old people and met at churches with
bad coffee."

"They usually do," she said. "That's why we formed this
one—we're more the happy-hour type, not the holier-than-thou
type. A few of us started it when we met through the hospice. It
just started kind of growing by word of mouth."

By the time I made it to my first widow(er) dinner, winter
was in full swing and the Christmas lights were already out. It
was about four months after Brad died, and I had driven across
town to a restaurant I had never been to, more nervous than I
had been in years. I mean, I'd always been a people person, but
widowhood had really put those skills to the test. What if I said
something wrong? What if they didn't like me and I was on my
own again?

What in the *hell* had happened to my life and *why* was I
doing this?

When I walked in the door of the restaurant that was decorated for the holidays that were not even on my radar yet, I
recognized Sally sitting at a table with a group of people who all
had cocktails in front of them.

So far, so good.

When she spied me, Sally waved me over, gave me an enthusiastic "hi!" and started making introductions.

We widows have such an odd language but we think it's perfectly normal. We'll plop down next to a new person in the group,
and the first thing we'll blurt out is, "So what'd he die from?" And
then we'll listen to some horrendous story about an accident or
an illness that lasted three grueling years, while munching on pot
stickers and drinking beer. After taking a non-widowed friend to
a group lunch with me once, I realized how strange we must seem
to the outside world. Because really all we ever talk about are sex
and death.

But I guess if you're looking at the big picture, what else is there?

As I glanced around at all of those faces on that first night, all I could think was, "My God. I'm not alone." And even if I didn't go to another event after that, that knowledge was worth the effort it took to get there.

Our once-a-month dinners eventually spilled over into other events and we became each other's go-to companions. Need someone to come with you to the water park with your kids? Email the group and see who wants to go. Need someone to talk to in the middle of the night? Email the group and see who's up. Need an entire group of people to fill a race team for the fundraiser you want to participate in to honor your spouse? We'll strap on our tennis shoes, pin that number to the T-shirt we're wearing from the race we were in last week for someone else, and we'll be there.

That group was vital to me because at a time in my life when I didn't even know who I was, they accepted me with no questions asked. I could contact any of them with the most insane ideas or personal issues, and they wouldn't even blink an eye.

I think I'm having a nervous breakdown, I texted Sally one night at about 1:00 a.m.

What's wrong?

Someone told me that P.S. I Love You was a really good movie and I should watch it. I've been crying for 4 hours.

Catherine! You need to check with me before you do something like that! And WHO told you that was a good movie for you to watch???

My hygienist.

I never thought I would leave that group. That feeling of normal. But after a while, I realized that it was time to move forward. The people I had "joined" with were like me—starting to get busy rebuilding their lives because they had come to terms with the fact that the old one was gone. Newer widows were joining the group, and while I felt a deep need to help them and let them know that life after a spouse's death was possible, going to regular meetings where the grief was so raw made me feel like I was backsliding a little.

I've often thought that there needs to be a Widow Support Group (for new widows) and a Widows Recovery Group (for widows who are a little further out). Those two groups need to meet on their own and then get together about twice a year for dinner. It's important for newer widows to see from the more seasoned professionals that they will get through it. That we're still grieving, but it's not all-consuming and we are able to get on with our lives at some point.

But it's difficult for the people who have overcome so many obstacles to be reminded monthly of how damn hard all of it really is. When we sit there and listen to someone who looks completely shell-shocked talk about how she can't get the sound of a beeping heart monitor out of her head, it's easy to remember where we've been. The widows who are a little further out have moved on to subjects like wondering if we can stretch our cash to take that cruise next year that we've always wanted to go on, and the newer widows are still concerned with whether they remembered to put deodorant on that morning.

I began to realize that my grief was progressing, but all that really meant to me at that point was more uncharted territory. It had always been on my radar that I would probably need to find a counselor, but I didn't really know how to go about it. It never occurred to me, before I lost Brad, that counseling would be something I would have to shop around for. I thought a professional was a professional. They're not all that different, are they?

Boy, howdy. Are they ever.

I have always, unfortunately, been a person who cares deeply about what people around me think.

That part of me has changed drastically over the years, but in those months after Brad died, I cared entirely too much about how the decisions I was making were going over with the people I knew. But there were so many changes and so many people that it was impossible for everyone to think that what I was doing was a good idea.

And that started to make me feel very prickly.

When something would come up—like dating or moving or just living this new life in general—and I would make a decision about which way to go, it was sometimes met with a disapproving look (or what I perceived was a disapproving look, but who knows? It could have just been gas). That would immediately make me want to not tell anyone anything that was going on in my life.

This left me in a very lonely place. And in the absence of people who would approve or agree with what I was doing, I thought it might be time to find someone I could pay to at least smile and nod when I told her I was thinking about dating a professional arm-wrestler.

There is a difference between grieving and depression, and although the line is blurry, it's still there. They both cause you to feel like life as you know it is over. But after a few months, when I started feeling myself sinking even further than usual and saw my life as one big, black hole that I would never climb out of, that's when I decided it was time to start talking to someone who might throw me a rope.

And because my time was at a premium, it made sense to me to look for a counselor who worked in my area.

What I didn't know was that location should have really been last on my list of criteria, or at least midway down. It really shouldn't matter if my therapist was in France as long as she answered her phone when I called and I felt like I could talk to her. I didn't realize when I was looking for a professional to help that the most important thing was to find someone I clicked with.

This was a lesson I was getting ready to learn.

I drove to my new counselor's home office in a neighborhood just five minutes from my own for the first time the winter after Brad died. It was gray and cold, and the sky was spitting snow. I'd left the kids with my mother, who gave me a hug when I left and an encouraging "Good luck. Don't rush back if you need a little time after the session. I've got everything covered."

Brad had been gone for about six months, and the problems that were pounding in my brain were getting to be too much to ignore. On my drive over, I was hopeful. I'd been to counseling before and, strange as it may sound, I loved the process. I loved how someone could ask you questions and make you think about your life in a different way. I knew that what I had been dealing with in the months prior was nothing close to what I'd faced before, but I couldn't help but be a little optimistic about the help I was sure I would receive.

I pulled up in front of her house and walked down the steps, through her side yard, and into the entrance of her office in her walkout basement as I had been instructed to do.

"Hello," she said, extending her hand as I walked through the sliding glass door. "I'm Dr. Weiss. I'm so glad to meet you."

I sat in her office looking around at décor that I think every therapist's office has. Really. I think they must all google "how to decorate an office to help crazy people" and the same picture comes up. Usually the walls are covered in soothing, pastel colors. There's an overstuffed couch, trifolded color brochures on a table about how you can take control of your life in one thousand words or less, and the obligatory table fountain somewhere in the room.

There's the chair in the corner across from the couch that the therapist sits in. It's always at an angle and never faces you head on. I don't know why. And then there's the yellow legal pad sitting next to the chair so that the therapist can either take notes on how crazy you are or work on her grocery list if your problems are not interesting enough that day.

I can't really put my finger on it, but there was something about Dr. Weiss that I wasn't happy about from the beginning. I've come to realize that those of us who have experienced loss—whether of a spouse, parent, or child—can sniff out those who have not. There was just something about her that hinted to me that the closest experience she'd had with death was when she put Fluffy down two years ago. But I was in such a fog at that point that I didn't trust my inner voice that said, "Walk away. Grab your purse, that useless grief pamphlet she just handed you, one more piece of cheap candy, and get the heck out."

"So, tell me what's going on," she began, which somewhat annoyed me from the start because I'd already told her over the phone why I was making the appointment.

"Ummm…well…my husband died about six months ago and I'm starting to feel a little bogged down with life in general."

"Uh huh," she said, pen scrawling across the page. "And what's making you feel bogged down?"

"Ummm…my husband's death?"

"Uh huh."

On and on this went. I left feeling like I had gotten nowhere but was willing to give it another try. After all, this problem was big. Enormous. Obese. Maybe she just needed a warm-up session until we got to the core of the problem.

But then at the next session, we talked about my life before I'd met Brad.

And then at the next we talked about when he and I dated.

By the time the fourth session rolled around, I was starting to feel so overwhelmed with my past that there was no way I was going to be able to deal with my present.

It took me two months to really figure out that this counselor and I just weren't clicking. And, even though I'd been willing to give her a try for a few sessions, the moment I realized this just wasn't going to work happened in an instant.

I stood up from the couch after I had just handed her my check and said, "Oh! I went out to dinner last week with an old high-school friend. He and I dated when we were teenagers. It was just kind of nice to be out with a guy."

Before I'd even finished telling her about my evening, she popped off with, "You're not ready to date. You shouldn't be doing that right now. Shall we go ahead and schedule your session next week?"

There was a moment of silence while I pondered what she had just said. I didn't exactly know what was wrong, but every ounce of my body was saying it wanted to get out of there. And to never come back.

"Uh. That's okay. Why don't I call you when I've had a chance to look at my calendar?"

After leaving her house, I sat in my car feeling completely shell-shocked. Not only was I back to feeling like I wasn't grieving right, but she had somehow implanted in my head the idea that I had done a bad thing. I felt cheap and dirty, like I had just cheated on Brad by going out to dinner with someone I had actually met a few times for lunch when Brad was alive (and told him about it). I drove and drove, taking the long, winding way home. Tears rolled down my face as I thought over and over again, "I can't be helped. I can't be helped."

And I quit going.

I felt utterly alone. Going to counseling was my last resort and now I knew, beyond a shadow of a doubt, that nothing was going to help me climb out of this grief hole. I would live a life alone, with only my crazy thoughts to keep me company. And eventually the grief would completely take me over.

I spent months feeling this way but kept my thoughts to myself. When my mother asked, "Do you need to make another counseling appointment? Let me know and I'll come over and watch the kids," I would be intentionally vague about my answer because I felt like I couldn't tell her why I couldn't go back.

That I was unfixable.

It was at lunch with Kristi one day, when she was talking about one of the networking luncheons she had been to for women starting their own businesses, that fate threw me a bone.

"You know, one of the women there was Beth, a counselor who works downtown," Kristi said. "I really liked her a lot. I got her card and I thought I'd pass it on to you, in case you know someone who might need it."

When I took Beth's card from my sister that day, I really didn't intend to use it. I meant to keep it in my purse until I met someone else who might need it, which was fairly likely with the circles I was running in at the time. But as I became more and more mired down, sinking further than anyone around me knew, I decided to give it one more try.

And that time, I hit the crazy-widow jackpot.

Unlike the previous counselor who'd spent several sessions completely steeped in the past and not dealing with my present problems, Beth just dove right in and started talking about my current state, which was exactly what my impatient widow brain needed. Through that process, other past issues did come up, but she didn't start out digging in so deep that I thought I'd never be able to claw my way out. I never left her office without feeling like I had made some sort of progress. And that's extremely important when you're on this journey.

Because if you're not moving forward, you start sliding backward at an unbelievably rapid pace. And that's the kind of thing that will get you drinking out of a paper bag.

I'd spent most of the beginning of my widowhood worrying that I wasn't grieving right, something that I felt my previous counselor had confirmed. I watched other people around me do it slower, which made me feel like I was either a shallow person or that I didn't love my husband enough. I watched others do it faster, getting remarried, buying new homes, and generally moving on with their lives, and I felt sure that I would never get to that place. I beat myself up, wore myself down, and generally didn't like who I was. All because I never felt like I was grieving the way I should be.

"I'm doing this backwards!" I wailed to Beth during one session, snotty tissues clutched in my hand. "I've spent months running around nonstop and now I don't want to get out of bed when it seems like everyone else has done it the other way around! I've been trying to convince myself that my marriage wasn't that great when I should be putting him up on a pedestal and thinking that no one will ever live up to how great he was! I should be doing what everyone else does! What is *wrong* with me?"

She calmly looked at me in a very counselor-like way and said, "Who says you *should* be doing that? You're doing everything you should be doing. In fact, I don't want you to use that word 'should' anymore. All you're doing is telling yourself that you're doing something wrong. And there is no wrong way to do this."

That idea opened up a whole new world for me, and ten months after Brad died, I began to slowly forgive myself for not being the perfect widow that I thought I "should" be. I began to grieve in the way I needed to, not as some meaningless pamphlet was telling me I "should." I stopped thinking that the way others were doing it was much better than my way and using it as a map that would never get me where *I* needed to go. I no longer felt guilty about times when I would tear up talking about Brad…and also the times I didn't. My emotions, in whatever form they came in, were no longer my enemy. They were something I began to accept as a part of who I was now. And that was okay.

It's important to feel like your therapist understands what you're going through. Nothing made me feel better than when I would tell Beth something that I thought only I did and was ashamed of, and she would respond, "Oh, people do that all the time!" Because no widow ever wants to feel like she's the only person who's ever thought about getting engaged six months after her husband died or that if she could abandon her children every weekend to just go sit in her car and cry for forty-eight hours straight she would.

And even if he or she hasn't experienced a loss like this (and if they have, they'll probably never tell you), you want to feel like, no matter what, your therapist won't pass judgment. It's a very delicate balancing act. A therapist needs to be somewhat sympathetic, but not over the top because you don't want to feel like your life story is the worst she's ever heard. I've had times when I've gone into Beth's office completely bent out of shape about some problem that seems massive to me at the time, and she will just calmly ask me a very important question.

"Why does that matter?"

She doesn't ask because it shouldn't matter. She just asks because she wants to know…and she wants me to know. And you know what? Nine times out of ten, it really *doesn't* matter.

After about a year of going to Beth every other week, I began to see the light at the end of the tunnel and regular visits weren't really necessary anymore. But the fact that we had established a relationship that allowed me to just go in for sanity maintenance was something that I never took for granted.

My "hot" time of the year usually hit the couple of months before the anniversary of Brad's death when I would stare at the pictures on my computer in wonder, thinking, "How could we have not known this was coming? Look at him! He's just sitting there laughing and feeding Sarah ice cream! You fool, *how could you not have known you would be dead three weeks later?*"

I even put together a PowerPoint presentation of pictures of him, complete with a sad song that was timed perfectly. Night after night, after the kids had gone to bed, I'd go sit in my office and play it, trying to get the tears out that I'd kept bottled up while I was with them all day, hoping for an emotional release of some sort.

I thought that if I could just relieve the pressure valve that is grief every once in a while, I would save myself from an explosion. And in a way it worked. But when a heart has been broken, it can't be healed by crying over a slide show for twenty minutes three times a week. I was, unfortunately, still under the impression that I could control my pain like I tried to control everything else in my life. Like a monster I had caged, I would let it out every once in a while when we were alone, hoping that that would be enough to appease it.

But grief cannot be trained. It will find a way out when it wants to. And when it does, it often happens when you least expect it.

16

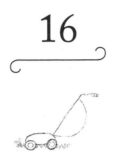

My mother swore that by learning how to use the lawn mower, I was putting my children in mortal danger.

"Catherine," she said in her stern, Southern mom voice. "Call a service. If you're outside mowing, how can you hear the children?"

My inner voice wanted to reply, "That's the point." I had visions of taking a lawn-mowing vacation once a week: forty-five uninterrupted minutes as I strapped on my MP3 and walked my lawn in a mindless pattern. Forty-five minutes of watching my children pantomiming tattles from the porch while I pointed at the mower and mouthed back, "I can't hear you!" and went on my merry way.

Forty-five minutes of lawn-mowing freedom.

Bet you never thought you'd hear someone daydreaming about mowing their lawn, did you?

It wasn't my mother's fault that she felt this way. I come from a long line of women who would rather sell the contents of their homes and hire a yard man than do it themselves. In fact, my grandmother used to go so far as to say, "Every time I see a woman outside mowing her own lawn, I just want to get out of the car and *smack* her! Don't you know she's just letting her husband sit around and watch the game while she does *everything?*"

In other words, in my family, women's liberation meant no female should cut her own grass. Ever.

I tried explaining to my mother that I could still watch the kids while I took care of the yard.

"I'll be outside, Mom. The kids can play in the yard while I mow."

"Well, don't you think that's *dangerous?*" she replied, looking at me in disbelief like I had just suggested they play with matches next to a propane tank. "What happens if you run over a rock and it shoots out of the mower and *hits one of them in the head?*"

Now, I'm sure that this is possible, and if it should ever happen to one of my children, I will have to swallow a big "I told you so" from my mother. But I honestly don't remember her sending my sister and me outside in helmets and pads while my dad mowed the lawn. So I figured I would take my chances.

Up until that time, I had relied on my dad to come over and take care of my lawn once a week, although a neighbor surprised me once with a spontaneous mow. But I was starting to feel like it was time to take control of my household.

All of my household.

Everyone was gone, and I was moving into that phase that most widows experience when they look around and think, "Hey! Where'd everybody go?" I was starting to realize that life would keep changing whether I wanted it to or not, and I'll be honest with you...that was a really painful feeling. And I can pinpoint, down to the moment, when I felt it.

"I'm pregnant!" my friend Christa said excitedly over the phone. "Due in June!"

"Oh, Chris!" I said. "I'm so excited for you!"

And I was. I truly was. At first.

But when I hung up the phone, it hit me. Christa was *pregnant*. She was going to produce this whole other person that Brad would never meet. This baby would come into the world and never really know Brad was in it. I started realizing that friends of ours would get married, divorced, move, and have countless monumental experiences...all without him here.

I know that life changes for everyone on the planet, but for widows it seems to happen at a rapid pace. The changes our friends go through seem to happen in fast-forward, and we can't even keep up with what we have to deal with personally. It feels like our lives are spinning out of control and we spend a lot of time either desperately trying to stop it...or feeling defeated because we know we can't.

Something uncontrollable had happened to my life, and I wanted to control the pieces that were left. I wanted to know how to do *everything* Brad knew how to do, and I wanted to know *now*. I needed to know how to mow, snow blow, and grill. I even remember, in a wild, delusional moment, asking one of his good friends to show me how to put a lift kit on a Jeep.

You know. Just in case.

I don't know if I was trying to convince myself that by becoming like him, maybe I wouldn't miss him. Or that by becoming him, I could keep a part of him alive. I *do* know that part of me was heartbroken that, because the kids were so little when he died, they would never really know how special and smart their dad was. I hated the fact that my son wouldn't get to work on a car with his dad. That my girls would never have the outrageous tickle fights that only he could deliver. That we would never all be able to lie in the backyard in one, big family heap under the stars and have the man who had been so obsessed with space since childhood tell us which constellations were which.

So I put a ton of pressure on myself to be him for them.

Have you ever tried to be something that you're not? If you have, you know how exhausting it is. There was a good reason why I didn't know how to do the things that Brad did, and it was mainly because my brain didn't work that way. I could put all of the expression in my body into playing Brahms on the piano, sing a pitch-perfect lullaby, and read stories with funny voices that made my children squeal with delight at bedtime.

But I didn't have a damn clue how to change my own oil, fix an electrical outlet, or do my taxes.

He did.

After about six months of running in circles, trying to be both of us and desperately failing, I stopped and came to terms with how utterly helpless Brad's death left me feeling. After getting married when I was twenty, I went straight from depending on my parents (the most dependable people in the world) to depending on him (who tied with my parents in the dependable category).

And then, for eleven years, I had been married to the smartest, handiest person I'd ever known. I knew that if the world should come to a crashing halt, Brad would go out in the backyard with a trap he had fashioned out of curly ribbon and paper clips and catch us dinner. I knew that if we faced a gas crisis, he would be in the garage making an alternate fuel source out of garbage like they did in *Back to the Future*. I knew that if I had a flat tire, I had someone I could call.

Brad was my rock. He embodied stability. If I could be sure about anything in my life, it was *him*. Just the fact of him. He was one of those people who could answer any question, fix any problem, and take on the world...all on my behalf. And I'll be honest with you, just his presence in my life allowed me to operate at about 30 percent of my capacity. Because I just knew that he would always be there to take care of me. There was not a doubt in my mind. *Nothing* could happen to Brad.

Confessions of a Mediocre Widow

And then he died. Which seemed to make everything I was sure about in my life turn from concrete to Jell-O within a seventy-two-hour time frame. Everything was left up to me, and I had a choice.

I could embrace it or fight it.

Of course, no one can get through this whole widow mess without some moments of extreme self-doubt. Daily. Hourly. And most of my moments of self-doubt are usually centered around my kids. 'Cause let's face it, I could default on my mortgage and have bad credit. But if I default on child-rearing, that's pretty hard to recover from.

Single parenting is not for the faint of heart. And although you'll hear many people say that there are a lot of "single parents" out there, there aren't. There are a lot of *divorced* parents out there, but there is a big difference. And let me assure you, I truly don't think that one is worse than the other.

That's like trying to compare whether it's more painful to have a boil on your rear end or the bottom of your foot. I can understand how painful it must be for divorced parents to send their kids off for a weekend with someone they dislike so much they can barely swallow the fact that that person has partial custody of their Tupperware, much less their kids.

But for the widowed single parent, the most single a "single parent" can get, it's pretty damn hard to do it all at once and all alone.

This didn't take me long to figure out. I was in the mode of trying to prove to myself and the kids that we could do this. That I could take on single parenting and that *Widowed Parents Magazine* would eventually feature me on their inaugural cover,

after all three kids had been accepted into Harvard on full schol-
arships, majoring in physics, with a minor in world peace.

And in my quest to become Single Mom of the Year, I think
I went a little too far trying to prove that I could do this…and
ended up doing things that I wouldn't have done even if Brad had
been here to complain to after they became epic failures.

A few months after Brad died, when the kids were six, four,
and two, I was having my usual midmorning conversation with
my mother and telling her our plans for the day.

"I'm going to take the kids out to lunch and a movie," I said.

"Are you sure you have this covered?" she asked me doubtfully
over the phone. "That sounds like a lot to handle all on your own."

"Of course!" I said confidently. "If I have any problems, I'll
just pack them all up and go home. It's no big deal. We have to
get out there at some point, right?"

"Still…" she said. "Why don't I just meet you for the movie?
I don't have anything going on today anyway."

"Okay. Whatever you want to do," I replied, slightly annoyed
at her for doubting my parenting skills.

Doubts that were, as it turns out, completely well-founded.

We met my mom at the front of the theater, and after we'd
bought our tickets, we all went up to the concession counter.

"Now, we just had lunch at Red Robin," I told the kids. "So
let's just get one package of licorice to split. You guys have already
had plenty of junk for today."

The girls nodded in agreement. But three-year-old Michael,
who must have had a near-death experience with licorice in a
former life, decided that this was *completely* unacceptable.

"I don't *want* licorice!" he screamed at me in front of the concession counter. "I *hate* licorice! I want M&M's!"

Now, I'd had my issues with Michael as a toddler. His constant
unexplainable meltdowns were the reason we left many a restaurant

with Styrofoam containers and red faces (until it got the point where I told Brad, "I'm not taking that kid out in public anymore. It's just not worth the money, and we might get sued the next time he beans someone in the back of the head with his pacifier").

But Michael's maniacal tendencies as a toddler had given way to the mellowest little boy you'd ever want to meet. Sweet-natured and quiet, he could sit contently with a stack of blocks for hours and you wouldn't hear a peep from him. Until all of that "mellow" would build up for a few weeks and he'd get mad about something completely out of the blue.

And then there was no turning back.

When my son would get pissed, he was *pissed*. And he wasn't like most kids who forget what they're mad about after a while and then go back out and play. He could scream his head off for half an hour, and when you asked him why, he could tell you every detail of how he was wronged.

That takes some focus and fierce determination in the grudge department, my friend.

"You take the girls into the theater," I said to my mom over Michael's wails. "I'm taking him for a time-out in the car, and when he calms down, we'll meet you in there."

She nodded and trotted off in the direction of the movie with the girls, picking up a booster seat for Sarah on her way into the theater. And I put myself into Super Mommy mode, picking up my kicking son and marching purposefully out the doors of the theater as all of the teenage employees watched in quiet horror.

I'm pretty sure they all took a vow of celibacy that day.

I stuck him in the car, shut the door, and stood outside with my back to him, determined not to give his bad behavior the audience it was looking for. As I leaned against my shaking, screaming minivan, I smiled and waved at the mystified people who were passing by. I truly thought that this would only go on for a few minutes and then I would open the door, have a nice, calm talk with him, and he would immediately realize that this was no way for a future general to behave. We would then share a hug, hold hands, and skip into the theater.

Imagine my surprise when I popped open the sliding door to the minivan, only to find out that in his licorice-hating frenzy, he'd stripped off *all* of his clothes. Except his socks.

So there I was, in the parking lot of the theater with my screaming, naked four-year-old, looking around wildly, expecting to see video cameras on every street lamp recording this lapse in my parenting. I was absolutely terrified that we would end up on some homemade YouTube video that resembled an after-school special on how *not* to parent your four-year-old.

I called my mom from my cell phone in the car as I headed home with a red-eyed, glaring Michael and said the words that no daughter *ever* wants to say to her mom.

"You were right."

What was I *thinking*? I can't do this on my own! If I can't even get my kid through an animated movie, how in the hell am I going to get him through his teenage years?

I put him in his room where he could continue his fit in comfort, and where I felt like I could safely walk away. I went downstairs and sat on the back porch to breathe in some fresh air and just…take a moment. And when I sat down on my patio chair, I realized something about Michael and his tantrums that I'd never thought of before.

I was jealous.

I could hear the sounds of an emotional train barreling through his room. And instead of wanting to run away from it, I stared up at his window in wonder and muttered, "Damn. That's a *good* one."

He was *mad*, and he didn't care who heard it. I could almost feel the head rush he must have had as he yelled with all of his might. And I thought, "How lucky is *he* that he can go up to his room, completely let loose, and kick the shit out of anything that isn't moving out of his way?"

I started daydreaming about doing it myself. Going into my room and screaming and crying until my head started pounding and I collapsed on my bed, completely spent. Slamming the door a million times if I felt like it. Swiping the contents of my desk into a heaping pile of junk on the floor and then stomping on it with all of my might. Who cares if the windows are open? Who cares if the whole neighborhood hears? Who cares if it makes someone feel uncomfortable?

Who the hell cares?

Many people talk about how resilient children are. And I think that's true. But that could be because we give them the emotional freedom to feel however they need to. The way they express their emotions when they're young is completely unshaped by the expectations of others and is, therefore, completely honest. But eventually, those tantrums at the store are met with a time-out. Crying, kicking, and screaming result in privileges taken away. Getting so mad they just want to hit something (or someone) is completely unacceptable.

By the time our kids are teenagers, they've already started to understand that having a nervous breakdown in public is "just not cool." And then if they experience a loss, we try and try to get them to express themselves when all the years before that, we basically said, "That's not okay." We've confused them by telling them all their lives that they need to keep their emotions in check, and then suddenly we start telling them that it's okay to be angry. It's okay to cry. It's okay to break down. When we've been telling them for years that it's not.

Once we hit adulthood, society's tolerance for emotional

outbursts is nonexistent. I mean, how many times have *you* screamed and cried in the middle of the grocery store? I'm guessing zero. And how many times have you wanted to? Probably too many to count.

I thought about that Volcano Room at the first group counseling I brought Haley and Michael to, where the kids could throw, punch, kick, and pummel anything they could get their hands on.

And where were the adults? In "discussion" rooms calmly talking about various topics related to grieving. What happens to *our* tantrums? What happens to our anger, our rage, our overwhelming grief about our situation?

It gets replaced with a smile, a nod, and an "I'm fine. How are *you?*"

And, not that the kids don't need an outlet to express themselves, but who do you think is *really* in need of a Volcano Room?

You can't see me right now, but I'm raising my hand.

I wanted to walk into a padded room and throw the grocery list, the bills, the back-to-school forms, the insurance paperwork, just chuck 'em at a wall over and over until the paper was crumpled and soft. I wanted to scream until my throat was raw. I wanted to kick at those padded walls until my legs were sore. I wanted to pull an *Office Space* and take a baseball bat to every appliance in my house that had the nerve not to work properly.

And sometimes I want to take my emotions out on an innocent teddy bear.

It's kind of funny to me now that that day at the movie theater was really the first time I started worrying about raising the kids alone. I didn't worry about it right after Brad died...I guess it was just too much to think about all at once. If I can be completely honest, one of the first things I thought was, "Who's going to stay up all night with the kids when they're throwing up *now?*"

I don't know why, but it was an unspoken rule that if one of the kids had a stomach bug, Brad would spend the night sleeping next to their bed. I never asked him to do it; he just took over. I got the colds, fevers, scraped knees, and bumped heads. He got splinters the size of small tree branches and the bucket next to the bed. This should give you an idea of what a stand-up guy he was. Or it's possible he remembered our college days when I had a weak stomach and the sight of someone paying the price after too much tequila sent me into sympathy vomiting and he thought he'd just be better off taking care of one little kid and not throwing me into the mix.

So, when he died one of my first thoughts was, "Oh crap. I have vomit duty for the rest of my life. I'm really going to miss that guy."

I think that's the brain's way of coping. You can't immediately think of getting all three kids through school without major incident, off to college, married, and having grandchildren he'll never see. You'd go nuts if you really thought about all of that in the beginning. You're better off pondering something stupid like, "Who's going to settle the kids' argument about Dairy Queen vs. Baskin-Robbins *now?*"

I also didn't realize at the beginning how hard it was to lose that person in your life who you could point to at any given moment and say "That's *your* child" when one of the kids does something bad. Because now it's all on *me*. I'll never forget sitting in the car with Sarah when she was about two-and-a-half years old and I quietly heard her say from her little car seat in the back…

"You're a butt."

Then, "You're a butt crack."

And finally, "You're a butt-crack sandwich."

To this day I can't remember what I did to incur her wrath, but it must have been a doozy. I mentally flipped back and forth between putting her in time-out and praising her for her creativity. And I missed having someone I could point to and say, "You taught her that, didn't you? You called someone a butt-crack sandwich during *Monday Night Football* and she picked it up! What were you *thinking?*"

Because if she didn't pick it up from him, that left me as the next logical culprit.

No one likes to have their parenting skills questioned, but when you're widowed, people seem to think it's their right—no, their *duty*—to point out what you're doing wrong. It's rather nerve-racking knowing that your kids and you are being scrutinized so thoroughly. Every time I accidentally sent one of my kids to school with their pants on backwards I thought I might as well be walking around with a sign taped to my back that said, "I just lost my husband, and studies show that childhood wardrobe malfunctions are a side effect."

Because I was worried about the long-term effects of Brad's death on my kids, too. I didn't need the public at large to point out that this could have a major impact on the rest of their lives.

I'll never forget the night I was watching a *20/20* special on some murders that had happened in Texas. The murderer turned out to be a teenage girl who, the show's host made sure to point out, had lost her father when she was a young child. This threw me into a panic because surely a two-year-old who calls her mother a "butt-crack sandwich" could have the makings of a teenage homicidal maniac.

As if worrying about the fact that I didn't have dental insurance wasn't enough, I suddenly felt like I needed to start checking my preschooler for concealed weapons.

And where was my backup? Gone. Even though Brad was physically out of town a lot of the time when he was alive, I knew that he had my back. That if I called him to complain about how Michael had made gigantic spit wads out of toilet paper and water from the commode and covered the powder room with them, he would commiserate with me from 1,500 miles away and read his son the riot act over the phone. That if one of the kids came down with some virus the doctors couldn't explain, he would be on the first plane home. And that if, for some reason, I had someone question my parenting skills in public, he would be the first to say, "What a bitch."

Which brings me to what I now refer to as "the Costco Incident."

I had taken Haley and Sarah to Costco one afternoon right before Christmas, killing time before we had to pick Michael up from preschool. In hindsight, I will say that this was not one of the smartest moves I'd ever made. Let's face it: I was nuts with grief, I had one of the most depressing holidays looming before me, and I found myself fighting a crowd that was buying large quantities of soup and zip ties. I'd had no sleep and was exhausted from trying to keep everything normal so that my family felt like everything was okay…when what I really wanted to do was stick my head in a punch bowl of eggnog and quietly end my misery.

That year, my Christmas "joy" was compounded by the fact that I was in a stabilizing boot up to my knee from pulling my Achilles tendon a few weeks earlier. I don't know if you've ever had to use one of those things, but the most annoying thing about them is that it's hard to find another pair of shoes that are the same height. Otherwise, you walk sideways like you're in an ongoing V8 commercial.

This was not helping my Christmas spirit.

After a few minutes of shopping, two-year-old Sarah decided to take off running in the freezer section of the store. And I hobbled behind her as fast as my crippled ass could go and managed to grab her by the hood of her coat (before she could get away and accidentally purchase a gross of oranges and a set of new tires). And then I picked her up and strapped her in the seat of the grocery cart.

I know. Lock me up, right?

As I walked through the store, Sarah started screaming at the top of her lungs, "*I wanna walk! I wanna walk! Let me out!*"

I tried everything I could think of to get her to stop...other than taking her out of the cart, which I believe would have sent the message, "The louder you yell, the quicker you'll get your way. Congratulations!"

I asked her politely to stop.

I ignored her and kept walking through the store.

I tried explaining to her why this was happening.

All the while, Haley was walking next to me, looking worriedly at my face, which I'm sure had turned bright purple by then.

Now, as a parent, you know that when one of your kids behaves that way in public...well...it's a little unnerving. You know that everyone is staring at you, and you're hoping that most people are thinking, "Wow. That woman is really sticking to her guns. That's a great mom. I bet by learning this valuable lesson so early in life, that child will grow up to be the leader of the free world."

In reality they're thinking, "Let her go first in line and get her the hell out of here as quickly as possible."

I finally made my way up to the checkout area, and I was waiting as calmly as possible while Sarah, never the quitter, kept screaming and screaming. Suddenly this woman walked up to me and quietly said, "Do you realize you're abusing your daughter?"

At this point I was so flustered that all I could think was, "Did I hit her or something and I don't even remember? Has it come to this? That I've taken out my grief on my child in the middle of a warehouse store?" Completely rattled, I turned to the woman and gave her the most sophisticated response I could come up with.

"Uh...what?"

The woman looked at me and said, "Why don't you just let her walk? I am a mother of four, and I can tell you this is unacceptable."

At this point I stood up straight, looked her in the eye for one solid second, and said, "I am the single *widowed* mother of three."

It would have come across a lot better if my voice hadn't been shaking and my eyes hadn't been filling up with tears.

"Why don't you try negotiating with her and tell her that if she stops screaming, you'll let her down?"

Negotiate? With a two-year-old?

Other women started to approach us, and I was immediately afraid that they were going to side with the resident Costco parenting expert while I was doing everything I could to keep Sarah from crying.

And then I heard, "She's doing nothing wrong."

"Why don't you leave her alone?"

"What else is she supposed to do?"

I didn't make eye contact with anyone as I loaded my groceries on the conveyor belt. The group of women behind me kept their quiet parenting battle going, defending me against my new blond nemesis while I did my best to function and not sit on the floor in a big, sad puddle. Sarah, of course, had started to watch all that was going on with an interest that had lulled her into complete silence, and she seemed to have completely forgotten what had had her so riled up in the first place. And Haley was cautiously fixated on my face as the cashier tallied up my items without saying a word.

I didn't even stick around to see who won the argument. I wheeled my cart out to the parking lot as quickly as possible and threw all of the groceries in the back of the minivan. Haley

silently climbed into her booster seat in the back and buckled her
seat belt while I walked around to get Sarah strapped in, glaring
at her in teary anger.

My hands shook as I started the car, and I could barely see as
I made my way through the maze of the parking lot.

"Mommy, are you okay?" Haley asked from the backseat.

"I'm fine, I'm fine. I'll be okay. Thanks, sweetie."

But I wasn't okay.

As I made my way onto the road to pick up Michael from the
preschool, I suddenly had a vision of a police car waiting at my
house, waiting to take my children away. I had no husband they
could call who would say, "*My wife?* You want to question my
wife? About what? She's the best mom in the world!"

I was utterly alone. With no one home to vouch for me.

I made a sharp turn into the first parking lot I could find, the
parking lot of a new apartment complex. And then I took my cell
phone out, told the girls to just stay in their seats, and got out of
the car to call my mom.

"Mom?" I said, hiccuping in hysterics and leaning on my dirty
car for support. "I think Social Services will be coming to my
house."

"Catherine? Where are you? Do you need me to come get
you? What happened?"

I gasped, moaned, and cried through the Costco story, while
the girls watched me through the slush-streaked glass on my car.
After saying the entire story out loud, I was sure that I should
probably just head for the border.

"Catherine, I think I need to come get you," she said when I
was done.

"No…it's okay. I'm okay. But what if someone is waiting for
me at the house? What am I going to do?"

And then in a final wail, "*How could Brad leave me here all alone?"* Anything—any bad thing that has happened to me in the years since Brad has been gone—can be directly traced back to his death. That I'm stuck in traffic. That I have to go to the grocery store for just one thing. That I have the flu.

Everything that has happened is really all his fault. Because he's not here.

Let me show you how it works:

Traffic: "I wouldn't be stuck in traffic right now because I wouldn't have had to go to a job interview if he were here. I would be at home, cooking dinner, waiting for *him* to get home because he's stuck in traffic."

Grocery store: "If he were here, I wouldn't have to pack all of the kids up and go to the grocery store for just one thing. I could leave the kids with him and just run out *or*, more importantly, I would have remembered that one thing because I wouldn't have widowhood draining all of my usable brain cells."

Flu: "I wouldn't have the flu right now if he were here because I wouldn't have had to go to the grocery store for that *one thing*... which is probably where I caught it."

See? It's called Widow Math.

The reality is that what happened that day at Costco probably would have happened whether he was here or not. Sarah would still be stubborn. I would still not have any clever comebacks until about a week after the incident because that's the way I've always been. And that lady would still be an idiot, free to roam and impart her damaging parenting tips to the unsuspecting.

I didn't sleep for at least two weeks after that happened, positive that the doorbell would ring at any moment and someone would show up and strip me of the remaining family I had left. That whole episode made me a little more sensitive to the fact that a stranger could turn me in at any moment for...well...parenting. And now that I was doing it completely alone, I felt vulnerable and exposed.

Because even those of us who provide loving, nurturing environments for our children have a fear of getting turned in by some nutty do-gooder who has nothing better to do than take the time to negotiate behavior with their toddler rather than just teach them what's right and wrong. And I'm too much of a sweet, Southern conflict-avoider to stand up for myself. I needed my husband around to say to that woman, "Hey! You go negotiate with your kids all you want! And when they grow up to be pot-smoking cab drivers, I'll tell my CEO daughter to tip them well!"

Sorry. That sounded a little bitter.

One of my favorite quotes is from Karen Kaiser Clark: "Life is change. Growth is optional. Choose wisely." And I don't think anything better embodies what she was trying to say than experiencing widowhood for the simple fact that once you enter into it, Normal exits at the same time. Which is a disconcerting feeling, to say the least.

I didn't know that Normal was only here for an extended visit. I thought that it was here permanently. I didn't mind that it didn't pay rent and never did the dishes. In fact, Normal lived so quietly in our home that sometimes we forgot it was even there.

Until it left.

Not one of us chose to have this life thrust upon us. But the ability to grow and change with it is within us all. It doesn't happen overnight. It's a long, slow process. I mean, I don't think many of us lie back in a relaxed pose after a long, hard day of widowing is done, pull out our serenity journals, turn on some sitar music, and say in a breathy voice, "Wow. What an interesting, yet life-affirming day. I'm so grateful that my garbage disposal backed up and my two-year-old has decided to use our living-room rug as her new potty. Now…what I have I learned from all of this?"

If you're doing that, I think you've been reading the wrong book.

I would guess that most of us flop down in exhaustion across our empty beds—after the kids have been put to sleep, five loads of laundry have been done, and we've spent the last half hour trying to stretch five hundred dollars over a thousand dollars worth of bills—and say the wise words of every widow on this planet.

"This really sucks."

I remember feeling incredibly overwhelmed with the fact that I would have to make every decision, every day concerning the welfare of my children and myself for the rest of my life *alone*. (Insert "This really sucks" here.) Every day made me feel like I was drowning.

Should I get the kids vaccinated for H1N1? But what about that girl in Texas whose face was paralyzed right after she got the shot? Should I move so that I have less maintenance, or would that be too hard on the kids? Should I start taking my prescribed Ambien that will help me sleep so that I can be less crazy during the day but that is also unpredictable and may cause me to raid my refrigerator and take a sleep-driving trip to New Mexico?

For someone who had been operating at around 30 percent her whole life, this was a lot to take on all at once.

It's really hard not having that person around whom you can bounce everything off. Oh sure, our friends and family say that we're not alone, and that they'll always be with us. But the bottom line is that we've lost the person who is as invested in our lives as we are. We can talk to people we know and ask them if they think we should refinance the house or change cable services or buy a new car…but those people aren't living with us and paying our bills with us every day. They can offer helpful advice, but as far as those decisions really affecting *them*…well…

They don't.

So that's the part of widowhood that really stinks. But on the flip side of the decision-making dilemma…

We can decide anything we want to. And there's no one at home to sheepishly look at when we've confessed that we spent one hundred fifty dollars getting highlights in our hair.

One day, I was having lunch with Kristi and she said, "Hey! You know what? You could go out and buy a big, floral couch for your living room and no one will say a word about it! We can make your whole house as girly as we want! It will be like our own clubhouse!"

Suddenly the heavens opened and a bright light shined upon me. I could hear angels singing as I envisioned all of the square footage of my house covered in shabby chic tied together with a pretty pink bow.

Well, not really.

But it *did* get me to thinking. Hell yes, making all of the decisions on my own was tough. But hey…*I get to make all of the decisions on my own.* If I want to move, I don't have to fight with someone about the floor plan. If I want a new car, I don't have to defend my choice because it's not "cool" enough.

Yes, parenting alone is tough…but so is co-parenting. Now I don't have to hear that I was too hard, too soft, that I shouldn't have let them watch TV that long, or that I should take a pacifier away from Sarah as he walks out the door for a two-week business trip, leaving me with a screaming toddler who won't sleep until the night before he gets back.

Yikes. Guess I have a few unresolved issues. And that stinks because they're with a dead man.

Anyway. The decisions, while daunting, were also all *mine.*

For the first time in my life, I felt like not only was everything left to me if I should fail, but it was also all up to me to make sure

I succeeded. I had visions of taking a cooking class, repainting the exterior of the house in a color I liked, joining a book club. I could have done all of these things with Brad here, but for some reason I didn't feel the true freedom to do it until I was forced to build a new life.

That's right. I said "forced." Because I could fight it. I could bury my head in my covers and stay in my grief cave for as long as I wanted to. No one could get me out of it but me. I could look at my life as overwhelming or filled with possibilities. I could focus on the things I'd never done before as daunting or a whole new adventure. I could build a life based on the fear that I would fail or the hope that I will succeed.

How I was going to build this life was entirely up to me.

Milestones

i'd rather pass a kidney stone
than a milestone

17

There's a saying about grief that I have found to be profoundly true.

If you're not feeling like yourself, take a look at the calendar. Because chances are something happened around that day that will subconsciously turn your world upside down.

I know this happens because I've experienced it firsthand. I would be sailing along, minding my own widow business, and then suddenly...

I would start to shake.

I would get dizzy.

My whole body would feel weak.

Then I'd look at the calendar and realize that that was the first time my husband had done something significant to my subconscious ten years earlier. And instead of experiencing what I thought for sure was a grief-induced stroke, I figured out I was going through something else.

Anticipatory grief. Also what I like to call pre-grief syndrome or PGS.

Anticipatory grief is something that most of us have heard of, and it's usually associated with the grief we experience when someone we love is dying from an illness. It's not pretty, it's not wanted, and, contrary to what most people think who haven't gone through it, it's really not that helpful. Despite the opinion of the public-at-large, it doesn't matter how long we've "known"…death is always sudden and somewhat unexpected. So, while pre-grieving is very real, its usefulness to the overall grieving process is somewhat of a myth.

What most people also don't realize is that anticipatory grief doesn't just happen when we are preparing for a death. It also happens when we know there is a milestone approaching and, unfortunately, it can also happen when we *don't* know that a milestone is approaching.

I've often thought that grief can just sneak up and attack you, but anticipating grief is more like a long, drawn-out hostage situation.

Anticipating a milestone is something that all widows have in common and something that we could all really do without. I mean, c'mon, it's bad enough that we have the *days* of all those milestones sucking the life out of us. Why does the feeling have to invade our bodies the entire month before as well?

I don't think anyone truly understands *why* we do this and, believe me when I say that just about any one of us would sell everything we own just to make it stop. We know the *day* will be hard, but very rarely do we see the week (or month) before that coming. If we could somehow anticipate anticipatory grief, I'm sure most of us would be willing to wear sandwich boards strapped to our bodies saying, "Stay away. I am armed with grief and I'm not afraid to use it."

Well, we would wear them unless we were curled up in bed. Which usually takes up about twenty hours a day during the pre-grief period.

And I'll tell you what makes it worse: we act like complete lunatics the entire week or month before a milestone and no one around us understands what in the hell is going on. And then on the actual *day*, we're perfectly fine, which cements our status as the "funny, but insane" person of our social circle.

I do it on the anniversary of my husband's death every year. I rant, rave, cry, and go completely nuts for about three weeks before. At some point during that time, every person in my life suggests that I get medicated; my parents start thinking about moving in and taking away my car keys; and even my dog won't come near me.

And then on the actual anniversary, I'm bubbly and personable and have no idea why everyone is looking at me like that.

"What? I'm fine! Never been better."

What makes this whole thing harder to figure out is that, as a widow, it can sometimes be difficult to differentiate between anticipatory grief and a hormone flare-up. I can't tell you how many times I've been crying, moody, and generally non-functioning, ready to blow the whole thing off as PMS, only to realize that I've been this way for an entire month and, unless I'm starting menopause in my early thirties, there must be something else going on.

I'm PGSing.

I've even had what I call "grief hot flashes," where I'm sitting in my car, getting ready to cry, and then this heat wave comes over my body and I suddenly start sweating like I'm going to spontaneously combust into one big, fiery grief ball.

Yes. It's just as pretty as you pictured it.

I have people in my life who, after a few years of riding this emotional roller coaster with me, can mark on their calendars with complete accuracy when my "time of the year" is going to happen. (Somehow they've figured it out and I never will. Maybe it's so they know when to plan their vacations.)

No woman *ever* likes it when someone tries to tell her she's PMSing. We get very defensive about it, mainly because what we're saying is something we've wanted to say all month, and we suddenly have the hormonal surge we need to get it out of our mouths. PGSing is much the same. My grief is there. It's been simmering for a while. All it takes is one good milestone to make it go from quiet to attacking a large metropolitan city.

And I don't want you to tell me that I'm doing it. About a month after it's over, I will have my "ah-ha!" moment and run around apologizing to everyone I've been in contact with for the last thirty days. But while it's going on, it's the perfect time for the people around me to practice their sympathetic nod technique.

And when it's over and I have a little clarity, then we can commiserate together on how completely insane I was.

Getting through the first round of milestones after Brad's death was tricky. Days that I didn't even know I cared about started to bother me. Like Labor Day. Or the Chinese New Year. They were all just a string of reminders that I was celebrating alone, mainly because they are considered "family days" and my "family" had been irrevocably altered.

For some reason, most widows seem to have a cluster of dates that make at least one or two months out of the year completely unbearable, and we're always shocked when we talk to others who go through the same thing. In my case, Father's Day, my birthday, the anniversary of his death, and our wedding anniversary are all within thirty days of each other, making summer my least favorite season.

I actually spoke with an astrologist once about this phenomenon, and she told me that most people are "clustered" like that and have been since the beginning of time. For many people, birthdays, anniversaries, and death all happen around the same period.

And while I'm sure that it should make me feel better that we're all in the same boat, it really just makes me think that we're all "divinely" screwed.

If you're wondering what a milestone is, I can sum it up for you fairly quickly. It's a day that "normal" people look forward to. It's a day that we couldn't wait for in our former lives. It's a day that everyone else is happy about…and we spend a good deal of the year wishing would never come.

Holidays.

Birthdays.

Graduations.

Anniversaries.

Weddings.

Flag Day.

New Year's Day.

Mondays.

Some of them are obvious, and some of them are hidden. Actually, most of them are hidden. Now that I think about it, most of them are not only hidden, but they're also wearing ski masks and waiting quietly behind a bush, ready to take anything we have to offer.

Milestones are complicated because they're different for all of us and that's part of what makes this journey so individual. Although we would all like to think that every widow goes through the same milestones at the same time with the exact same type of mental breakdown, unfortunately that just ain't so.

If that were the case, bars would only have to be open on certain days of the year and the world would only need one book about grief.

Since Brad died during the summer, my first holiday hurdle was Thanksgiving. I know you're thinking, "What happened to Halloween?" but he traveled all the time and was rarely around for Halloween. I was usually alone trying to get all three kids bundled up for Colorado-style trick-or-treating in twenty-degree weather. Anyway, during the first Thanksgiving without Brad, my parents made the decision that the best way for us to get through the holiday would be to pack everyone up and head to Louisiana to spend it with the rest of my extended family.

Let me rephrase that.

They decided it was a good idea to pack everyone up and *drive* to Louisiana. From Colorado. Locked in the car with my parents and my three children. Two days there and two days back with a four-day tropical vacation in the area of the world where they film *Swamp People*. The Texas leg of this trip alone would probably make the ordeal of Brad's death pale in comparison.

This was a good plan.

Looking back, I'm not sure it's the best idea to take someone in a state of extreme grief and manic confusion to a ten-block town with a drive-through daiquiri stand. This was a very risky move on their part. It sounds like the beginning of a bad reality series: "Widows Who Drink Daiquiris from Recycled Gallon Milk Containers and the People Who Love Them."

After spending two days in the car with the kids constantly asking, "How much farther until we stop for lunch-dinner-snack-world's largest prairie dog?" while I tried to figure out what seemed to be an impossible algebra equation involving travel time versus movie time ("We'll stop when *Monsters, Inc.* is done"), we stepped out of the car at my grandmother's house and breathed in the sweet, fresh Louisiana air.

Actually, we stepped out and breathed in the thick, chemical-filled Louisiana air.

It had been a long time since I'd spent Thanksgiving at my grandmother's house. In fact, the last time we had been there was right after Brad and I got engaged. During that trip, he and Sean formed a tight bond, sticking together as the two Yankee future grandsons-in-law (and believe me, the way my extended family says "Yankee"…it's not a compliment), which sealed their friendship from that day forward.

Kind of like war buddies.

They marveled at how the tap water fizzed in a mysterious way. They could drink twice as much beer below sea level. And although everyone seemed to be speaking English, they couldn't understand a word anyone was saying.

Of course, I didn't realize that that was the last time I had been to Grannie's until I got there. And from the moment I stepped out of the car, all of those memories came flooding back and threatened my already wavering equilibrium. That was my first lesson in how going places you've been to before with your spouse and then being there for the first time without them is tough. And it sneaks up on you. You don't realize how hard it's going to be until you're there. And once you're there, you're stuck.

With fizzy water.

I spent what seemed like the entire trip walking. I left the kids playing in my grandmother's yard with my cousins and parents on alert, plugged in my MP3, and listened to angry music while I pounded the cracked pavement. I probably walked three times a day for miles. I don't know what I was trying to accomplish or where I was trying to go, but I had this feeling that if I could keep moving, I might just make it through.

"Do you always walk this much?" my cousin asked me after a few days.

"I do now," I replied, expecting the fact that I couldn't sit still for two minutes to make perfect sense to someone on the outside.

By the end of the third day, I could give an exact house-to-trailer ratio in that town and tell you who was frequenting the B&B Bar at nine every morning. (And, no, it wasn't me.) When Thanksgiving Day rolled around, I actually thought I had outsmarted, outwalked, and outmaneuvered my grief.

Until the turkey was brought out and I suddenly found myself sobbing in my aunt's childhood room, crushed by loneliness in a house full of people who loved me.

After getting through that first Thanksgiving as gracefully as I possibly could, I could see Christmas looming before us. The holiday that had always been my favorite and so magical for me had suddenly turned into something that I would have sold one of my children to avoid.

Not really. Well, maybe. But only if I get to pick which child.

First on my to-do list was my Christmas card. Now, this is a challenge for new widows and most of them don't take it on.

I don't blame them.

But I had been so overwhelmed right after Brad's death that I often found it hard to keep up with the people who called or emailed to see how we were doing. Not only that, but I was still stressed out about that whole thank-you note business and wanted to do something that just let everyone know that we were okay (or at least let them think that) and how much we appreciated the generosity of our friends and family that year.

Hoping to take something off my plate in the weeks after Brad's death, Kristi had suggested, "Why don't you just send a Christmas newsletter in a few months and let them all know how you're doing?"

What sounded like a good plan during the summer became a huge source of stress in December. The upshot was that I finally had enough information about my year to write an entire newsletter, something that I'd never considered our lives to be newsworthy enough to do. The dilemma was, how do you write a cheerful Christmas card that includes the death of your spouse? I mean, who wants to read something like *that* while eating cookies and drinking hot cocoa?

Of course, the crazy widow lurking deep inside me just wanted to write something like:

"Hope you enjoy your holidays with your loved ones!
My husband died and I now have a well-used loyalty card at
    the local liquor store!
Merry Christmas and Happy New Year!"

Instead, I'll give you a better idea of what I came up with:

2007 has been an amazing year.
In 2007, I lost an amazing husband, friend, and father of my
    children.
In 2007, I learned how amazing the people around me are.
    The support I have received has meant more to me than
    anyone will ever know.
In 2007, I figured out how amazing my children really
    are...

And on and on with news about the kids and how we were doing. This, complete with a picture of all of us in which I look like there's no way I could possibly concentrate on a camera much less my life, summed up our "amazing" year.

Many experts suggest that, to make the holidays a little easier, you should take the traditions you had with your spouse and alter them a little. I don't know about making it any easier, but I do think there is some truth to changing things so that the absence isn't quite so glaringly obvious. Like, go get a different tree topper so that you're not constantly reminded that it was always your husband who put that exact star on the top of the tree. Do a pork roast instead of a turkey. Switch from Bud Light to Coors Light for your beverage of choice while putting together all of the toys.

Just something simple.

When I set out to get the house ready for Christmas that first year, I was determined to make the most of my newfound single state and decorate the house *my* way. You see, Christmas decorations were always a source of tension between Brad and me. He was colored racing lights and I was stationary white lights. He was tinsel. I was bows. He was tacky. I was not.

I'll never forget our first Christmas as a married couple. We were living in Florida where Brad was working at Cape Canaveral on the Titan rocket and, because the Air Force is so especially helpful when it comes to scheduling, he had a launch scheduled right after Christmas. This meant that no one from the squadron was allowed to go on leave, and I think I can safely say that neither one of us was thrilled with spending Christmas away from our families. We were pretty tense and took to fighting about the pettiest of things, both of us wanting to carry on the traditions we had had growing up.

The problem was…our traditions were polar opposites.

We spent weeks arguing over what would top our tree. I always had a beautifully traditional angel when I was growing up, and he had a blinking star that looked like it belonged on the top of a Vegas stripper's tree. To me, it seemed to say to Jesus, "We're over here! Bless us! Bless us!"

I remember standing in the middle of one of those nauseatingly Christmassy stores in the mall a couple of weeks before our first Christmas Day as a married couple and, in keeping with the Christmas spirit, arguing.

"Why in the world would we get that?" Brad asked, looking

in disbelief at the plain angel I held in my hands. "It doesn't even light up!"

"Exactly," I said. "I don't think that a traditional Christmas in Bethlehem was spent watching a star that spins, blinks, and plays 'Jingle Bell Rock.'"

I still have pictures of that tree. There's nothing on top.

I always used to tell guests over the holidays that our Christmas tree turned into the symbol of how we compromised and made our marriage work. I made a string of tinsel with fabric mixed in so that Brad had a little sparkle and I had a few bows. We found colored lights that had ten different settings, one of which was a faint fade in and out. We mixed those in with our white lights.

When the kids were finally old enough to help with the decorating, they added their own touch by only decorating the bottom two feet of the tree that they could reach with ornaments. I finally gave up on the angel and we had a non-blinking star adorning the top of the tree. It was completely original and no one would ever know about the ten years of fighting that got us to that point.

And it was the perfect definition of compromise because I don't think either one of us really liked it.

On my first Christmas alone, I was determined to decorate the tree how I'd always wanted it. I covered it in white lights and coordinating ornaments. I bought traditional decorations that I could picture in Martha Stewart's home. Everything was spaced out perfectly and centered in the front window of my house.

And I didn't have nearly as much fun decorating as I had when there was someone there to roll their eyes and tell me that those decorations were flat-out *boring*.

Haley, Michael, and Sarah had to come to terms with the fact that the main gingerbread-house maker was gone. Being an engineer, Brad couldn't rest until the prepackaged, do-it-yourself gingerbread house looked exactly the same as the picture on the box. Believe me, if there was one gumdrop missing from that kit, he was probably the only person in the entire country who noticed that the path leading up to the house was incomplete.

"Why does the gingerbread house lean to one side and have a crack in the roof?" Haley asked, eyeing the first gingerbread house I'd tried to construct on my own.

"I'm trying to remember those affected by Hurricane Katrina," I said, attempting to make excuses for my dilapidated house. "If you can go cut me a little piece of blue fabric, we can stick it on the roof and cover that crack."

Buying presents wasn't quite as much fun after he died, either. When I used to shop for the kids, one of my requirements was to find at least one thing that would be impossibly complicated to put together. This was part of my Christmas gift to Brad. He liked nothing better than staying up until 1:00 a.m., cursing the packaging engineers put here on earth for the devil's entertainment and constructing a toy workbench for a three-year-old with directions that only came in Japanese.

Not that he looked at the directions anyway.

During my first Christmas without Brad, it suddenly occurred to me, as I was doing my shopping, that it would be my father and me putting together whatever toys I bought. And if there's one thing my dad and I have in common, it's impatience with anything that has directions, no matter what language they're written in. Finding toys that needed to be constructed wouldn't be considered "fun"…it would be more like an excuse to open that next bottle of merlot.

The kids got a lot of stuffed animals that year.

The other difference was not having a present on my Christmas list for Brad and knowing that there wouldn't be anything special for me under the tree. And let me tell you, that was a big deal. Not only have I always been a big kid around Christmas, but Brad was the best Santa Claus *ever*. Actually, he was the best Santa Claus with a huge penchant for procrastination. This was something I knew was hereditary, because very often we wouldn't receive our Christmas presents from his family until around Easter. And the one year he didn't put off shopping and got it done early, I ended up with an Oral-B toothbrush and a collectors' set of CDs that he wouldn't let me open and play because they'd lose their value.

Clearly it worked out better for me if he shopped under pressure, with a sprinkling of guilt for good measure.

The fact that Brad was such a procrastinator in purchasing gifts for any occasion both irritated and intrigued me. I hated feeling guilty every time he'd rush out the door at the last minute to go get me something, but I was always curious what he would find at the zero hour. It got to the point that his presence at home wouldn't be expected on Christmas Eve. I swear that if the stores were open Christmas Day, he would have waited until then.

He was the kind of customer that retailers count on to make their last-minute Christmas quota and the entire reason they stay open until midnight. Believe me, I'm sure the salesmen were salivating as he ran through the dealership door in a panic the Christmas that he surprised me with a car. I've often wondered since then if he actually went out to buy me a sweater and realized they were out of my size so he got flustered and exclaimed, "To the Honda dealership!" in the middle of Macy's.

Until he died, no one could convince me that there really wasn't a Santa. Because until he was gone, Santa always visited me.

When Christmas was over and the rest of the world had gone on their normal, merry way, returning to work and back into their routine, I stripped my house of all of the holiday decorations that made me cry every time I looked at them and tried to do the same. While most everyone else had the post-holiday blues, I actually felt a little lighter, knowing I had gotten through that first Christmas without him. I looked at the calendar and thought, "Smooth sailing until Easter. I got this."

And then I got broadsided by Valentine's Day.

I'll never forget it. I had just stopped at the intersection of Winter and Spring, and then—*wham!*—it hit me from behind.

I guess part of me knew it was coming. I had just finished helping my kids put the finishing touches on their Valentine's Day cards, so it's not as if the day was a complete surprise. They were at home with a babysitter the afternoon of Valentine's Day while I ran a few errands, and at the last minute, I decided that I should stop at the grocery store and pick up a gallon of milk.

I stood completely still at the entrance of the store, watching men hurriedly pick up flowers on their way home from work to bring to their significant others. I was overcome by a feeling I just can't explain. It was kind of like a combination of sadness and abandonment…mixed with an urge to trip every one of those guys as they walked out the door.

So I skipped the milk and bought a bottle of wine instead.

The truth is, I don't even know why I cared. Brad had always hated Valentine's Day. The thought of some executive at Hallmark demanding that he show affection for his wife on February 14 every year just really chapped him. I remember having many conversations with him about how he didn't need anyone else to remind him to give me flowers or send me a card.

Of course, his end of the argument would have held up better if he actually *did* things like that any other day of the year.

I'll never forget our first Valentine's Day as a married couple. I was on the phone with my mother, sobbing to her about how

I'd made a huge error in judgment by getting married because my husband had abandoned me on Valentine's Day to go to happy hour with his Air Force buddies.

"I've made a huge mistake!" I hiccuped to her. "What was I *thinking*? How could he not come straight home on *Valentine's Day*?"

"I know, sweetie, I know," she said soothingly. "Men just don't think of these things. But if it makes you feel any better, you'll get used to it."

By the time Brad actually stumbled through the door, I was about ready to draw up divorce papers and stick them in his Valentine. I didn't feel much better when he handed me my Valentine's Day present, which consisted of a dozen wilted roses, a twelve pack of Bud Light, and a dartboard. Little did I know that as the years wore on, that would be one of the more romantic Valentine's Days I would have.

When Brad decided to rebel against something, he did it big time.

That was when I began to figure it out. It wasn't just the holidays we enjoyed that I missed—it was *everything*. All of the memories of times past and the knowledge that we wouldn't be making new ones together. To actually feel nostalgic for that first Valentine's Day that we were married, the one when I was so annoyed with him that I thought for sure I wouldn't speak to him until the next February 14, made me even sadder. I had no idea that not only would I miss the great days we had had together, but I would miss the bad ones as well.

The good, the bad, the disappointment of a dartboard for Valentine's Day, or the surprise of a car for Christmas—they made up a *life*. Our life.

My life.

In the beginning, every day was hard because every day *was* a milestone. Every "normal" day was a day I would never have again. And I missed it.

The year before Brad's death seemed to play in my mind like an old home movie as I relived what we had done, day for day, memory for memory, the entire first year he was gone. I still can't explain it, but somehow my widow brain could remember an entire year in detail...yet I couldn't remember what I'd had for breakfast (or if I had even eaten) that morning.

(Shaky sigh.) "One year ago today, we sat with Michael on the toilet for three hours straight, waiting for him to do a number two. What I wouldn't give to relive that day!"

During the first year it seemed like I was in a constant state of emotional agony. The whole damn year was hard, and getting through every day was a milestone. As soon as night would fall, I would grab a chocolate out of my Days of Grief Calendar, grateful that I had made it through another one. I tried to keep myself as busy as possible so that I wouldn't have time to dwell on what was going on, but it seemed like every night, I would sit with a photo album in my lap and flip through pictures of a man I just couldn't believe was actually *gone*.

As I crept closer to the anniversary of his death, I felt proud. Yes! Proud. *I had done it.* I was almost there. All of those firsts were behind me. Never again would I have to say I hadn't lived through a Christmas without him. Never again would I have to say I hadn't made it through a spring without him. Never again would I have to say that four weeks was the longest we had ever been separated.

Three hundred and sixty five days of widowhood. And I was still standing. Most of the time.

As I was approaching that one-year mark, my friend Sally came to a session of group therapy for the kids puffy-eyed and looking like she hadn't slept in weeks.

"Sally? Sally...*are you okay?*" I asked.

She looked at me through bleary eyes and said, "I'm trying to get off Prozac, and a part of me thinks that I've been on it so long...I've never really allowed myself to grieve."

And then she said it.

"Year two is the *worst*."

Ah, yes. The words that strike fear in the heart of every widow. That whatever year we haven't gone through yet is "the worst"...when we can't imagine anything worse than what we're going through. And to think I was so proud of myself for making it through that first horrific year! I hadn't totaled my car, gambled away my insurance money, or torched my house. The kids were doing well, and I was even starting to occasionally get them to school on time.

So when Sally said that, I sat there stunned, unable to imagine anything worse than what I was going through right then. Year two is the *worst?* Then what the hell have I been *doing* all of this time? If someone had told me that from the beginning, I would have just hung up my Kleenex box and retired as a rookie!

To distract myself from the impending doom of the second year that I now felt hanging over me, I began thinking about what I wanted to do for the first anniversary of Brad's death. Did I want to be alone? Did I want to be with people? Did I want to be alone in my room with people downstairs? Did I want to lie in my bed and let people come up to my room one at a time to pay homage to a great man and the woman he left behind? Did I want to assign everyone their own pager so that they would be on call to bring me comfort, sympathy, or something containing alcohol?

Really. It's a complicated time for any widow.

"I'm going to invite everyone over!" I told my mom. "Everyone I can think of! Then we'll have a big balloon release in the backyard. It's going to be so much fun!"

Pause. "Are you sure you want to do that? It sounds like a lot of work," she replied slowly.

"No! It's perfect! We'll make it an annual event! I won't go overboard. I promise!"

Ha.

It was as I was grocery shopping for the party that it suddenly came to me: *I'm going to put a party together that involves everything that Brad loved.* I started wheeling my way through the grocery store getting more and more excited about this idea, picking up huge bags of Snickers, chips, mozzarella sticks, pizza, and ice cream. Anything with grease, sugar, or marinara sauce made its way into my cart. It was overflowing by the time I made my way up to the cashier, and as I started loading everything onto the conveyor belt, he gave me a worried sideways glance.

I think if I had added a box of tampons and a gun to that order, he probably would have called security.

Okay. So now I've got the food. What else do I need?

Liquor.

"This is it," I thought, completely rationally. "I'm going to get *all* of the stuff Brad liked…from the moment he turned twenty-one to the day he died! It will be a stumble down Memory Lane!"

Miller High Life, Mad Dog 20/20 (yes, we really *were* that classy), and Busch Light were dumped with a clank into my cart. Bud Light, Fat Tire, and Rolling Rock were piled on top, commemorating his later years when he could afford beer that was more than two dollars a case.

"Having a party?" asked the clerk as he rang up my purchases.

"Oh, yes!" I replied, brightly. "It's the first anniversary of my husband's death. We're going to party it up big time!"

Silence. "Oh. Well. Have a good weekend, then."

I raced home to get everything set up. I preheated the oven for the pizza and cheese sticks. I put all of the candy into bowls, opened up all of the chips, and iced down the beer. I brought everything out to the back porch table while trying to fend off my kids who were desperately trying to dig into the buffet of their dreams. And when I got it all set up, I looked at it, expecting to feel complete pride at the zit fest I had provided for my friends and family.

But instead I felt…defeated.

I sat down on my back porch chair with a thump, tears rolling down my face as I looked at all of Brad's favorite food sitting there on the table.

Why isn't he here? Why am I doing this alone? Why don't I feel better now that the first year is finished?

What is that smell coming from inside the house?

And at the time, I could only answer one of those questions.

That smell was a year's worth of dust burning in my neglected oven.

In many ways, holidays are the easier milestones to get through because there are usually traditions surrounding them that we know are not going to change. Christmas trees usually still need to be purchased, Easter eggs need to be hidden, and sparklers on the Fourth of July still need to be lit.

But birthdays and anniversaries (wedding and death)…those are a different story.

The problem with those milestones is that there isn't a set of rules that outlines how we are supposed to acknowledge them. I would say that beyond the dating questions, what widows ask each other the most is how we "celebrate" those days.

Because we have no idea what the hell we're supposed to do.

We can always try the typical balloon release, where we go out to the destination of our choice—an open field, a cemetery, or the parking lot at McDonald's—and each person lets go of a helium balloon. Now, most widows have done this at one time or another, whether they have kids or not. And I'm sure there is a good, therapeutic reason for doing it, but I think the main reason why most of us release balloons is because we can't think of anything else to do.

While we excel at grieving, we're not the most original bunch.

I truly wish that whoever came up with the balloon release had decided on something else, mainly because I've had very few go smoothly. And I worry every time one of these goes awry that I will have to take out a second mortgage on my home to pay for the therapy that my kids will need in the future.

Balloon releases can go wrong for all of the obvious reasons. You know…trees, electrical lines, and just the random pop. And all of these obstacles impact our need for healing. Unfortunately, there isn't a children's book that deals with the loss of a balloon after the loss of a parent. I could really use something like *Daddy Still Knows You Love Him Even Though Your Balloon Is Caught on the Neighbor's Satellite Dish*.

Now, the good news about the whole balloon idea is that every time we pass a Toyota dealership and they happen to be advertising a sale with tons of balloons, my kids get excited and think that the manager is remembering their dad. But when the kids were little, balloon releases seemed to be unreasonably complicated. I'd always have to have a big build-up as I jollied them along and convinced them to let go of a helium balloon they'd rather keep anyway.

"I know it's a pretty pink balloon. But don't you want to send it up to Daddy and let him know that you love him? And no, I can't explain why you get to keep the balloon you get from Red Robin but I'm making you let this one go."

As the kids got older, they started writing notes to Brad and sending them up with the balloon. Now, I thought this was a great idea but eventually I started worrying about the fact that they were so fixated on it. I began wondering if the note attached read something like, "*Help!* You left us here with this crazy woman and she has no idea what she's doing!"

I'll never forget one Father's Day a couple of years after Brad died when I packed the kids up for a trek to where his ashes are buried in Buffalo Creek. I stopped at the local grocery store (the last piece of civilization before we hit the official Middle of Nowhere), and after I'd waited…and waited…and waited for someone in the floral department to come along and help me with our grief balloons, I finally made it out to my minivan where I carefully opened the back hatch to put our purchase away until send-off.

As I let go, a gust of wind blew through the car, sending one balloon up in the air. This, of course, sent me into a panic, so I quickly slammed the hatch shut, popping a second one.

The wails of my children could be heard across the parking lot as I desperately tried to comfort them.

"It's okay, it's okay!" I said in my brightest voice. "Daddy will be happy with just one family balloon! All he wanted this year anyway was for us to make a big family wish and send it up to him!"

Quick thinking, right? Yeah, they didn't buy it, either.

We've also always released balloons on Brad's birthday, and not once has it gone well. Actually, when I think about it…very rarely does Brad's birthday go smoothly at all.

You see, I came up with the idea of Brad's birthday being "Daddy Day." Daddy Day consists of me taking the kids out of school for the day, doing things that are completely frivolous and fun, and eat as much junk food as we can get our hands on.

Now, I know that therapists around the world are shuddering at the idea of doing something so flippant to remember something so significant. But I know that playing hooky to go bowling and eating fried cheese is something that Brad would be proud of. So I'm sticking with it.

The best part about Daddy Day is that it has made Brad's birthday something that the kids look forward to. The bad part is that usually when you merrily anticipate something so much, it very rarely lives up to expectations.

It wasn't until our third Daddy Day that I started wondering if Brad was trying to mess with our day for his own birthday enjoyment. Up until then, I just thought it was such an emotional day for me that it would be impossible for it to go perfectly. But on that Daddy Day I realized—you can't have a day *that* screwed up without getting a little help from above.

We were heading up to the mountains yet again to visit Brad's headstone, the kids blissfully silent thanks to the in-car DVD player that I rarely let them watch. I was happily sipping my Starbucks, enjoying a moment of peace, when there was a burst of noise from the third-row seat of the minivan.

"MOM! She drew on the seat with *marker*!"

Sure enough, I would find out later, four-year-old Sarah had decided to make her own permanent seat covers by doing some sort of abstract drawing of a "zebra playing catch with a fish while driving a semi." Now, what *I* was expected to do about it while going seventy-five miles an hour on the highway, I still do not know. But it sent Michael into a frenzy of reprimanding her, never mind that he had actually *stamped* his own name (in permanent ink) on the backseat the previous year.

But in a super-mom attempt not to let a little artwork get in the way of Daddy Day, I decided to let it go. The kids went back to their movie and I went back to my Starbucks, and as we neared our final destination, I thought I should be proactive and stop for a potty/lunch break, even though Michael had assured me that if he had to go to the bathroom, he could find an obliging tree. Feeling that peeing in the middle of a cemetery might be frowned upon, I pulled off the highway and spotted a Qdoba, the only restaurant in town that didn't involve fries.

"Can I sit next to you?" Haley asked as we waited in line for our food.

"Sure," I replied, not seeing the shit storm that was building. Because at that exact moment, Michael suddenly decided that sitting next to Sarah was akin to having lunch with fifty pounds of plutonium. And he proceeded to throw a complete fit.

And I mean a *fit*.

"I don't want to sit next to Sarah!" he yelled in the middle of the restaurant. "I want to sit next to you!"

"Haley asked me first," I said, trying to defuse the situation. "But you can sit across from me and that way we can talk to each other easier!"

Nice try, Mom.

I learned a very valuable lesson that day. My desire and determination to "make it a good day" was no match for the temper of a six-year-old boy. He yelled. He cried. He stomped his feet. I gave him "the look." I gave him that scary mommy-angry under-the-breath voice. People stared. They shook their heads, knowing they could handle this situation better than I could. And unaware of the embarrassing situation he was creating and the nervous breakdown he was about to make me have, Michael screamed.

And screamed.

And screamed.

"Can I help you to your table?" asked the woman behind the counter, trying to be heard over Michael's tantrum.

"No, thank you," I replied, trying to stay as calm as possible and handing Michael his lunch. "He can carry this and I've got the rest."

At which point Michael gave his feet a final stomp.

And his lunch slid to the floor.

Seeing what I'm sure looked like my eyes spinning around and smoke coming out of my ears, the wonderful woman at the cash register looked at me and said cheerfully in a thick Spanish accent, "We can clean this up! Here's a free quesadilla! And here, chips and guacamole! It's okay! I have children!"

Michael sat at the table, all cried out and hiccuping. The girls were silent, knowing that one false move could send me over the edge. And I sat at the table, next to Haley as promised, a lump in my throat so big I couldn't even eat.

What was I *doing*? Were the "powers that be" trying to tell me that I couldn't do this alone? Was some divine force trying to make me miss him even more?

Why didn't I pick a restaurant that served wine?

Later that afternoon, after we had released our balloons at the cemetery in Buffalo Creek and, thankfully, only one of them got caught up on a telephone pole, we made our way down the mountain. I felt drained and weak, as I always did on Brad's birthday, and was somewhat zoned out as we made our way into downtown Denver.

You see, in order to make it the *perfect* Daddy Day, I had promised the kids that we would go see the new 3D IMAX movie on the Hubble telescope, and I knew it was playing at the Denver Museum of Nature and Science. With our day pretty much wide open, I felt sure that we would be able to make it to the 4:00 p.m. showing with plenty of time.

I just had no idea that the entire downtown work force was going to be released at exactly 3:00 p.m. that day.

I sat in gridlock traffic, watching the minutes tick by on the clock on my dashboard. I inched my way closer and closer to the theater, willing us to get there on time, knowing that you can't breeze in late to an IMAX. Those educational people are real sticklers about promptness.

I squealed into the parking lot and pushed the kids out of the minivan. We ran through the entrance of the museum, and I breathlessly said to the man at the counter, "Four tickets to the Hubble show."

"That started two minutes ago, ma'am. Last show of the day."

Really?

The kids and I walked slowly back to the car.

"What are we going to do now, Mom? Where are we going? Daddy Day isn't over yet! *What can we do now?*"

"Just be quiet for a second while I think," I said, as I laid my head on my steering wheel.

"Can't we just go to a different movie?" asked Haley from the backseat.

Deep breath. Pick up head.

"Okay. Just let me look at my phone," I said, punching in a movie website. "Well, you guys have already seen the only kids' movie that's playing right now. But...wait...what is this?"

That's when I saw it. *Another* IMAX was showing the Hubble telescope movie. *And* it was closer to my house.

Choosing to ignore the fact that I was dumb enough not to check this in the first place, I felt for the first time like Fate was offering me her hand and saying, "Here. Let me help you. I'll make the traffic heavier going the other way and I'll even get you there early. You can grab some pizza with the kids before the movie starts. In fact, let me buy you a Bud Light for your trouble."

As we waited for our pizza at the restaurant across the street from the theater, the man at the next table leaned over and asked, "Excuse me? Do you know where the IMAX is?"

"Yes! It's right across the street! We're headed there ourselves to see the movie on the Hubble telescope. Is that what you're seeing?"

"No," he replied. "We're seeing a movie about migration. Gosh, I didn't know they had so many theaters."

As he turned back to his dinner, I suddenly had a sinking feeling. I couldn't have this wrong, could I? I dug out my phone and checked trusty old Yahoo! Movies and sure enough, Hubble telescope. November 19, 6:00 p.m.

We finished our pizza and made it to the theater right on time. I pulled into the loading zone, flipped on the hazards, and told the kids, "Wait here. I'm going to double-check and make sure it's playing."

I ran in the front doors and looked up at the listing.

Sure enough.

Migration.

In all my life, I had never known a movie listing to be so completely wrong. I wanted to run up to the ticket counter, shove my phone in the teenager's face, and say, "This says Hubble, so, by God, you're going to *play* Hubble. Look at me! My husband is dead and the only thing that is keeping me from having a complete nervous breakdown is watching something float around in space and not listening to my children for one blessed hour! I don't care if you don't have it here. Make it happen!"

Instead, I wheeled around, slammed through the theater doors, and made my way back to the minivan. I plopped myself back into my seat, rammed the gear shift into drive, and yelled, "*Home!* Pay-per-view movie!"

This declaration was met with noisy applause from the backseat.

I *almost* made it home when it hit. Complete hysteria. I'm laughing. I'm crying. I'm laughing so hard I'm crying. I may have snorted a couple of times.

The kids were suddenly very quiet in the backseat until finally, Haley said quietly, "Mom? What's so funny?"

"Oh, sweetie. This was just a bad day. I mean, not all parts of it were bad. We did some fun things. But sometimes things get so bad they're funny. Remember how I always tell you that if you're getting bullied, the best thing you can do is laugh right in the bully's face? Well, today bullied me."

And all I could do was laugh.

18

A nd so as year two started, I waited and waited for it to get worse, certain that Sally's second-year breakdown meant mine was imminent. It was as if I was watching the skies, just knowing that grief was going to drop a bomb on me that I would never recover from. I waited and waited…and the bomb never came.

What happened to me was more of a slow transition in the grieving process. When Sally said that year two was harder, I was expecting exactly what had happened in year one only much worse. But what year two really meant for me was the beginning of the shift from the life I'd had into the life I was developing.

It was then that I learned a very valuable lesson.

I should never listen to or read about what another widow is going through and think it's absolutely going to happen to me.

And there's a very simple reason for that.

Because they're not me.

Our hardest times are as different as we are. Not only that, but how we express these milestones is also individual. I used to feel so inadequate when I would hear other widows talk about the anniversary of their husband's deaths as a matter of weeks or months, when I couldn't *wait* to get far enough out from my husband's death so that I could say he'd been gone for years (mainly because the awkward silence after telling someone what happened gets a little shorter when you can attach the word "year" at the end). And I felt like I didn't love him as much as the other widows loved their husbands because I couldn't calculate down to the minute how long he had been gone.

"Today is so hard. My husband died one hundred four weeks ago as of 5:04 p.m."

"Really? Wow. I just passed my two-year mark."

As I moved into year two, the pain of loss had dulled a bit, which was a good thing, but without the overwhelming ache of grief every day, the milestones were so much sharper. By year two, most of the people in my life had returned to their day-to-day routine (as they should have), comfortable with my loss even though I wasn't. A transition was happening in my life, one that I didn't feel ready for but had to make anyway.

Most of my days were better, but every once in a while I would start crying and not be able to stop. This would usually happen in my car and not only alarm my occupants but the people behind me who were honking and trying to get me to "move the hell out of the way." (I think that's how they put it.)

And many times it would happen and I wouldn't even know why.

I had been so proud of myself for getting through that second year, and I felt sure I had the second anniversary emotionally under control. I thought I knew by then how to anticipate my grief, how to read the signs when I needed to take care of myself, and how to manage on my own. I had it in my head that by that time, I had conquered all of the "firsts" and that I should be living a life that I miraculously had all of the answers to.

As you can imagine, if you set standards like that for yourself, you're bound to be disappointed.

As the second anniversary approached, things that I hadn't witnessed during Brad's accident began to bother me as much as the things I had. Picturing what he was seeing, through his eyes, the moment he hit the driver's door of the Jeep turning left in front of him. Then suddenly, my imagination would take me to an aerial view of him lying bleeding and helpless on the road, his body twisted in an unnatural way and his head, heavy with his helmet, lolled to the side. The ride in the Flight For Life helicopter, which for years after his accident made me nauseous every time I heard a chopper just checking the traffic…and then relieved when I would pass the local hospital and see a helicopter perched and waiting for its next rescue.

"It's there," I would sigh quietly with relief. "Everyone's okay tonight."

Those visions haunted me every day, along with the things I'd actually seen, until my mind was so paralyzed with fear that I didn't want to think about my past at all. A vision of Brad laughing and smiling would end with him lying unconscious in the hospital bed. Remembering when we first met and how much fun we had would melt into a nightmare of him riding blissfully along to work on a summer morning…only to crash into an abyss of permanent darkness.

It was time for a sanity tune-up. So I went to Beth's office, the anniversary of his death looming before me like a rogue wave, and sat down on her well-worn couch. I knew she could see the anxiety all over my face.

"Are you doing okay?" she asked.

"I'm scared," I said tearfully. "Memories of the hospital scare me. I try not to think about them, but it's like they're in the back of my mind, just waiting to bring me down."

She shifted in her seat a little, her pen at the ready. "Have we talked about EMDR?"

Sniffle. "No. What's that?"

EMDR, or eye movement desensitization and reprocessing, is not something that every counselor does. Like hypnotism, it's something that you have to be trained in and something that affects everyone differently. Beth explained to me that I would have to come in for four sessions, at least one a week, because the therapy could not be spaced out over a long period if it was going to work, and that each session would last an hour and a half. She said that we would actually do very little talking; it was more about me envisioning what had happened while I sat there with instruments in my hands that pulsed back and forth. And then every once in a while she would ask me what I was seeing.

"Now, I have only done this with a handful of people," she said. "But so far, the results have been amazing. Very few of them have needed all four sessions."

I won't say that I was skeptical, because I have a fairly open mind when it comes to stuff like that. What I was...was terrified I had spent two years doing everything I could not to think about those three awful days in the ICU, and I didn't think I had it in me to sit in her office and think of nothing *but* that.

But my fear that those memories would someday, somehow jump out of my brain and attack me outweighed my fear of sitting with someone I trusted to bring them out, pacify them, and then put them in a cage where they belonged.

And so I agreed to do it.

With the first session set for a Friday afternoon, my parents insisted that they would not only watch my kids during the appointment, but for the weekend as well. Thinking that this wouldn't be necessary, but always one to welcome a little break, I dropped the kids off at their house on my way downtown. Dressed in comfortable sweats, my fingers clenched on the steering wheel, my heart racing with every mile I covered, I made my way to Beth's office.

After getting me settled in my usual spot on the couch, Beth placed two palm-sized oval objects in my hands and asked me to close my fingers around them. They began to pulse back and forth, back and forth, in the center of my hands until I almost felt like my body was rocking with them.

"Now, picture you're in a train," she said softly. "The images out of the window are the images from the hospital. They don't have to be in order. Just envision them as you would frames in a movie. You're on the train. You're in a safe place. Just watch the visions as you pass them."

For an hour I sat that way. I envisioned myself on a gray passenger train traveling around dusk. Sometimes I could see myself in the window, almost as if I were a ghost traveling alongside the train in a passenger cabin with the lights on, watching the landscape. Then the view would shift and I would be in my body, seeing the scenes unfold in the window as if watching the frames of a movie. Every once in a while, Beth would ask me about the vision I was seeing, and somehow she seemed to know to ask when I was stuck with one moment I couldn't get past. The trauma room. The radiology waiting area. The ICU with every tube imaginable keeping the man I loved alive.

After she slowly brought me back around, I sat on her couch feeling like I had just woken up from the most vivid dream I'd ever had. I left, promising that I would see her the following week, and I drove home, not really remembering the journey.

Every limb, joint, and hair was limp with exhaustion. I climbed into my bed fully clothed and lay there feeling like I was out of my body. I couldn't move. I don't know if it was the experience of remembering so many things all at once or the sweet release of just *letting it all go* that had me feeling like my body didn't even matter at that point, only my mind and the soul I felt like I was starting to reclaim.

During the week in between the first and second sessions, I felt like a different person. Yes, the memories were sad, but the fear was gone. The two EMDR sessions that followed weren't nearly as intense, and by the end of the third one, I felt like a weight had literally been lifted from my shoulders.

I had remembered it all. And I had come out the other side.

It was then that I realized that the more I fear my grief and the more I push it away, the bigger it becomes and the more control it has. That fight, that denial, is often more exhausting than actually feeling what I'm going to feel. The battle to remember or not remember pieces of my life is one that really can't be fought. Not successfully, anyway. I don't know if I will ever be able to welcome grief into my life.

But I know now not to be afraid of it.

After a few years, the birthdays got easier. My Christmas spirit returned.

But my throat would still catch when he missed something. And it was usually some small, everyday occurrence. During the first six months after he died, I tried to get the kids to church every Sunday. Eventually, though, I had to quit going. Now this is something I have never understood because, when he was alive, there were plenty of Sundays I would get the kids to their various Sunday schools and then go sit in the sanctuary on my own while he was out of town. In fact, I looked forward to it. With Brad gone so much, that hour on Sunday was often my only break during the week. But for some reason, after he died, I just couldn't do it.

I would drop the kids off in their classes, find my usual spot on the pew, listen to the sermon…and cry. After I stopped going regularly, I would try and get us there every once in a while so that I could have a test run and see if it was still a problem. And it always was. Maybe it was because I was being forced to sit there for an uninterrupted hour, and even though I tried to focus on what was being said, I couldn't help but look around at all of the men with their arms planted firmly around their wives' shoulders. Maybe it was because, while I had never been raised in a very religious family, going to church was just so *Brad* that it made it hard. Or maybe it was going to the place, every Sunday, where I said my final good-bye.

After months of struggling with this, I finally went to speak with Pastor Teri about it, certain that she would have an answer for me.

"I don't think I can come to church anymore," I said, somewhat embarrassed to be saying this to a pastor. "I don't know why, but it's just too hard."

She leaned over and gave my hand a quick pat. "Don't you worry about it," she said. "When my husband died, it took me four years to come back to church. You'll come back when you're ready."

I don't think she could have said anything more comforting to me. All that time I felt like I would be letting Brad down if I didn't bring the kids every week. And here was this woman, this widow, who had gone through something similar but had not only found her way back…she had become a pastor in the process.

And she was right. Three years later, I did start going back. I was ready. I announced to the kids that we were going to start going to church, and my goal was to get us there every other week.

"But *why*?" ten-year-old Haley groaned. "Why do we have to start going?"

"Because it meant something to your dad," I replied. "His

church community was extremely important to him growing up, and I know that he'd like for you to have that. And so we're going to try."

And sometimes just trying is the best we can do.

I still anticipate the days that I know will be hard. Even though I was hopeful that the passage of time would make my cluster of dates in June and July easier (and in some ways it has), I've learned by now that it will never be *easy*. By the fourth year, I knew to clear my calendar of important things for at least three weeks and forgive myself for the days when I just needed to stare at a blank wall. I journal, cry, and don't even attempt to explain to the people around me why, years later, there are days when it feels like he was just here, playing in the yard with the kids. And that there are days when it feels like yesterday that he was suddenly taken from all of us.

I know that when Haley and Sarah get married, I'll wish with all of my heart that he could be there to walk them into their new lives.

I know that when Michael graduates, he'll be wishing his dad was sitting in the audience cheering him on because he knew he could do it.

I know the first time one of them has a baby, I'll be looking into that little face to see if I see a resemblance to their grandfather.

And you know what? *That's okay.*

Knowing these things and acknowledging the fact that there will be times that I will miss Brad for the rest of my life will never stop me from finding a life that I can be happy with. What has been one of the greatest "healers" for me is attempting to live my life as fully as possible so that my new memories are just as happy as my old ones. I laugh when I think about all of our misguided Daddy Days. I get a smile on my face every time I see my dad curse over a Christmas present that has five hundred pieces he has to put together. I can acknowledge my grief and smile through my tears, wishing that Brad could be here but being happy at the same time.

My life is not just about the old milestones.

It's also about enjoying the milestones yet to come.

Dating

mom...don't read this part

19

I'm just going to get this out of the way right now.

I started dating early.

The reason I wanted to come clean is because questioning whether to date, or when, are usually some of the first things that people think of when they lose their spouse. And it took me a while before I was able to tell myself one simple phrase.

It's okay.

It's okay to wonder just days after your husband died if you will ever fall in love again...or even if you *want* to. It's okay to be curious about whether you still have it in you to be attractive to another man. It's okay that you suddenly start paying attention to bare ring fingers much more than you ever used to...and then are curious why you even care.

It's okay. It's okay. It's okay.

My wonder and worry about dating pretty much started right after the funeral. I suddenly became painfully aware of how middle-aged and motherly I had allowed myself to become, something that I think Brad was comfortable with but that probably wouldn't go over well with someone new. Much of what I thought about when I was out on those long walks, trying to out-maneuver my grief, was that I'd better start paying more attention to how I looked to the outside world and get my shit together. Otherwise I would be alone for the rest of my life. Around and, around my neighborhood I would go, convincing myself that I was improving myself and that love, a stable relationship, and, therefore, some kind of inner peace were just around the corner.

I know. It doesn't make much sense. But there you have it.

Part of the lure of dating was that I wanted someone I had never met before to be attracted to me. When you've been married for a long time and your spouse has seen you give birth and suffer a bad case of food poisoning, you sometimes feel like the magic is gone.

I wanted to meet people who just knew *me*...and not the "me" that was attached to "us" for so long.

When you're suddenly on your own, it's tempting to try and find someone who will work for your attention. Who will notice when you've had a pedicure (or five). Who might tell you that you look nice every once in a while without being prompted. Who will wait until he's outside to pass gas so that hopefully you won't notice...rather than doing it in the car with the windows locked so that, much to his delight, you can experience the ultimate Dutch oven.

I've never liked being alone. And, up until that point, I had never been on my own. I moved out of my parents' house right into a house with my husband when I was twenty years old. So at the time it seemed perfectly natural to try and take my old life, mesh it with someone else's, and get on with things.

My method of grieving was also a contributing factor. When Brad died, I remember saying to my sister, "I can't wait until it's a year from now and people won't think of me as a widow anymore."

I don't know *why* in the hell I thought that, but part of

putting this whole annoying widow business behind me was finding a new relationship. And I thought that if I could find the right person to hang out with, people would stop thinking of me as a widow.

I honestly thought the first guy I dated a few months after Brad died had been put in my path by a higher power of some sort and, therefore, I trustingly stumbled right into the arms of the wrong relationship. Chad was someone I had known since high school and who I considered my first boyfriend. We'd kept in touch off and on for fifteen years…through marriages, kids, moving, and growing up.

The main reason why I got in touch with him was because he was a cop in the county where Brad had had his accident, and I was desperately trying to get the accident report so that I could send it on to the life insurance company. Thinking that Chad would have an inside edge and might be able to get it quickly for me, I called him to see if he could.

"Hello?"

"Hi…Chad? It's me, Catherine."

"Hey! How are you?"

"Well, I'm doing okay except Brad-died-a-few-weeks-ago-in-El-Paso-County-and-I'm-trying-to-get-the-accident-report-can-you-help-me-and-how-is-your-family?" I said without taking a breath.

Long pause. "Say that again?"

I concentrated on slowing down and told him the abbreviated story of what had happened. At which point he replied, "Oh my God. I'm so sorry."

And then he dropped his own bomb.

"My wife just served me with divorce papers."

I knew…I just *knew* that this was meant to be. At that moment, I thought that we were purposely being thrown together into one big, depressing, codependent mess that only we would understand. And you know what? *I felt better.* I felt like someone was looking out for me and telling me that I wouldn't have to go through life alone. That the independence I said I was okay with but secretly feared would only have to happen for a little while and then I'd have someone to take care of me all over again. I'd spent weeks not being able to envision my future at all, and suddenly I could see getting remarried, being a stepmom, and living happily ever after.

And with someone I've *known* half my life! Not just some wacko off the street. How lucky was I?

What followed should have been made into an informative video on how *not* to start dating after the death of a spouse. Two people who were both digesting the fact that life wasn't turning out as it was supposed to, both raising kids and imbalanced. As he was reeling from his divorce, I was alternating between running myself into the ground trying to keep busy and lying on my couch, staring at the wall, and thinking, "This is not my life. Is it? Is this really my life?"

I was so desperate to fill the void in my life that Brad had left. My partner had been stolen from me—yes, *stolen*—and I wanted him back in any form I could get him. I wanted my relationship with Chad to speed up past the beginning stages when you're not sure of where everything is going, past worrying about whether he would call, past wondering if I would have a date on Friday night. I wanted to know that he was going to call at 5:00 p.m. and ask how my day had gone. I wanted him to come over on Saturday night so that we could just sit in comfortable silence and watch TV. I wanted to fight about what couples who have been together for years fight about.

And I wanted it *now.*

That feeling of desperation, combined with Chad's inability

to cope with what he had going on in his own life, was a deadly mix. I would call and text him, only to have him not return any messages for a week. And just when I would come to terms with the fact that he just didn't want to have anything to do with me but didn't have the balls to say it, he would call and ask me if I wanted to go to dinner. Then that dinner, where he said over and over how important I was to him and always would be, would be followed by two weeks when I wouldn't hear from him at all.

I would sit on the floor of my bedroom looking at pictures of Brad and asking him over and over, "*How* could you leave me all alone here to deal with this?" I was terrified that this was what dating was like, and I knew I didn't have it in me to handle it. I didn't have the self-esteem at that point to say to myself, when I didn't hear from Chad for a couple of weeks, "Screw it. There are other fish in the sea." Because at that time, I didn't know there were. Or if there were any fish who would want *me*.

After three months of this off-and-on communication, I stopped by Chad's parents' house to drop something off for the holidays. Since he and I had been getting together, I had seen them a few times, and from what I could understand, they seemed fairly happy that I was back in his life. Of course, I was under the impression that they knew we were dating. That's because I was under the impression that we were, too. I think the only person who wasn't was Chad. Because on that last visit to their house, I'll never forget one sentence:

"Why can't Chad date someone like you instead of Tammy?"

That's right. In the middle of my feverish optimism that I had found someone who would save me from living a life alone, it turned out that he was seeing someone else all along. I felt manipulated and confused. Desperate and alone. Hysterically laughing at the situation I found myself in while writhing on the floor in complete agony. Stomach churning with the knowledge that I wouldn't be attractive or worth anything to anyone else but Brad, who was gone and never coming back, I am still amazed that that relationship didn't send me completely over the edge at that point in my life.

And he never got me that damn accident report.

꩜

It was around the time that Chad and I started dating (or whatever the hell it was that we were doing) that I decided to take my wedding ring off. I don't know…maybe it was the idea of dating while also wearing a ring symbolizing my lifelong commitment to my husband that didn't sit well with me. I couldn't imagine someone else holding my left hand tightly and feeling the ring that Brad had given to me crushed between our palms, or sitting at dinner twirling my engagement ring around while I tried to make small talk with another man. Basically, I felt less disloyal by taking it off than I did if I wore it out with someone new.

I was never much of a ring wearer anyway. I know that there are many people out there who would never consider taking that ring off. I've seen the gold bands embedded into their skin like the rings have become a part of their bodies. The grimy prongs of the diamond that never gets cleaned because the wearer would never consider taking it off and handing it over to a jeweler. The gold bands of the men that looked scratched and beaten up, signifying a long commitment…and a love of working on cars.

I was not like that.

In fact, up until I got engaged, I had lost pretty much every ring I had ever owned. Which is why, after I agreed to marry Brad, the first thing he said was, "I've already insured the ring."

Very romantic. And practical.

So it wasn't uncommon for me to take my wedding ring off.

If I was gardening, sleeping, or chopping garlic, that ring would be sitting in its crystal holder, waiting for me to put it on again.

The other reason why I took it off soon after he died was because I was tired of the questions. I mean, what's the second question you ask someone wearing a ring when you first meet them?

"So…what does your husband do?"

And my only honest answer to that after he was gone was, "Oh, you know. He just lies around all day."

At least when I didn't wear it, people assumed that I was something normal, like divorced, and knew not to ask. People walking around with small children and no ring…they come across as complicated. I know I've always thought so. Any time I see a man with a four-year-old and a two-year-old sitting alone in a booth at McDonald's on a Friday night, his bare left hand picking up a chicken nugget, I think, "I'll bet there's a story there. And I'll bet it's not pretty."

I've always thought that becoming a widow should involve some sort of jewelry that announces our new title to the world. I know that there are "widow rings" out there, but the truth is that not a whole lot of people know about them. It's not like a single diamond solitaire on your left ring finger, which everyone knows means you're engaged. What the widow ring *should* be is about five carats of something that comes in a FedEx box with our first Social Security check. It should be placed on our right middle finger so that when people ask if we're married…well…we can show them our status in a way that we see fit.

See? It allows us to answer complicated questions without even opening our mouths *and* it vents a little frustration at the same time. Marketing gold.

The idea of taking off that ring is difficult for so many. And it should be. It's a *huge* step. In one motion, you are saying that you might be able to imagine your life differently. You're owning your widowhood. You're telling the world that you're no longer attached by jewelry (which has nothing to do with the attachment you hold in your heart).

I never really thought of taking off my ring as entirely permanent. It was something I could test drive. I could leave it off for a few hours and see how I felt. If it didn't send me into therapy, I'd leave it off for a few more hours. If I felt like I needed to start breathing into a paper bag in the condiment aisle of the grocery store, I'd put that sucker back on.

Years later, I still sometimes wear my wedding band. I can't explain it, but sometimes I wake up in the morning and just feel like I need it and am completely insecure without it...like I'm getting ready to walk out the door without wearing pants or something. Sometimes I need the sense of attachment and the confidence that comes with it to get through the day. I thought I was the only person who did this until I met another widow at a retreat and realized that she did the same thing.

"I know this going to sound crazy," I started off slowly. "But when I feel like I need a little courage, I wear my wedding ring on my right hand. It's like a security blanket or something and I get a little extra boost. I don't do it all the time, but sometimes I really need it."

"I do, too!" said Diane in amazement. "When I need to feel my husband with me, I'll put it on. I thought I was the only one who did that!"

Believe me. When it comes to widowhood, no one is the only one who did *anything*.

⟨꜠⟩

Just because I can deconstruct my dating timeline and make sense of it now doesn't mean that it did then. I don't think it's possible to describe how guilty I felt. I felt like I had let my husband down by not wearing black and living like a hermit in my house for at least five years. Even though I talked a good game about how I didn't care what anyone thought about my personal life, I worried constantly about what people would say. And when they didn't say it, I felt sure I knew what they were thinking. A few things along the lines of: "What is wrong with her? Ohhhh… she's making a huge mistake. Who is that guy she's with? What is she *thinking*? If I were in her situation, I would *never* do that."

In short, I was projecting all of my own insecurities about dating on everyone else around me and assuming that I didn't have their support.

I knew that if I started dating within the first year, half of my friends and family would have thought it was too soon. And if I didn't start dating until five years had passed, they'd wonder what in the hell was wrong with me. Everyone had different ideas about how I should go about this, and then I realized…I wasn't going to please everybody. Hell, I probably wouldn't please *anybody*. But if going out on a date on Friday night gave me something to look forward to on Monday and made it easier to get through my week, I don't know why anyone should care about it but me.

I've often thought that there are people in my life who wanted to see me married but didn't want to see the process that I had to go through to get there. I think they would have been perfectly happy if I had shown up at their doorstep with a middle-aged, childless, never-been-married billionaire and said, "Guess what? We were married last night in the Bahamas!"

Well, okay. I would have been happy with that, too.

Then there were people like Kristi, who just flat-out said, "Catherine. I don't care if you hook up with someone every night of the week, dammit. Just stop feeling guilty about it."

Sound advice.

And then there was the other group, the friends and family

who I knew wanted me to be happy but had no idea how much my dating life would impact them and their own grief over losing Brad. For a long time, I watched my friends proceed with caution any time I introduced someone new to them (which wasn't often). Oh, they were friendly. But as they shook someone's hand for the first time, they couldn't keep that look out of their eyes that seemed to say, "I'll give you a chance, but if you hurt her, I'll kill you."

I know that my dating life was painful for some of my closest friends because we were set. We were a pack. If there was anything we were all sure about, it was each other. Getting together was effortless and it had taken years to get to that point. Now, anytime someone new was around, we didn't have the same old conversations that picked up in the middle of where we'd left off. Our gatherings took work as we all tried to make the significant-other candidate comfortable and assure each other that we would weather this storm together.

I don't know if they truly felt this way or if it was something I was insecure about and projecting on them, but a part of me thought that even if I got remarried and that marriage lasted fifty years, my marriage to Brad would always be considered the "real" one. He would always be my husband, and whoever came along after would always be considered somewhat of a stand-in.

But I was so eager to not be alone. Too eager. Something I didn't do during those early days of dating, even after the nightmare of my first "dating" experience, was really ask myself what I wanted. What did I want in a new relationship? What was my goal? Did I want to get remarried? Did I want someone to go to dinner with every once in a while? Or did I want to just meet up for a roll in the hay and a handshake as I got in my car twenty minutes later?

What did I *want*?

If I had asked myself that question, I probably could have saved myself and several other people a lot of time and beer money.

20

O ne would think that after that experience with Chad, I
would have shied away from the dating world for a while.
That I would have learned my lesson: that I needed to figure out
who I was and bulk up my confidence a little before I set out
again. One would think that I would have been so worried about
being hurt again that I would have stepped back and tried again
in say…oh, twenty years or so.

Yes. One would think.

But in fact, my experience with Chad did the exact opposite.
I felt the need, more than ever, to prove that I was still desirable.
That I could rebuild my life. That I could move forward and be
happy again. And even though I have since learned that I can do
all of those things without being "attached," at that time they all
seemed to be related to being in a relationship.

The idea of getting remarried was never my prime motivation
for dating again. It's quite possible that what I was trying to do
was fill the void of intimacy in my life that had been left by the
early exit of my husband. See…this is *why* we're not supposed to
lose our spouses until we're in our nineties, when everything is

"dried up" and the fear of breaking a hip is larger than the desire to have sex. We're not supposed to lose them when we're young enough to miss that part of the relationship.

But obviously God and Cupid didn't get that letter from Dr. Ruth. Because spouses still die too soon. And we are left with nothing to "intimately" fall back on.

Many of us go through the desire for intimacy. The need to be held, comforted, nurtured, kissed, and told that everything will be all right. Yearning to feel skin on skin in the middle of the night, even if it's just the touching of hands. The fear that that part of our lives might be over because we don't know how (or even if we *want*) to get it back.

The fact that the need for intimacy doesn't get discussed as much as it should has widows around the world feeling shallow and lost because they think they're the only ones. I know I did. When we think about being with another man—not even necessarily loving another man because we don't know if we're capable of that anymore—we feel slightly sleazy and, unfortunately, this is not something you can talk through with your "normal" friends. We think that missing out on the physical part of our relationship should be the least of our worries...and that we should be more concerned with other aspects of widowhood.

I had a new widow ask me once, "So...did you feel like a complete hooker after your husband died? I feel like I just want to have sex all the time! I don't know what's wrong with me!"

After talking to both men and women who have lost their spouses, it seems like we all go through this stage at some point. Some act on it and some don't, and either way you're not wrong. The need for physical intimacy prompts widows who, before their husbands died, would have blushed and shifted uncomfortably in their seats when the subject of "friends with benefits" came up, now seriously looking at their contact lists and wondering if anyone in there might be up for a little action.

It's a dirty trick.

When we're the least capable of sustaining a healthy relationship because we're reeling from the one we just lost, our bodies are crying out for the same level of intimacy (if not more) that we shared with our spouses. And what *really* stinks about that is: even if we are fortunate enough to find a good relationship when we're looking for it, usually that level of affection and someone knowing exactly what "pushes your buttons" is something you have to build up to. It may not happen for years.

Missing out on the intimacy of marriage is all part of losing the benefits of a lifelong partner. *Of course* it will be missed. Of course we want it back! I know I've had to bite my tongue several times listening to married friends who complain about having to "give it up" every Tuesday night on the dot and who are avoiding their husbands by rolling over and giving them "the back."

And all I want to say is, "Girlfriend, you don't know what you have till it's gone and you're facing the possibility that you'll never have it again. So roll back over and get 'er done."

So what do we do? Well, there's a choice to be made. Either we decide that we're just not ready and take up kickboxing, or we acknowledge that this is something we want, take the plunge, and find some sort of relationship.

After the whole Chad fiasco of 2007, I started looking for love (or at the very least a little foot action under the table). All of my friends were married and knew of no single men. I had been a stay-at-home mom for years, so I didn't have a ready opportunity to have an affair with the CEO of my company. (Hey, every woman should have a sugar daddy at some point in her life.) And my weekly outings usually only involved multiple trips to Walmart (limited sugar daddy opportunities) and visits to the nail salon where, unless I decided to make a huge lifestyle change, the chances of finding a relationship were pretty slim.

I didn't like the bar scene in the short time I was in it. I don't know how I ever imagined that I would have any sort of meaningful connection with a stranger as we shouted over an '80s cover band and sipped (or gulped) watered-down well drinks. But it didn't take me long to figure out I wasn't going to find Mr. Right that way. It got to the point where even if a guy *did* make eye contact with me, my mind immediately went on the defensive.

"You think you can pick me up, just like that?" I would think, giving him the evil eye. "I'm not just some girl you can pick up in a bar!"

So, one night I was at a dinner with my young widows' group and talking to two friends, one of whom was recently married and one who had just gotten engaged.

"How did you meet your spouses?" I asked, nonchalantly. (Actually, I was probably foaming at the mouth a little bit.)

"Online dating!" they both exclaimed at the same time.

Alrighty then.

Online dating opened up a whole new world for me, and I have come to the conclusion that I have a different view of it than most women. A lot of my friends found it appalling the way men would pick up on them via email or proposition them in a chat room. They found most of the men beyond unattractive and the ones who did look cute looked *too* good and like they could possibly scam them out of their life insurance money.

I, on the other hand, loved it. Not the picking-up part, but the looking at profiles part. It was like people-watching from the comfort of my own home, one of my favorite activities. I could put on my flannel pajamas, light a fire, and enjoy endless hours of entertainment while I looked at pictures of men with mullets who had user names like "Lookin4DDs."

All of my married friends started to enjoy their daily email updates on how my online dating experience was panning out. The guy with the user name "DUIOffender" who was out there looking for his soul mate. Or the one who forwarded his picture and, much to my dismay, had a rockin' set of bangs to go with his tank top. The email I received with words that I didn't understand, but I think the upshot was that he was offering to make me a princess in a country I'd never heard of. And then, my personal favorite, the one who was "climbing the corporate ladder" but couldn't spell "am."

He spelled it "aim." Three times. In one paragraph.

Hope he's in accounting.

My friends made me promise that, on the off-chance I *did* find Mr. Right, I wouldn't give up my subscription.

Another bonus to online dating is that you can look at someone's personal résumé before you even respond to them. This way, the guy already knew that I was widowed before he shot me that deep, meaningful email that just said, "Hola." It really is such a time-saver. Think about it: wouldn't it be great if you could walk into a bar and glance at someone's "criteria" (which has been conveniently stamped to his forehead) and know immediately if you had a shot at making this work before you even said, "Nice tattoo?"

For example, if his stamp said that he has "4+ kids" and is excited about having more, you would know right away to down that mojito and bolt.

After a few weeks of enjoying "interesting" profiles and receiving emails that sounded like form letters asking if I was interested in a one-night stand, I began to wonder where all of the "normal" men were. How in the world did my friends find men they wanted to go bowling with…much less marry?

I began to get discouraged and wonder if I should save myself the sixty dollars a month and just use it toward extra pedicure appointments (which, apparently, no one would notice because I would never find anyone to whom I felt close enough to show them my feet), when Kristi told me a tip she'd heard from a friend.

"You need to change your profile," she said. "If you sound too nice, you'll get emails from all kinds of weirdos. My friend told me that you need to write your profile so that it will offend at least 85 percent of the people who read it. That way you'll really get what you want."

It may sound crazy, but it worked. As I deleted my profile and began to work on the new one, I thought of all of the *men's* profiles I had read. They weren't shy about saying what they wanted. They didn't beat around the bush. The women, doing anything and everything they could to hook a new fish, would write, "I love walking in the rain in a white T-shirt and rubbing my man's feet." They would have three paragraphs detailing how they could be any man's dream woman.

The men, of course, were more direct (as men have a tendency to be). In one paragraph they would say how they liked skiing, biking, drinking microbrews, and watching *Duck Dynasty*. Anyone who didn't like that stuff need not apply.

So, I began to write like a man, detailing what I wanted and what I didn't. I was straightforward and didn't hold anything back. And this is what I came up with:

So, this is what most people seem to be doing...a list of things that you are completely honest about when looking for your next friend or significant other. To quote Joe Public out there...if you fall into any of these categories, we probably won't get along: if you have ever spelled fashion "fation" or if you spell "am" with an "i" in the middle; if you are constantly going to compare my cooking to your mother's; if sleeveless, big-hair rock T-shirts are a staple in your wardrobe; if in our first conversation on the phone you ask me about my cup size (I like to have fun as much as any other girl, but come on!); if your previous wedding had a NASCAR theme (I can tell you that story later); if when you go to a party with people you don't know you stand in a corner and look miserable; if your idea of romance includes a bottle of Mad Dog 20/20; if you can't handle life's little curve balls with a little grace and laughter.

Now, if any of the following DO apply to you, we will probably hit it off: if when you put in your profile you are comfortable going to a dive bar or going to the theater you actually meant it; if I ask you if my ass looks fat in these pants, you don't even blink before you say "no"; if you understand that women just don't find bodily noises as funny as men do (this is just a fundamental difference, I can't explain it); if you enjoy people-watching (and can tell the difference between fake and real); if you can balance watching WWF Smackdown with a little HGTV; if you are looking for an independent woman who likes to have fun, whether it's quietly sitting at home in front of a fire or going out to one of the millions of amazing places that Denver has to offer (and this may include someplace that has more than wings and nachos on the menu, but don't be scared).

Think about it. What I wrote was entertaining, but I basically said, "If you're going to take over the remote, make me eat bar food all of the time, never take me anyplace nice, or have the grammar skills of a goat, please don't contact me." Some "goats" will slip through the cracks and you might hear from someone who wants to make you one of his wives. It happens. But I definitely saw a decrease in the number of goats.

And I started to see some possibilities.

To give the guys out there the benefit of the doubt, I'm not saying it's always easy dating a widow. But our faults are not where you think they are. I think most men have a fear that they will be competing with a "ghost" for the rest of their lives, and I know very few women who put their new relationships through that. Well, any more than anyone else. The truth is, no matter how you became single—whether it's through death, divorce, by choice, or by force—we all bring our life experiences with us and they have some influence in the next relationship.

Hey. If *you* can talk about your ex-wife or girlfriend and the things you liked and didn't, how is that any different from me talking about my late husband?

Dating a widow with young children can be a hard adjustment, too. Because then your date has to deal with the fact that you don't have "custody." You *are* custody. Plans must be firmed up at least forty-eight hours in advance to ensure a babysitter. I once had a guy ask me constantly, "So, do you have your kids this weekend?" He could never really grasp the concept that I had my kids *every* weekend. I never got why this was so hard to understand.

The good news about dating with children is that you can actually put a monetary value on a date. I could sit there and ask myself, "Is this guy worth ten an hour?" More often than not, the answer was no. And if you don't have kids, I'll offer up this helpful tip: if at any time during the date you start feeling sorry for his ex-wife, it's best to just cut your losses and run.

One of the things I disliked about the beginning stages of dating was how all of my memories and funny stories seemed to tie back to my husband in some way. It wasn't intentional, but you spend thirteen years of your life in a devoted relationship, and that's where your stories are. After a few dates when even *I* was sick of hearing "my husband and I," I decided that I needed to make more of an effort to get out and live a little so that I would have something else to talk about.

At the very least, I thought I should peruse a *Sports Illustrated* every once in a while so that I could beef up my conversation skills a bit.

I spent some time emailing back and forth with a few guys, sometimes even getting as far as texting back and forth (which meant that I'd taken the risk of giving them a phone number), but very rarely did I actually make it to the date. I was fairly picky. Once, I was close to what I think would have been a disaster in the making when I had been emailing back and forth with a guy who seemed funny and nice and had a little potential. I made it as far as an actual phone call with him where he told me that he was pissed that he was out of sick days at work.

Yeah. It was the end of January.

Next.

I had a pretty good experience overall. Sure there were guys that I would take a chance on and meet, only to figure out that we had no chemistry. But none of them lied. In fact, on one date, the very nice looking, professional guy I met immediately sat down and said, "I've got no game."

Well, not necessarily what I wanted to hear at the beginning of a date. But at least he was honest.

For the most part, I kept my dating life on the down-low. I knew the friends who were entertained by my stories and the ones who were uncomfortable with the whole concept. I did the "responsible" thing and told at least one friend every time I was going to go out on a date with someone new so that if they didn't get the "you'll never *believe* my evening last night" email the next day, they would know to come sniffing around my house to make sure I was there.

Knowing that my parents hated the idea of me dating almost

as much as I did, I kept my reports to them to a minimum unless I thought I was getting close to introducing them to someone. In fact, I basically used the same rule with them that I did with my kids.

Never introduce your kids or your family to a possible "significant other" until you've been dating for at least three months.

Think about it: at three months, you have a better idea of where the relationship is going and if there is even a possibility it might last. You're starting to come out of the "honeymoon" phase a little and figuring out that at Week One this guy was perfect and at Week Ten…not so much. At three months, you might have found one understanding friend who will go on a double-date "test drive" and tell you what they really think before you take the chance on confusing your family.

As I weeded through emails, avoided texts, and occasionally met people I knew would not become the future Mr. Catherine Tidd, I started to lose confidence that I would find my love connection. Or even just my happy-hour connection. And just as I started to give up…

…I met Billy.

After emailing back and forth with Billy a few times, I found it hard to believe that I might have found the one engineer in the world who had good grammar. Courteous, nice, with a good job, Billy seemed worth risking a lunch. And as I made my way through the door of the Mexican restaurant in downtown Denver one sunny spring Sunday, he greeted me with something I hear from people all the time.

"Wow. You're taller than I thought you'd be."

I'll never forget that first date because, as I was driving

downtown, the oil light came on in my little sports car. Now, Brad had always been overly diligent with our car maintenance and since he'd been gone, I'd become paranoid about car trouble. I know that a normal person would have thought, "Eh. I'll get the oil checked next week." I, on the other hand, started panicking and wondering if this guy would think I was completely psycho if I asked him to work on my car on the first date.

The hostess led us to a booth that was against one of the exposed brick walls of the old building. We were pretty much the only people in the place since the restaurant did a hefty bar business and most of its usual customers were probably still sleeping off the night before. We sat there making small talk (me, wondering the entire time how I could bring up this whole oil light business), and even though I didn't feel the need to grab his hand and elope to Vegas, I did think he might be worth a second date.

Billy was sweet, smart, fun to be with, and five years younger than me (which actually made me feel less like a "cougar" and just really old). We lived on the complete opposite ends of town from each other, which made things inconvenient, but we both seemed determined to see where this would go.

We would go out and meet his friends for trivia at a bar near his house. He would meet mine at parties and dinners. And after a couple of months, I introduced Billy to my kids and, even though I could tell that this was uncharted territory for him, he seemed to enjoy hanging out with them.

I realized fairly quickly that time was on my side. I know that all kids operate differently when it comes to their widowed parents dating, but mine never thought of my going out as shopping for a new "daddy" for them. And honestly...I didn't either. I had complete confidence that I could raise these kids on my own and enough outside support that when a male influence was needed, plenty of guys would step up and help. I wasn't dating *because* of my kids, because they had begged me for a new dad; I was almost dating *in spite* of them, trying to keep it as quiet as possible.

Even though I'd heard that some of their friends had asked their mothers, "Will Haley, Michael, and Sarah get a new dad?" my kids never asked me that question, and to this day I don't know why. All I know is that sometimes what I proudly labeled as resilience should probably have worried me because it may have been awfully close to denial. So, even though I would sometimes fear what was going on in their little heads, eventually I realized I needed to let it go a little bit. After all, I had them in counseling. I thought we spent a healthy amount of time talking at home about Brad and what had happened. If they weren't worried about getting a new daddy or what that might mean, who was I to force that concern on them? I just had to learn to take each issue as it came.

Being the social person that I've always been...Haley, Michael, and Sarah never really thought twice about new people coming in and out of the house. To them, Billy was just another face in the crowd or another adult they waved to as they walked out the door to play with their friends. He would bring his dog over, and the kids were *much* more interested in it than him.

We would grill, play Frisbee in the yard, and take the kids to the water park. In fact, they probably really enjoyed that time in their lives because Billy was so concerned with impressing them and winning them over and I was so concerned with how they were doing. When we were around the kids together, our attention was focused entirely on them and their needs. What more could three kids want?

But it was hard for me to relax. I was so worried that it was too much for Billy that I felt hypersensitive to how he was doing when we were all together. Sometimes I wanted to make things as easy for him as possible, and sometimes I wanted to test him to make sure he was a keeper. There were days when I would pray for no whining or fighting, and then some when I'd want the kids to let go with all the bad they had in them just to see if he would run away screaming.

And I was constantly watching the kids, just waiting for a sign that one of them wasn't doing well. I paid close attention to what Billy said to them and how he would interact, ready to abandon the whole thing if for one moment it looked like he was crossing the invisible widowed-mother boundary I had set up. It was exhausting.

For the first time, I really started to understand how difficult it is to date with children. It was hard enough to have a moment alone when I was married, but back then, I was hanging out with Brad so he was just as much to blame for those lovable interruptions as I was. But when it's a *date* who doesn't have children and therefore doesn't have a clear idea of how *wonderful* (yes, yes… wonderful…that's it) they can be, it can lead to some uncomfortable moments.

I remember sitting on my couch with Billy on a snowy night, enjoying a postcard setting: snow falling in big flakes, a roaring fire, a little hand holding, a few stolen glances. Right at that moment, my youngest daughter decided to add her own touch to the romance by shouting from the top of the stairs…

"Hey, Mom! Guess what? I have a *vagina!*"

This declaration was then followed by my son running through the room, completely naked except for a strategically placed sock.

But Billy handled everything with a sense of humor, and I could tell that he and the kids were really starting to bond. Which made how I felt that much harder.

On paper, Billy was everything I wanted. Seriously, it was like I had made a list, handed it in, and a higher power said, "Okay. Here you go. He's all yours."

On the first anniversary of Brad's death, he had the compassion to say, "Do you want me to call you this weekend? Or do you need to be left alone?"

I know. Perfect, right?

It didn't seem to matter to Billy how crazy I was—and I was pretty bat-shit crazy right around that time. Anything could set me off without warning. All of my emotions stayed right at the surface and I think what really made them bubble over was the fact that I had found someone who cared enough to hear about it and still look me in the eye the next day. It seemed like I could do no wrong with him, and I had never been in that position before in my life.

Oh, I know with complete confidence that Brad loved me, but he was always ready and able to disagree with me about the big things (which I needed) and was sometimes impatient with me when I would get emotional and needed to talk. Billy, on the other hand, never seemed to tire of hearing about how I was doing, good or bad, and we didn't fight once.

After six months, Billy and I decided to take a trip. I had vowed, when Brad died, to start traveling more, but I was scared to go alone. So, when Billy asked, "Have you ever been to the Bahamas?" I immediately replied, "Nope! Let's go!"

It was beautiful. The hotel was amazing, the setting was like a postcard, and we ran around like kids, playing in the pool, going down countless waterslides, and lying on the beach. Everything was perfect.

Except me. Because I wasn't happy. And it was on that trip that I started realizing that if I couldn't make myself happy and find some sort of peace with who I was as a person, the perfect guy, the perfect relationship, and the perfect place wouldn't make me happy either. This situation was *actually* when the whole "it's not you, it's me" thing applies. It *wasn't* him. It was completely me. And for the first time, I realized, I wasn't ready. I wasn't ready for any of it. I didn't know who I was. I was slightly confused about whom I had been, and I had no idea where I was going.

And if I didn't know where I was going, I knew it wasn't fair to ask someone else to come along for the ride.

In a move that I will forever feel guilty about, I broke off our six-month relationship in an email, the action of a true coward. But never one to handle conflict well and feeling so overwhelmed with the grief and guilt I didn't know what to do with, I couldn't bear to even have the actual conversation that would probably strike him from out of the blue. Because I didn't understand it myself.

"This just isn't working for me."

The kids were told that Billy wouldn't be coming around anymore, and they seemed to take it in stride. But realizing that by embarking on a new relationship, I was risking not only my broken heart, but the kids' as well, made the whole thing seem less like a fun "adventure" and more like a dangerous expedition. And I knew as they got older and more aware, it would get a little scarier for us all.

After that experience, I understood that I had no business dating for a while. I had gotten exactly what I wanted and I still couldn't make it work. I needed to overcome my fear of being alone and the only way to do that was to be…alone. I needed to concentrate on the kids, go to therapy, and generally just dive into a project that I should have taken on a long time ago…even before Brad died.

Figuring out who I was.

21

You may not believe me after reading the previous dating stories that ended with me sitting at home on Saturday nights with my favorite fluffy socks and a good book that I couldn't concentrate on, but widows have the upper hand when it comes to dating.

And I'll tell you why.

Many of us have been (or are embarking) on a journey of self-discovery that most people won't ever experience. And even if they do, most people don't experience it before they put themselves in a position of being in a committed relationship. I'm not saying that death is a good thing. But it does completely open our eyes to the world around us, and we tend to see things unfiltered and for what they really are.

We have a new level of appreciation that life is short. So we'd better do what we can to make the most of it.

At some point, the death of our spouses has us questioning who we are and what we want, when most people won't do that once in their entire lives. We are forced into a world that we don't want to be in…and then given the opportunity to change it into a world that we can live with.

In a twisted sort of way, it's a gift.

When Billy and I broke up, for the first time I stopped questioning whether *I* could be loved and asked whether I was capable of loving another person. As I examined our relationship, all I could find fault with was my lack of ability to move forward. I started questioning if it would ever be possible to find that "spark" again or if that part of my life was over.

I'd worried about the prospect of being alone for the rest of my life right after Brad died, but that was because I was so insecure about whether anyone would want me. It never occurred to me that I could be indefinitely single because I chose to be. And I knew the only way to get on with my life was to make peace with that possibility.

I began to sit quietly in my bedroom…and just be. I wouldn't talk on the phone. Occasionally I would watch a movie. But I did my best to become friends with being alone rather than constantly slamming the door in its face or running away from it. As I've said before, alone is something you choose to be; lonely is not. And as I chose to spend more and more time alone, I became less lonely.

I had spent so long trying to like what someone else liked, say what they wanted me to say, and mold myself into someone that another person would want to be with that I had no idea who I was anymore. I think a big part of me even did that with Brad. I didn't like fighting with him, so I would usually do my best to keep the peace and go with the flow. I would do things he wanted to do because it was easier than pushing for what I wanted. It took me a long time to realize how much of my relationship with him was bleeding over into the new relationships I was trying to create.

You can't be with someone that long without getting into relationship habits that are hard to break. Brad, I think, had a touch of attention deficit disorder, which served him well in his professional life, but had contributed to a lot of the communication problems we had as a married couple. After thirteen years together, I had conditioned myself to say what I was thinking in two sentences or less. Otherwise he would get distracted and I would get frustrated. He wasn't a cold person...far from it. He was just *busy* and always thinking about the next thing. And for the first time, I started dealing with how neglected that had made me feel.

And how much I feared feeling that way again.

I dug deep and really tried to get to know myself, and in a way, I met myself for the first time. I started thinking about what *I* wanted and ignored the part of myself that was constantly asking, "How can I be more attractive to him?" or "What kind of person would *they* want me to date?"

I don't want to watch sports all of the time.

I like going to the theater.

I'm not good at pool.

I like movies that involve someone speaking with a British accent and wearing uncomfortable clothing.

I knew I had made it through a huge turning point when, one night, as I buried myself under my covers, smack dab in the middle of my bed, watching *The Golden Girls*, one thought entered my mind.

"This feels pretty damn good."

This evolution turned me into a person who not only couldn't be changed but didn't want to be. I was good with myself. I could recognize the perfections and imperfections of my marriage and admit that I had a part in both. I discovered that I could hold on to my old memories while I made new ones. I started realizing that I could love Brad and still make enough room to love another person. That I could accept us—*all* that was us—and make peace with the beauty and defects of our relationship.

It also made me realize that I had no interest in changing anyone else. Losing Brad had left a huge hole in my life, a hole that, in the beginning, I just wanted to fill. I'm sure that I could have quickly found someone, anyone, to fill it. But that wasn't good enough for me, and that shouldn't be good enough for anyone else. No one should want to "replace" my husband and no one should be asked to do that. No one should mold themselves into the person I wanted if that wasn't the person they were to begin with.

If this was going to work, I would have to find a new space in my life. If I was going to find the right relationship, it would have to be with someone who was just as sure about himself as I was. If I was going to be happy, I would have to accept someone else's imperfections and he would have to accept mine as well.

Would this put me on the path to the "perfect" relationship? No. But it would take me in a new direction.

22

I 've heard many widows say they had an amazing marriage and that they will never find that again. And they're right. It *is* completely impossible to find that exact same relationship again.

It took me a while to figure out that wasn't necessarily a bad thing. I mean, I'm not the same person anyway. When something this huge happens in life, it's impossible not to change. We all change *tremendously*. I've often said that if I met my husband now, he may not even recognize me. Hell, he may not even *like* me.

And that's okay. Because the old me was perfect for him.

The new me is perfect for someone else.

The chances of us finding the relationship that's just right for us, well, they're slim. It's a miracle when we find someone we can sit across the table from for two hours at dinner, much less entertain the idea of spending the rest of our lives with. Someone who makes us smile when we think about him. Someone we can't wait to hug when they walk through the front door. Someone who makes our hearts jump in a good way when we see their name on the caller ID.

But the chances were *always* slim. They're slim for everyone, loss or not. And I found it once.

Who's to say it would be impossible to find again?

After spending some quality time with myself, I started feeling ready to try dating again. I realized that I had finally answered the question "What do I really want?" with "I want to meet new people." This new outlook had me going back to the online dating scene with a different outlook. The pressure was off and I wasn't going to take it so seriously. Who cares if I go out with someone and I end up not ever seeing them again? Who cares if the date is a total dud? Who cares if he "has no game"?

If I had a good time, great. If I didn't, well, I can turn just about anything into a funny story for my married friends. And that was when I started looking at going out as part of the journey and stopped focusing so much on the end result.

I had a new requirement for this next round of dating. It had to be with someone who either had a hobby I knew nothing about or a job that sounded interesting. That way, even if we had no chemistry, we'd at least have something to talk about. And in a world where every man is in IT, finance, or sales, this was a lot more challenging than it sounds.

When I told my old college roommate what I was doing, she said, "Great. Good to see you're treating your dating life like trading cards. 'Well, I don't have that one, so I guess I'll go out with him…'"

I tried to find the balance between finding someone to spend time with and getting in enough "me" time, which I had come to enjoy. I began a pattern of going on about one date a month. It was almost like an addiction. I would be alone for a while, and then I would need a "hit" of male conversation. Then that need would be satisfied for about a month and I would curl back up with my *Golden Girls*.

A month later, I'd be out on another first date.

In a short series of dates, I met a guy who liked to hang glide, a guy who had traveled around Western Europe for a year, and a chef. During all of those dates, the chemistry wasn't brimming over, but the conversation was always interesting. I looked at going out as brushing up on my people skills since, as a stay-at-home mom, I spent so much time alone. I knew that at some point I would want to go back to work and, just as sorority rush in college helped me hone my people skills and prepare for job interviews after graduation, dating seemed like a way to dust off those abilities that I had shelved for years.

After a few months, I started emailing back and forth with a guy who worked on a NASCAR team…the only team in Denver. Through his emails, I could tell he had a sense of humor, and by the time I agreed to go out on a date with him, I had decided that if Brad were here, he'd probably be dating him himself. Eventually, it came time for my "one date" that month and it was between Mike, the NASCAR guy, and someone else I had been emailing back and forth with at the same time.

"You want to get together some night?" he emailed me.

"Sure," I replied.

"How about Dave & Busters?"

Since Mike had unknowingly suggested something that had been high on my list of preferences for a first date—go someplace where you can *do* something rather than just sit across a table and stare at each other—I took this as a good sign. And if the date was a complete failure, at least I could work on my Skee-Ball skills.

It wasn't until I was driving to meet Mike that I realized I had never even talked to him on the phone, something that was always a requirement for me. And knowing that I was about to meet someone who worked on a NASCAR team, I had no idea if he was so redneck that he might need subtitles. So when I pulled into the parking lot of Dave & Busters, I started chuckling to myself that I was actually even *on* this date.

Brad loved NASCAR. In fact, for a while, *he* wanted to quit his job and try to get on a team as a mechanic of some sort. But since NASCAR racing did nothing for me but put me to sleep with its constant white noise, when he mentioned it, I gave him my "you wanna do *what?*" look and put that notion to rest.

I'm sure Brad was watching me walk up those stairs to the front door of Dave & Busters thinking, "If you had paid attention to me for thirteen years, you would know what in the hell this guy is going to talk to you about."

I was late, which I always am. I walked in and recognized Mike from his picture, sitting at the bar with an enormous beer and looking slightly embarrassed that he was there. After being stuck in traffic for the past forty-five minutes, I sat down on the stool next to him with a thump and said something that apparently endeared me to him right away.

"I'll have one of those, too."

We started talking with complete ease from the very beginning. And although I had no real interest in hooking up with someone who spent his weekends covered in grease and hanging out with 200,000 people who say, "Hold my beer and watch this," on a regular basis, the longer the evening went on, the harder I laughed and the more fun I had.

I found out that he had three kids who were around the same ages as mine at the time—seven, five, and three—and that we could easily commiserate with each other on potty-training stories and how we both worried that our youngest daughters might end up on "Wanted" posters someday. Through the course of the conversation, I found out that he usually traveled about thirty-eight weekends a year and he learned that I was used to crazy schedules like that because Brad was gone all of the time, too. As the conversation took us from appetizers to dinner, we both seemed to forget that we had just met.

"I've always wanted to go to one of those places with the swim-up bar," I told him as we paid our check. "I think that looks like fun."

"Oh, you don't want to that," he quickly replied. "I brought my kids to Mexico once and my son and I watched those people sit there at that bar for hours, and you know what we noticed?"

"What?" I said.

"No one ever gets up," he said. "How can they drink that much and *never* get up to go to the bathroom? Makes you think, doesn't it?"

When he told his coworkers the next day about what he'd said, they all replied, "You talked to her about peeing in the pool on your *first date*? What is the *matter* with you? No wonder you're single!"

But honestly, that comment—that had me laughing so hard I couldn't talk for five minutes—and his face, red with embarrassment, appealed to me. By the end of the date I was comfortable enough to mention that if I had known we were going to play basketball in the arcade, I would have worn my sports bra. And even more shocking to me was that I was okay with getting a quick kiss as we parted ways.

And the sweet sting I felt surprised me so much that I couldn't stop thinking about it for days.

Who knew I still had it in me?

For those people who are waiting for the "right time" to start dating after loss, I have some bad news for you. Yes, you should be self-aware, know what you're looking for, and be in the healthiest place personally that you possibly can be. But, like child-birth, even if you have all of your ducks in a row, chances are you're going to go through some growing pains.

And many times, also like childbirth, things will happen when you least expect it.

The truth is, there are certain things that you can't work out before you're in a relationship. There are things that you have to work out while you're in it. Even if you've talked yourself out of feeling guilty, once you feel truly committed to the next person, those feelings might temporarily surface again. Even if you know with all of your heart that your first husband would really want you to move forward, there is a part of you, when you're with someone new, that just *doesn't want to.* You start realizing all of the things about your spouse that you loved and wish you had back, and then you start liking new things about your significant other and wonder why your husband never did that.

By the time you're dating the second time around, chances are the person *you're* dating is also on his second time around. He could be widowed himself, divorced, or have just ended something long-term. Dating later in life means that everyone comes with some sort of baggage, and part of the process is figuring out if you can help each other carry what you both have without sinking under the weight.

The bottom line is: we all have something to work on when we've lost something we were once invested in. And it involves patience from both parties.

I had no idea how abandoned I felt by Brad's death until I was in the thick of my relationship with Mike. And I don't think he knew how abandoned he felt after going through an agonizing divorce until he met me. We went through a long and painful phase of alternately pushing each other away.

Just when I would think things were going well, Mike would

somehow upset the apple cart and make me doubt why I was with him. And just when I could see that he was getting completely comfortable...*Bam!* I'd step in with a whopper of my own. I'd push, force him into fights that were completely unnecessary, and generally turn his world upside down when he least expected it. I'd cut off communication suddenly and without reason, blindside him by telling him I needed some space, and through it all, my subconscious seemed to be asking him one question:

"Are you sure you *really* want to be here? Because I've gotten past the point of being easy to commit to."

I'll never forget the first time Mike told me that he loved me. It was late at night in the summer of 2009, and we were sitting in the dark on my back porch. One of the things I loved most about our relationship was how we could just rattle on like two friends who hadn't seen each other in years, even though at that point we were talking multiple times a day.

We never seemed to tire of telling each other things about our pasts, both funny and painful, and learning new things about each other was our favorite hobby. I remember looking at him, his face half glowing from the light shining through my kitchen window. There had been a pause in our conversation, and he suddenly looked at me a little sheepishly and said, "There's something I have to tell you."

I'd like to say that I had no idea what was coming, but I did. Women usually know when a man is getting ready to tell her that he loves her. We try and act surprised, but believe me, most of the time we're not. We're either dreading it because we're still not sure about how we feel, or we're hoping for it because we didn't want to be the one who said it first.

I fell into the latter category.

"What's up?" I said, trying to look innocent but really feeling like a fisherman who knows he's finally caught the big one.

"I...I think I'm in love with you," Mike said, his face turned down a little and his eyes looking up at me.

Now, I know a savvier woman would have been more collected at this declaration. She would have said, "Oh. Well. I'll need some time to think about that. But thank you for sharing your feelings."

Not me. I stood up from my chair, walked over to his, and hugged him around the neck.

"Thank *God* you said it first!" I exclaimed. "I've had to catch myself so many times before I've said it when we hang up the phone! What a relief it will be to just be able to *say* it!"

Mike hugged me back and we began chattering away again, talking about when we first thought we fell in love with each other. We talked on and on and I'm not sure when that switch was flipped in my head, but I think it happened somewhere around midnight.

"In *love?*" I thought. "What am I doing? I can't be in love! It's too risky! I have too much at stake! The kids...my sanity...my heart. Nope. Nope. Back it up."

And so I did what I always did to Mike. I picked a fight about something random, something out of the blue, and something that really didn't matter. And Mike, who was suddenly having similar fears of his own after realizing that we had shared something that made us truly committed, fought right along with me.

On and on we went. I don't even remember what it was about, it was so insignificant. It was probably something years and years down the road that I was worried about. All I know is that at two in the morning, it ended with me kicking him out, telling him to go home, and that I wasn't sure how I felt about him anymore.

How's that for an ending to that romantic story?

As we always did, we cooled off, and by the next afternoon, everything was okay. We were back to talking and texting, nothing resolved because for some reason we were both thinking that our fight actually had something to do with what we were fighting about and that it would figure itself out later, when in reality, our fight had nothing to do with our discussion. It had to do with our fear.

What if I left him as his wife had? Where would that leave him? And what if he *died* on me? Was I *ready* to take that chance again?

I kept the arguments that Mike and I had to myself, not really talking to anyone about them, and for the first time, I felt like I couldn't talk to my friends and family. Oh, I knew that they would listen. In the years that I had been married, my friends and I had all shared with each other the problems and annoyances that we had with our husbands. But Mike wasn't my husband. He was my boyfriend…something that my friends had never had "later in life." So there was a part of me that felt like they either wouldn't understand or that they would dismiss these issues because he wasn't my husband.

My voluntary solitude with these problems was made worse by the fact that my kids were getting so attached to Mike. They would crawl up into his lap, hug him constantly, and generally couldn't get enough of him. Every time I worried that the relationship might be too much or that I might want to back away, I'd look at those faces, happy in anticipation every time they asked, "When is Mr. Mike coming over?"

And that scared me even more.

It was during a particularly heated insignificant battle when Mike finally raised both his hands and said, "Wait, wait, wait, wait, *wait*. Do you want to be here?"

"Of course I do!" I replied, ready for an argument.

"Are you committed to us?"

"*Yes!*"

"Well, so am I! So what in the hell are we arguing for?"

It's amazing what fear of the unknown can do to a relation-ship. I had to understand that yes, it was a possibility that he could die on me. But knowing that didn't outweigh how much I loved him and how much I wanted him in my life. I started realizing that even though losing Brad was by far the most painful thing I'd ever been through, I wouldn't trade the happy years I had with him, even if that meant I wouldn't have had to go through the pain of losing him.

I had to accept the bad with the good. The fear with the secu-rity. And I had to learn how to love all over again.

23

I was more than two years into widowhood, and I felt like things were finally coming together—that my life was starting to shape up into...well...a life. The kids were doing well, going to school and becoming small people who provided me with company, as opposed to toddlers who just gave me a headache. Firmly entrenched in my relationship with Mike, I felt like I was moving forward as I should be. But with the kids developing their own lives—in their own activities and constantly on the go with friends—and Mike on the road most weekends, a question kept popping up in my brain.

What was I going to do?

I could see the children becoming more and more independent. Mike had a life outside of our relationship that kept him busy and fulfilled. And so that question—about my future and where I personally wanted to go—would keep me awake at night and generally not leave me alone. I wanted something that would allow me to make my own schedule so that I could be around for the kids, something that was important to Brad and me. I wanted something that didn't require going back and getting a master's degree (something I felt sure that I didn't, at the time, have the attention span to do). I wanted something that was my own.

I had a sudden flashback to a conversation Brad and I had had years earlier about my going back to work someday. "You ought to look into getting your security clearance and work on proposals," he said. "Contractors make good money, and they can pretty much make their own hours."

"What in the world would I do, working on proposals?" I said, laughing. "I'm no engineer."

"No, but you can write," he said. "They're always looking for technical writers."

So, after thinking about it for a few weeks, I decided to email Brad's boss, Mary, and see if she had any insight on how I could get into writing as a consultant.

Do you know how I can get involved in working on proposals? Brad mentioned something about it a while ago and I thought I would ask.

To which she immediately replied:

Yes. I'll put you in contact with a company you can work through. I'll hire you through them.

For the next few months, I worked on getting my security clearance, taking a class on writing for business to brush up on some skills, and waiting for an email saying that they were ready for me to work. And that email never came. Later, I read:

We want to work with you, but all of the proposals we're working on are on the East Coast. And we know that you can't travel.

Even though I should have been discouraged to find out that

my current life situation made it impossible for me to work a job I thought was a sure thing, I wasn't. At that point in my widowhood, I had gotten fairly good at taking things as they came at me and really not panicking about anything. I felt like even though they didn't have a job for me *yet* didn't mean that they never would. And I did my best to hold on to that thought every day as I got the kids ready for school and did my usual tasks around the house.

I didn't realize it yet, but by preparing myself for that job—taking classes, doing research, and generally dusting off the skills I already had—I had been unintentionally working toward something I'd always wanted to do. I had been reminded of how much I loved to write and why I'd gotten that degree in English in the first place. I loved the process, the thinking behind it, how one sentence had the ability to make you laugh, while the next could have you in tears. Like putting together a puzzle, even the driest, most technical sentence can be configured just right so that everything comes together and makes sense. And I enjoyed figuring out a way to make that happen.

After coming to the conclusion that this whole proposal-writing thing wasn't going to happen, or at least not in the near future, I was back to "now what?" And even though I didn't have a firm answer for myself, I felt a new idea right at the edge of my brain. And the answer came from a most unexpected place.

People magazine.

I was lying on my living room couch reading the book reviews to see if there was anything interesting that I wanted to pick up. I was reading a review for a memoir—and to this day I can't remember which one—when I literally sat up and said out loud, "I can do that."

I walked down to my basement office that day and began to write. Not a book...I just started writing. Somehow, in that one moment, a voice was born and couldn't be silenced. I wrote about all of the funny stuff that had happened to us that I knew would come as a surprise to a lot of people. All of the transitions the kids and I were going through. The good, the bad, the life affirming, and the life altering. It all came pouring out of me like it had been waiting there all along.

"You know what you should do?" Mike said a few months after I showed him a little of what I had written. "You should start a blog. I mean, it's free and you never know who might pick up on it."

And so I did. Completely confident that not one person out there would read it. But I underestimated myself.

My mom and my college roommates never missed a post.

I loved it. I loved writing about what we were doing, what we had done, and where I thought we were going. It became a diary of sorts and a way for me to process all that was happening. I made a promise to myself that whatever I wrote would be positive or at least end in a positive way so that even if no one else ever read it, I might be inspired by all we had done and how far we had come. Putting that goal in front of myself forced me to think about even the worst situations in an upbeat way. I contacted the Donor Alliance and told the volunteer coordinator there what I was doing, and she promised to spread the word and asked if I would start speaking for them as the wife of an organ donor. And even though I wasn't getting paid a dime, I couldn't help but feel that I had somehow found my calling.

By the summer of 2010, Widow Chick, as I called myself on Facebook, was getting hits from people all over the world. I watched in amazement as other widows and widowers would try and connect with each other through comments and posts on the blog site and on the Facebook page. People who thought like I did. People who needed the same connection that I was looking for. People who wanted others to listen to them, laugh with them, cry with them, and ultimately say three magical words to them.

"You're not crazy."

It was all-consuming for me and I loved it. But there was a part that I couldn't quite put my finger on…that just wasn't enough.

It came to me, as most of my good ideas do, while I was driving down the road in my trusty minivan. And when it came, it all came in a rush, complete with goose bumps and an optimism I can't explain. I suddenly saw my life unfold before me in a way that I never had before and I knew—I just *knew*—exactly what I was supposed to do.

"A website," I thought. "Someplace where people can come together at any time of the night and talk to each other. Where they can search for each other and find people they have things in common with—maybe even meet for a cup of coffee. Where they can talk to other people about issues like funerals, sex, dating, and dealing with in-laws without having other people who might not understand judge them or what they're going through. This is it. This is what I'm meant to do."

I've since read articles from other writers about a "moment of obligation"—that instant when you realize that you need to stop waiting around for someone else to create or start something that you wish you had. I had no experience with websites. My technical abilities consisted of turning on my computer and checking my Facebook page. I could never even remember to update my virus software. But I remembered those early months of widowhood—before I had found my young widows group—when I thought, "Why doesn't someone start something so that we can all find each other?"

And two years later, that someone was me.

I met with graphic artists, attorneys, and, of course, my ever-faithful financial planner, Kristi. After six months of meetings and late nights, copy and code, www.theWiddahood.com was born—something that I never knew I had in me to create—and in the months following, I saw people coming together, grateful for this place where they could find unconditional support.

A place to come together.

A place to connect.

A place where, no matter what self-doubt plagues us on this journey, someone will be there to say what we all need to hear.

"I believe in you. And I know you can do this."

Everything was falling into place. I felt alive and like my life was being driven by something that was bigger than me. I could work on the website and my writing on my own schedule. When the kids were on break from school, I could drop everything to spend the time with them that we all needed. Mike and I were spending more and more time together as a family—including his kids—which left us both exhausted, but in a good way. There were days when I found it hard to believe that this was my life because it was something I had never imagined before.

And as if on cue, when everything was going well, Fate stepped in yet again to test me.

It started out as a small limp. But then it grew into a bigger one. And finally the pain was so bad that Mike couldn't sleep. He could barely walk. He couldn't even sit comfortably, and his diet started including massive amounts of Tylenol just to get through his day.

Mike had fallen in January during a NASCAR test in Daytona, Florida. When he described slipping on the oil, I couldn't help but laugh and say, "Oh, how I wish I had been there to see that!"

But then his hip started hurting.

A couple of months went by, and finally he couldn't take it anymore. He made an appointment with a workers' comp doctor to have the hip looked at. When the initial x-ray showed nothing, the doctor told Mike to make an appointment to have an MRI. And when the film came back, it showed something.

A big something.

"Now, I'm not a doctor," the technician told Mike, pointing to a huge mass on the upper part of his femur bone, "but in all the years I've been doing this, I've never seen anything like this."

And then he said the words that completely turned our world upside down and shook it.

"You need to make an appointment with an orthopedic oncologist immediately."

When Mike came to my house with the MRI results in his hand, my stomach dropped to my toes. As he held the film up to the light in my breakfast room, I could see a white blob covering the entire top of his femur, five centimeters in length…basically the size of a baby's fist, leaving almost no bone. We pored over the results, looking at the film from every angle, hoping that between his engineering degree and mine in English we would somehow be able to say definitively, "Well, *that's* nothing to worry about!"

No one wants to hear "I need to make an appointment with an oncologist."

And, I daresay, a widow wants to hear it even less.

Now by that point, I'd been hanging out in The Widdahood long enough to know that there is no quota on bad luck. I'd seen enough through the website to know that just because one bad thing has happened doesn't mean that you are immune for the rest of your life. I'd read posts from people who struggled with the deaths of parents mere weeks after the death of their spouse. People who had lost children and were trying to figure out ways to cope because the person they would have leaned on—their partner—was gone, too. And just because you've lost one person you love doesn't mean you won't lose another one. Fate doesn't look at your chart and say, "Oh wait. She lost her husband in 2007. She's not due to lose another one for at least sixty years."

My hands were shaking so hard I could barely type as I sent a message to a friend who had just lost *her* husband the month before. And would you like to know how they found out he had cancer?

That's right. A tumor on his hip.

Do you have the name of an orthopedic oncologist?

Why? What's going on?

Mike has a tumor on his femur.

OMG. Go see Dr. Brown. She's the best. Keep me posted.

With the doctor's name and number in his hand, Mike left for work the next morning and called me around lunch to tell me that the first appointment he could get was in two weeks.

Two weeks?

I had no idea that time could go by so slowly. A million different scenarios ran through my head. What if this *was* cancer? What if it wasn't and he was going to have major surgery and a long recovery? What if this was something that would leave him crippled?

And what is my role in all of this? We weren't married, but I couldn't picture myself anywhere else but by his side. With him being an only child and his parents not financially able to come to Colorado and take care of him, chances were that the caretaking responsibilities would fall on me.

What if I didn't have it in me to do this?

When the day of his appointment finally arrived, I dressed very carefully. I was petrified that the same thing that happened with Brad would happen again: that I would leave for a hospital expecting to bring someone home, but that something so bad would happen and that someone would never come back. I put on layers and comfortable shoes. I didn't wear my favorite jeans—I wore jeans I thought I could sleep in if I had to. I packed my purse with a book, a phone charger, and a few granola bars…anything I could think of that I might need for the next twenty-four hours in case I couldn't get home right away. I debated on whether I should wear a scarf that would look cute with what I was wearing and could double as a pillow later if I needed it.

I tried to discreetly prepare myself for the worst while simultaneously trying not to scare the crap out of Mike. And it didn't occur to me until later how sad it was that I couldn't take him to a doctor's appointment without worrying that he might never come back. I told the kids that Mr. Mike had to have surgery and was grateful for the fact that we had had so many surgeries within the family during the past year—knee replacements and minor foot surgeries—that they really didn't think much about my making another trip to the hospital.

I could tell that my parents were just as afraid as I was about what might be coming and as confused as I was about my place in all of it. My mother tried her best not to dig too deeply into my business, but every once in a while she would sneak a question in that let me know that they were concerned.

"Now, who will be taking care of Mike after the surgery?" she asked.

"Well. That would be me."

"Uh huh."

The day of Mike's first appointment with Dr. Brown, I sat fidgeting in the waiting room as he filled out paperwork. Neither one of us said much, both of us afraid of scaring the other even more than we already were. But finally he looked up and asked a question that would forever, in my mind, change the nature of our relationship.

"Can I put you down as an emergency contact?"

Ask any widow: their *least* favorite thing to do after the death of their spouse is to fill out paperwork that asks that question. We *know* that we have lost the person we can turn to immediately in our time of need, but there it is in black and white, staring us in the face. What that question seems to really be asking us is: "You're completely alone, aren't you?"

"*Me?*" I asked, my eyes filling with tears. "You want *me* as your emergency contact?"

If anyone around us was watching this scene unfold, they probably thought Mike had just asked me to marry him. And in my own weird widow way, it was kind of like he had.

"Well, sure," he replied, not really understanding the significance of it. "You're the person I'm the closest to. If anything happens, I want you to be making the decisions."

Sniffle. "I'd be honored."

Mike handed his paperwork in and we made our way into the examination room. Dr. Brown, a woman who exuded medical competency, strode in and threw Mike's film up on the light box.

"There," she said, pointing. "Right there. You have a tumor and very little bone left. My main concern is that if you fall again, the top of your femur could completely break off and you'd be in a whole mess of trouble. We need to get in there and take it out and rebuild the bone. Now, I won't lie to you, this is going to be painful and the recovery won't be easy. But if you don't have it done, the consequences could be much worse."

"But...what about cancer?" I asked, surprised that she didn't mention that right away.

"I can see some fluid around the tumor and that makes me pretty confident that it's not," she said. "But I really won't know until I get in there."

We immediately started pooling our calendars, trying to come up with a time that would work for the surgery. Mike knew that he could come off the road at any time and that the NASCAR team would understand. My schedule was a little more complicated, trying to work around the kids and everything else I had going on as a one-woman show in my household so that I would have the time to take care of him when he was released.

"All right, guys," Dr. Brown said when everything had been worked out. "See you in a month."

We left that day feeling a little better, but I knew I wouldn't be able to sleep until I saw her walk out of that operating room and say, "It's not cancer." In the weeks leading up to the surgery, I did my best to keep my panic at bay by staying busy, but I know that there were times when I was short with the kids for what seemed like no reason at all. While they knew that his leg was hurting, I didn't think it was necessary to tell them how worried we were about the Big C. I found myself constantly apologizing and telling them frankly, "I'm sorry Mommy's so cranky sometimes. I'm just a little worried about Mr. Mike."

Which I'm sure made them worry a little as well.

At night I would lie awake, envisioning the worst. I couldn't help but think about those first few hours in the hospital with Brad, before he'd had the stroke and we thought he would just be coming home with a dislocated knee. Thinking about preparing the house for someone who couldn't do stairs and putting my life on hold while he recovered, I couldn't help but let my mind go to that dark place that wondered if Mike would ever come back. And during that time, I'm afraid that I had every selfish thought known to man.

Why is this happening to *me*?

What have I done to deserve this?

Can *I* do this?

Notice how none of those thoughts had *anything* to do with the actual patient.

Mike went to work and was extra cautious, knowing that one false move could give him an injury he might never fully recover from. I kept going, doing things with the kids and explaining to them over and over again that they needed to be careful with Mr. Mike because he hurt his leg. Our conversations centered around benign topics like how our days were going and what was the latest gossip around the NASCAR shop. Neither one of us dug too deeply into what was really going on, but every once in a while, we would both look at each other with tired, watery eyes and pale faces, and I knew we were both feeling the same thing.

Scared shitless.

When the day of the surgery rolled around, I hired a babysitter to come to the house and watch the kids at 5:00 a.m. so that I could get Mike to the hospital and prepped for surgery. We got him checked in and tried to keep things as light as possible, given the circumstances. I took pictures of him in his "shower cap" before he was wheeled into surgery and threatened to text it to all of his coworkers. And eventually I gave his hand a hard squeeze and watched as the nurses wheeled him away.

Hospitals. The smell. The beeping machines. The way they all have the same damn carpet.

Without Mike still in front of me to jolly along, my worst fears bombarded my brain all at once, making it hard to breathe. I had been to several hospitals since Brad had been gone, almost forcing myself to "get over" my issues with them. I never wanted to be the friend, daughter, or sister who couldn't help because she was too afraid. My first experience was during my dad's knee replacement surgery the year before. My mother and my sister had assured me that I didn't need to come, knowing that it would be hard. But I didn't want to be that person. I didn't want to be the person who couldn't be there for others. And so I went.

When the nurses wheeled my dad into his hospital room after his surgery, hooked up to monitors with oxygen running out of his nose, he looked at my mother drowsily and said, "Can I have some Jell-O?" just as Brad had said to me years earlier before he fell permanently asleep.

And I calmly went into the bathroom across the hall and threw up.

There is a part of me that knows I will never be as useful in a hospital situation as I once was. Up until Brad died, hospitals had actually been nothing but a positive place for me. They were where I happily gave birth to my three children and where the people I loved went to get fixed. Brad was the first person who couldn't be, and I'd seen enough of life to know that he wouldn't be the last. And that day, leaving Mike in the hands of the nurses, I hoped that I hadn't come to that next unfixable moment already. As I left Mike in the surgery prep area, I looked around at all of the patients in the room, getting ready for surgery, and wondered whose life was going to be changed.

I just hoped it wasn't going to be mine.

I walked out and immediately got lost on my way to the waiting room. I find every hospital I have ever been in so unnecessarily confusing, and I hoped with all of my heart that we wouldn't be there long enough for me to make sense of the maze. And when I finally made it to the area that would be my home for the next few hours, carrying my laptop and a million other things in my backpack, prepared for a long wait...I walked through the swinging doors and saw them.

My parents were sitting there waiting for me.

We have a rule in our family that no one—friend, family, neighbor, or acquaintance—should ever sit alone at a hospital.

I've known my mother to give up days at a time, waiting with someone she may have only met once because she'd heard that they didn't have anyone going with them for whatever procedure they needed to have done. And when I saw them there, my mother stood up and gave me a hug and said, "If you have to make a hard decision, we didn't want you to have to make it alone."

God, my parents should be cloned and every family should have a set.

Minutes later, Kristi walked in the door, armed with the latest *People* magazine to distract me, and the four of us sat there and waited for what we hoped would be the magical answer we wanted to hear. I looked at the three of them, sitting in uncomfortable waiting-room chairs, and had a flashback to all of us sitting in a hospital, waiting together, just a couple of years before.

Waiting for the magical answer that never came.

Two hours later, Dr. Brown briskly walked through the swinging doors of the waiting room, still wearing her surgical scrubs.

"It went well. Couldn't have gone better. The tumor is benign, and I've put in three screws and a plate. The cement I've put in will dissolve as the new bone grows. He's going to be just fine. You can see him in about an hour up in recovery."

I'm sure that woman had no idea why I was shaking and crying as I shook her hand. Not only had Mike weathered this storm, but so had I. Months of waiting, worrying, and assuming the worst would happen because it had before had all led up to this moment.

That this time everything would be okay.

And even though I knew that could change tomorrow, on that day, I could breathe the sigh of relief I wasn't able to years before.

I once asked a woman who had not only lost her husband, but also her fiancé (her potential second husband), if she was ever afraid of getting into another relationship. And while, at the time, she seemed as if she wasn't actively looking for one, I was surprised when she said she was still open to it.

"I was put here to love and be loved," she said. "And every time I do it, I do it even better than before."

Bad things happen to good people. And we widows don't have the luxury of pretending that they won't.

But life is meant to be *lived*. We are meant to be loved... and to love someone else in return. The fear of loss will always be there. It has to be accepted and dealt with. But the fear of loss should never paralyze the ability to love and live fully.

And sometimes the key is to find someone who will help you both live your life...and love your past.

I had no idea that I could have a relationship with two men. But now I do. That was a lesson that Mike taught me: that it is possible to love two people at the same time.

I think of it as a very spiritual three-way.

Brad will always be the father of my children and the first man I really, truly loved. By having that relationship, he showed me what was possible. And by taking that relationship with me, I made it possible all over again.

I grieve while I laugh. I laugh while I grieve.

I'm happy.

I cry because I wish Brad could be here to share this with me.

Mike accepted that Brad would always be a part of my life. He wasn't jealous and seemed to understand (and not take offense) when I missed my old life. He gave me space when I needed it and hugged me fiercely when I asked. He allowed me to have it all, in my heart, without feeling guilty or feeling like someday I'd have to let Brad go.

At the beginning of our relationship, I tried to walk the widow tightrope with care, unsure of how Mike really felt about my life. I worried that he would be like the men I'd been warned about, who would have no patience for listening about my past and would feel threatened when I talked about my husband as if I still loved him.

Because, even though he's not here, I do.

There are very special people in the world who have no problem accepting our past and present love of our spouses while accepting what we have to give to them...and I stumbled onto one of them. Mike let me know early in our relationship, in his own way, that my life was perfectly "normal" and that he was ready to be a part of it. And that moment came after we had been dating for about three months and had an uncomfortable milestone looming before us.

Father's Day.

Mike was at loose ends for the weekend, and so awkwardly I said, "Well, the kids and I always go up to the cemetery for Father's Day. I'm sure that's not how you want to spend your Sunday, so we can just call you when we get back, if you'd like."

And he surprised me with, "Actually...I'd like to go."

So we packed the kids in the family truckster and headed up to Buffalo Creek to visit Brad.

The entire drive up there I could *not* believe this was actually happening. Taking a *date* to the cemetery to see my *husband*? While I tried to make normal conversation, I worried for an hour and a half about what Mike could possibly be thinking, certain that this date (Can I even call it that? Three kids and a cemetery plot?) would probably be our last. I tried not to think about how Father's Day was one of the hardest days of the year for me because I didn't feel like I knew Mike well enough to have a complete nervous breakdown in front of him.

Could he later sue me for the therapy *he* would need after this date?

After we parked in the dirt parking lot, the kids jumped out of the minivan and started running down the path toward Brad's plot. Mike and I slowly got out of the car, uneasily not making eye contact. And then we both spotted it at the same time.

There was a construction vehicle parked on the mountain right next to Brad's plot. They were digging a grave…not for an urn…a full-on *grave* in the spot next to Brad.

This made me nervous for two reasons. First, I didn't want one of my kids to run around and take a flying leap into a hole that was six feet deep, although that would make it a Father's Day to remember. ("Hey, Mom! Do you remember that time I fell in the grave?")

Second, it made the outing a little less peaceful and a lot creepier, and I wasn't sure how Mike would handle it.

But as we walked down the mountain toward Brad, Mike slowly turned, looked straight at me, and with a little twinkle in his eye he said one thing.

"That's not for me, is it?"

I started laughing. It burbled up from my gut and came out of my mouth as my eyes filled with tears at the sheer *ridiculousness* of it all.

And suddenly my heart felt lighter.

Laughing with someone else.

Absorbing that I could love someone else.

And suddenly life's possibilities seemed limitless.

Moving Forward

time to pull on your tights and
become your own superhero

24

For the first few years of widowhood, I tried everything I could think of to find my old normal. I wanted to get back to that place where I had the same problems as everyone else I knew because those problems seemed a hell of a lot more normal than the ones that I now had. (Who knew that it was possible to wish for "normal problems"?) From attempting to be both Brad and myself for the kids to trying to recreate a life with someone else that would fit the idea of what I thought life should be like (there's that dreaded "should" word again)…not only was it exhausting; it was impossible.

But that was a lesson I needed to learn in my own time.

I put a lot of pressure on myself when it came to figuring out my life on my own, especially when it came to parenting. I thought that no one would notice if I went a little crazy and no one would really care if I did…as long as it didn't affect the kids.

I constantly worried that the girls would pick up on the fact that I was incapable of doing everything by myself and that Michael wouldn't get enough "guy time." However, I do believe that with all of this female influence around, he'll make great husband material. About a year after Brad died, I noticed that he had the most amazing ability to remember things I'd looked at in the mall, and before we left, he'd remind me about them.

"Mom? Didn't you like that purse? Don't forget you wanted to buy that before we left."

I mean, who wouldn't want their husband to do *that*?

When he did that kind of stuff I was as proud as a dad watching his son score the winning run at a Little League game. Because, really, what are the chances that he'll make it to the big leagues? Reminding a woman to go buy accessories is a skill that will serve him well for the rest of his life.

There are always things that catch you off guard in single parenting, and in my case most of them have to do with my son. Oh, I know that there will be some "lumpy throat" moments with the girls. But I'm good at girl time. I'm good at relating to the girls, even as they go through various changes. Most of my "I'm not sure if I can do this" parenting moments have to do with Michael and worrying that just having a mom around won't be enough.

And that was never truer than when, four years after Brad died and Michael was entering the first grade, he decided to join the Boy Scouts.

I had mixed feelings about it before we even made it to the meeting. I was worried about the time commitment, and I had heard horror stories from my sister, who had had to drag my nephew to every meeting and do just about every project for him during the six months he tried on the Boy Scout uniform.

But for the most part, I was sad. I was really proud of Michael that he wanted to do this, and knowing how he operated, I was sure that he would make a great Boy Scout. But this was Brad's deal. Brad had been the Boy Scout. Brad had been the *Eagle* Scout. Brad had volunteered with the Boy Scouts before we even had kids.

And now he was missing out on his own son participating.

I had reached the point that every parent looks forward to: when the kids are old enough to actually *do* stuff—not just sit in a stroller chewing on a pacifier while we walked through the zoo—like throw a ball, ride a bike, and discuss what had happened at school that day over dinner. Brad in particular looked forward to that time when the kids would be more interactive and he could show the girls how to ride their bikes and Michael how to fix a Jeep. We were just getting to that point with Haley when he died, and in the months before the accident, he loved taking her to the local go-cart track to watch the other kids race, hoping she would catch the bug.

"Now, I think we need to make a deal," I said the second time he took her. "We won't put the kids in activities unless they *ask*. We're not going to push our own agendas on them."

Of course, I said this secretly hoping they would all beg me for piano lessons on each of their sixth birthdays.

And now he was missing the magical time he'd always dreamed about as a father. That in-between time when they were searching for independence and but still needed to see your face in the crowd. When they showed off because they knew you were watching and actually cared. When they tested their boundaries because your opinion still mattered. When they wanted to go sleep someplace overnight…but still held on to you for a minute when you left.

I sat in on those meetings as the leaders told us all that Boy Scouts was a "family" organization and that the moms were just as involved as the dads. But the moment the leader said, "You'll have so much fun showing your son how to use a saw and all of your power tools!" I thought…

His dad should be here doing this with him.

I spent the entire first meeting with a huge lump in my throat and "I can't do this" rolling around in my head. I mean, for crying out loud, I couldn't even sew on the patches. Brad was the one who fixed our buttons and sewed in shoulder pads. (Yes, we were married in the '90s when shoulder pads were oh so slimming.) So not only could I not do the "manly" part of what was expected in the Boy Scouts, I couldn't even be a successful *mom*.

That night after the first meeting, I went home and sat on the edge of my bed, softly crying while the kids put their pj's on. "Brad should be here," I thought. "I'm the one who should be gone. He would be handling all of this so much better than me."

Just then, ten-year-old Haley walked into the room and I quickly wiped my cheeks with the sleeve of my sweatshirt.

"Mom?" she said softly.

"What's up, kiddo?" I asked, taking her into a one-arm hug.

"I...I need to talk to you about something."

"What is it?"

"I...I think I need a...a..."

"What, sweetie?"

"A bra."

An image flashed into my head of Brad sitting there instead of me. Of Brad taking her to the store to try on bras. Of Brad eventually figuring out the best way to tell his daughters how to use a tampon. (I would imagine it would go something like, "The directions are in the box. Here's your grandmother's phone number in case you have any questions.")

And then I realized: there's no right way to do any of it. All we can do is work with what we have.

Brad is very much a part of their lives, but in a positive way. For the most part, what they want to talk about when it comes to their dad is how much they remind me of him. I don't do it too often, because I don't like to center their lives around what they've lost, but every once in a while, I'll tell Michael, "Oh, you think so much like your dad!" Or to Haley, "Pizza is your favorite food? So was your dad's!" Or to Sarah, "If you don't stop that, you're always going to be in trouble...just like Grandma says your dad was."

Okay. So that last one wasn't very positive. But if there's anything Sarah has inherited from her father, it's his mischievous streak.

When your kids lose a parent at such a young age, it's hard to find the balance between keeping his memory alive and forcing memories and grief on them that they may not even have. I watch my kids very closely and take their lead on when we talk about their dad. I don't randomly grab them in a group bear hug and wail about the fact that they've lost the best father and they'll miss his presence for the rest of their lives.

That will pretty much guarantee that you will be paying for an extra ten years of children's counseling.

Still, I'm all about emotion and sharing feelings, and I'm very upfront with my kids. If I'm crabby and one of them asks why, I'll flat-out say, "I'm really missing Daddy right now, and sometimes I'm angry he's not here." Or when they do something great I'll tell them, "I wish Daddy could have been here to see that."

And I know that even though they were young when he died, my kids wish that Brad could have been around to help me out a little. For years, they would hear me say daily, "How many hands do I have? And how many of you are there? Can you see that I can't make your lunch, put in a movie, and wipe someone all at the same time?"

I'll never forget when, a couple of weeks after Brad died, I was trying to get a car seat strapped into my minivan, which was never my skill area. Even though most people deal with this sort of thing every day, when I suddenly found myself alone, something as simple as child safety became completely overwhelming.

As I started nearing the fifth anniversary of his death, I felt myself going through what I now call growing pains: I knew that things were about to be different. I didn't know exactly what they were or where I was about to end up, which was torture for a planner like me. But I'd gotten to the point where I could sense it coming, like the darkening sky before a tornado. I would stand there and hope it would pass me by, but as life has a tendency to do every once in a while, change would pick me up, swirl me around, and leave me stunned in a place I didn't quite recognize.

And I would be left to pick up the pieces once more.

25

I n the fall of 2012, five years into widowhood, I found myself in the pedicure chair once again. The RX8 had been sold, the house needed a new roof, and I was single again because Mike and I had broken up after three years together. Needless to say, I was not in the mood for brightly colored "Big Apple Red" on my toes. I was into more of the darker hues like "Midnight in Moscow."

It would be easy for me to say that I sat there, vibrating in that chair that had become so familiar to me over the years, wondering, "What has happened to my life?" But I didn't wonder. I could link every decision I ever made that had gotten me to that point—from saying "I do" to Brad, to sadly nodding my okay when he bought that motorcycle, to dating and meeting Mike, and to ultimately saying the relationship wasn't working for me anymore—and I take responsibility for them all.

Because all of those decisions, the good and the bad, had led me to where I was and had shaped who I had become. And if I couldn't accept all of it, it was as if I was saying I couldn't accept myself.

I have discovered that the worst kind of breakup doesn't come in the heat of the moment, during a fight, or because you can't stand the thought of seeing someone ever again. The worst is actually when both people are good, kind, and caring. And when one of them decides that it's just not working anymore in spite of all of those things.

My decision to try life on my own again came as a surprise to many, including the kids. They had spent years with Mr. Mike a part of their lives, and it didn't occur to them that it wouldn't always be that way. Since Brad's death, I had always tried to stay ahead of the three of them emotionally, doing my best to antici-pate their needs before they even knew they had them. But on the day I told them that Mr. Mike was going to be in our lives just as a friend from then on and that we wouldn't see as much of him as we used to...I'll admit that I didn't see what was coming.

The kids had weathered the storm of Brad's death so well that I underestimated how hard this breakup would be. That, in fact, it would be another loss to them and hit them at a time in their lives when they were old enough to truly understand what was gone but maybe not old enough to understand *why*. I watched in horror as tears began to flow down Haley's eleven-year-old cheeks. Michael's face twitched as if trying to hold everything in, and Sarah started to sob.

"This is the worst change we've ever been through," she cried. And I realized how naive I'd been, assuming that she would remember how hard our lives became in 2007 when she lost her father...when she was really too young to remember it at all.

I held my children that day and cried along with them. That the pain they were experiencing was a result of something I had done—and not because of some outside influence I had no power to control, like death—was something I almost couldn't take. We were careful around each other the rest of the day as if one false step might break the balance that was now just the four of us again. The kids were quieter than they had been in a long time. Which gave me more time to digest what I had done.

The next day, I packed them up in the car for the sole purpose of getting us out of the house. Our faces were drawn and tired, but I had hopes that if we could just get out in the fall sunshine, the world would look a little brighter to us all.

"We're going on a short hike," I said as I backed out of the driveway.

While I drove, the kids pointed out the blinding fall foliage. They had a conversation in the backseat about how Halloween was in just a couple of weeks and brainstormed about costumes. They hopped out of the car when we reached our destination, a trailhead not far from our house. And as we hiked, my son taking the lead at a breakneck pace while my daughters and I struggled to keep up, Sarah took my hand.

"I don't like change," she said.

"I know."

"But life would be weird if we didn't have it," she said after thinking about it for a minute. "I don't think I would like it if nothing *ever* changed."

"That's true."

"At least we have each other," she said.

After saying those wise words, she dropped my hand and raced ahead to join her brother and sister. I watched them as they chatted and occasionally slowed down to help each other scale a boulder or cross a stream. I realized that the changes that we had been through—both the good and unthinkable—had made us who we are as a family. Maybe fearful of the unknown at times but confident that together we would make it through because we'd already proven that to each other.

And that's something I hope will never change.

I catch myself wishing, quite often, for the past when life was less complicated…when I could just look to the person lying next to me in bed and ask what he thought we should do about breakfast, buying a new car, or fixing the microwave…when people still looked at me funny (because I've always been on this side of crazy), but I was blissfully ignorant as to why…when the good and bad times in my relationship seemed to be the problems that everyone else in my life was having, too. And the truth is, those days seem less complicated *now*, but at the time there were still things that were difficult to get through.

Getting married and moving when I was so young.

Dealing with different relationship dynamics.

Quitting my job when Haley was born and feeling terrified about our finances and making it on one income.

Life is *complicated*. It's complicated for everyone. Every time I wish I wasn't dating, I remind myself that married life wasn't always perfect either. Every time I'm trying to navigate a new path with my in-laws, I remind myself that my best friend is doing the same and her husband is alive and well. Every time I feel like I'm alone, I remind myself that there were times when I felt that way before Brad died. That life wasn't ever as perfect as I would like to think it was. That Brad and I loved each other, but we also had hard times. That raising kids alone is hard, but raising kids is hard *period*. That even though the relationships I have with my friends and family are constantly in transition, the truth is that they always were.

My mom has a saying that she loves and I think of it often: If you had everyone you know put their troubles in a paper bag and you hung all those paper bags on a clothesline and someone told you that you could exchange your paper bag with someone else's, chances are you'd take your own.

I know that I have troubles. I know that I've had loss. But I've had a lot of wonderful things happen, too…before and after Brad died. *I* was the one he chose to spend his life with. *I'm* the one who gets to have all of the wonderful memories of him that I do. *I* was the one who grew from our fights, who benefited from his love, and who has the honor of raising our children.

So would I choose to change my "paper bag" for someone else's if that I meant that I wouldn't have to be a widow? And risk losing all of the wonderful things I've experienced before and since then?

Not on your life.

I miss Brad every day. *Every day.* And I have come to understand that I always will. It's not something that will ever go away. There will always be things that remind me of him. There will always be things that I wish he could be here to see. And there will always be times that seem more difficult because he's not here.

I think most of us, when we begin our journey into widowhood, think that loving our husbands is an "either or" proposition. That to move forward, we have to move *on*. Move on from what? Our lives? Our experiences? Do you know *anyone* who can do that, loss or not? 'Cause I'll tell you right now…wherever I'm going, I'm dragging the rest of my life with me. And that means that Brad's coming along for the ride.

But there comes a point in every widow's journey when she has to make peace with what has happened and finally accept that, yes, this has happened to *her*. Most of the widows who seem to all of a sudden turn a corner have one thing in common: they stopped fighting widowhood and started to work with it. Because it takes a lot more time and effort to deny yourself the grief you feel than it does to work to accept the life—including the grief—that is now yours.

CATHERINE TIDD

The people who have experienced losing a lifelong partner and who have successfully come out the other side…well, they're carrying a secret. They have the miraculous ability to pay attention to their journey. And appreciate it. They watch for signs, for meaning, for something that speaks to them, and then they act on it, knowing that life is short and that they alone have a special path, one that no one else has taken. They cry when they need to. They feel everything and welcome it into their lives rather than fighting it. And once that self-awareness happens, so does a certain inner peace. It doesn't matter if anyone else understands.

We do.

These moments of clarity are, of course, counterbalanced by self-doubt. No one can possibly navigate life successfully without sometimes questioning why they are where they are and if what they're doing is right…and that's true for anyone, widowed or not. It's that questioning, that quest for insight into ourselves and where our lives are going, that keeps us growing.

Who am I now?

What do I want to do now?

Chardonnay or merlot tonight?

One thing I know for a fact is that no one has the perfect life that they seem to. You may be looking at your married friends, envying their "normal" lives, and have no idea the struggles they have been through or go through every day. You may be looking at someone who has more money, a bigger house, or kids that seem better behaved than yours…and have no idea whether they truly think their lives are fulfilling. Heck…*they* may not know if their lives are fulfilling. They may not have taken the time to even question it.

I know that I've found odd things about my own experiences with widowhood amusing. I'm somewhat proud of myself that I've kept my sense of humor through some of my darkest moments and experiences. But the truth is…I know I'm not alone. I've never laughed harder than when I'm with a group of widows. We embrace our craziness, laugh through our tears, and heal through humor. Our bond is almost always immediate, and our ability to comfort each other cannot be matched.

It was with a group of widows, years after Brad died, that I found comfort in something I thought had officially forever cemented me as the most mediocre widow that ever lived. Something that only a handful of people in my life knew about. And something that I didn't truly find funny until I told it to a group of widows…and they laughed right along with me.

A few months after Brad died, I took on the task of finding just the right headstone. Now, this turned out to be more complicated than I thought it would be because I had something very specific in mind for his peaceful spot on the side of the mountain. I wanted something natural and beautiful. Something that would look great in the mountains and that would reflect his personality.

I settled on getting a boulder—not a stone, a *boulder*—which I knew would be a little pricey, but I wanted to do this right. After all, how many husbands was I going to bury? I decided to have Brad's name, his dates, and the phrase "When in Doubt, Look Up" engraved on it…which I thought was perfect, given Brad's love of space and the need we all have sometimes to look to the heavens for divine intervention.

I was very picky about the look and wanted three stars near the beginning of the quote. And after reviewing the proofs several times, I gave the company the go-ahead to get it done.

After a couple of weeks, I was surprisingly excited when they called and said that it had been completed and installed in its new home. I mean, this was no small task. Brad was buried on the side of a mountain, after all, and this was a huge rock. The company had to lay a cement foundation so the boulder wouldn't eventually roll down into the river, and then they had to hand-carry that sucker in.

So, when I heard it was finished, I immediately packed the kids up and drove them up to the cemetery. I stood there in misty silence, admiring my handiwork, which really was a thing of beauty. In fact, I was so proud of how it turned out that I took pictures to send to my in-laws in Pennsylvania.

When I got home, I immediately downloaded the pictures. I sat there and just stared at them trying to digest, once again, that this had really happened. That he really was gone. That I was sitting there on my couch, surrounded by three small children and looking at my husband's headstone. And for some reason I couldn't get over the fact that there was something not quite right about the boulder.

Then it hit me.

His birthday was wrong.

I thought I was going to throw up. I ran to my office and found the proofs that the company had sent, certain that there was no way *I*, the woman who at that point was determined to be Wonder Widow, could have possibly made such a monumental mistake. I shuffled through page after page, looking at the stars that I had been so adamant about looking perfect...and the birth date I had signed off on that was completely wrong.

I immediately called Kristi in a hysterical panic and told her what I had done.

At which point, she started laughing so hard she couldn't speak.

This, you can imagine, did not help at all. It's like laughing at someone when they tell you they're pregnant again, on accident, for the fourth time, and they just found out that it's going to be twins. The story may be cute and funny later, but at the time... not so much.

"Oh, Catherine," she said, trying to catch her breath. "You

can't tell me you don't think this is funny. You can't tell me that *Brad* wouldn't think this is funny."

"But what am I going to *do*?" I asked, trying to decide if I was going to start laughing with her or hang up on her. "How can I possibly fix this? It's a rock! A *boulder*! It's immovable at this point! This was the last thing I could do for Brad…and now I've screwed it up!"

"Whatever," she said dismissively. "The last thing you're going to do for Brad is raise his three kids. Believe me, this is not that big of a deal. Do you think anyone will even notice?"

"Uh…I think his parents will notice if they ever come to visit. *I'll* notice every time I go up there, and it will be a huge reminder etched in stone of what a terrible widow I am!"

"Well, just take a Sharpie up there the next time you go and turn that one into a nine so that it says the nineteenth instead of the eleventh," Kristi said in her infinite wisdom. "No one will ever know!"

I guess there's a reason why she works in finance and not for a memorial company.

Eventually the headstone got fixed, thanks to a couple of men with a grinder and the ability to re-etch the number. I came to the conclusion that if they had the ability to fix it, surely I wasn't the only widow in the world who had made this mistake. And I learned two very valuable lessons that day:

1. You can try all you want to be the perfect widow, but all it takes is one typo on a tombstone to blow your cover.
2. There's no such thing as the perfect widow.

I've never been perfect, and it's quite possible that I've never been "normal." And I don't know why, when I lost Brad, I thought widowhood was the ideal place to start. It took me a while to realize that those imperfections are actually what make life interesting. I'll never have a moment when I've done something idiotic (which is daily) that I won't wish that Brad could be here to share that laugh with me.

But…that doesn't mean that I've stopped laughing.

I have a card that I look at every day that says, "A truly happy person is the one who can enjoy the scenery on a detour." Since I don't know of a bigger detour in life than widowhood, I'm doing my best to enjoy the scenery along the way to wherever it is that I'm going. Which I think Brad would appreciate. Because even before he died, he knew that I always thought the best way to find my way around when I was in a new place was to get lost for a little while.

And that, eventually, I would figure out the best way to go.

Tips for Widow(er)s

and those who support them

Widowhood

when normal becomes a fantasy

Tips for Supporters

Assess, ask, and act. Take a moment to assess the situation and find out what's needed—don't just jump in with what you think you would want. Ask if there is anything you can do, and don't just make a hollow promise—follow through on your commitment. Don't wait for your widowed friend to call you. Figure out your strengths (Are you good with her kids? Can you help with her in-laws? Are you good at organizing meals?) and act.

Set up a phone schedule. Do this with her mutual friends so that you know someone is calling to check on her, and put two people on it twice a week for six months minimum.

Set up a meal schedule. Go to Take Them a Meal (www.takethema-meal.com) and set up an account.

Send cards. You could put her on a "card schedule." Give her a stack of greeting cards and put on the envelope when she's allowed to open each one. This gives her a small something to look forward to.

Set up a "kitchen table club." Let's face it. When the going gets tough, we want our girlfriends around us. Gather a group of four close friends for a regular monthly gathering to just catch up with each other. There is a great book on how to do this called *This Is Not the Life I Ordered* by Deborah Collins Stephens, Michealene Cristini Risley, Jackie Speier, and Jan Yanehiro.

Don't give your support an expiration date. When we go through a huge transition, we're often surrounded by people in the beginning, and then we don't hear from anyone a few weeks later when we really need it.

Widow(er) Tips

Immediacy is your friend. Do your best not to "borrow trouble," and take each problem one at a time. Your immediate well-being (and that of your children) is the only thing you should be worrying about now. The rest can usually be dealt with later.

Ask for help: Believe me, everyone around you wants to do something. Put them to work if you can. It makes them feel useful.

There is no right way to act. Feel like you're not responding to your spouse's death the right way? That's because there is no "right way" to respond. There were many things that I found funny and surreal when my husband was dying in the hospital, and I felt so guilty and like I wasn't acting "widow" enough. But eventually I figured out that there is no right way to cope.

Memorializing

if i get the casket without the four-wheel drive, how much will that run me?

Tips for Supporters

Pay attention to what needs to be done. Are you a really organized person? Take over the organization of the food that everyone brings (make sure dishes are labeled with names and dates of drop-off, and so on) and make notes of who brought flowers. Are you crafty? Offer to put together photo albums for attendees to look through during the service and reception. Think of your strengths as a friend and use them behind the scenes.

Listen. Most people mistakenly think that because our spouse is gone, it's too painful to talk about them. In reality, most people love to remember their spouses with anyone who will actively listen to them. Asking questions like, "How did you meet?" and just listening could save a lot of embarrassment from saying the wrong thing. (For more tips on what to say to someone after the loss of a spouse, please reference the end of this document.)

Widow(er) Tips

You can't please everyone. This can be a really sensitive time for everyone, and although it is sometimes hard to see past our own grief, we have to remind ourselves that we're not the only person who has suffered a loss. If you want to have more control over your situation, consider these options:

1. If your spouse is being cremated, consider splitting the ashes between yourself and your in-laws. That way, you can do whatever you wish with yours without worrying about pleasing them.

2. If you suddenly see the funeral getting out of control and know that this is not something you want to participate in or that your spouse would have been happy with, consider letting others in your family do what they wish for a memorial service…and then plan something on your own with close friends (a party, a trip, or an intimate gathering) to remember him or her on your own terms.

Just remember that a lot of relationships change after a loss, and it's partially up to you how things end up, something that's hard for *everyone* to remember in the throes of grief.

Coping/Changes

an all-inclusive trip to the island of crazy

Tips for Supporters

Don't leave us hanging. We are bombarded with support the first two weeks after our spouses die, but then everything gets quiet when everyone leaves. Can't come to the funeral? Tell your friend that you're planning a trip to see her the month after. It will give her something to look forward to. Throwing a party? Ask your widowed friend. She may decline fifty times, but it could be the fifty-first time that you ask when she really feels up to it.

Call her. Even if she doesn't answer or call you back right away, I promise that she appreciates your effort. Don't give up.

Changes. Remember that your widowed friend is experiencing changes at such a rapid pace that she can barely keep up. And many times, when she talks to you about them, she's not asking for your approval; she's asking for your support. (Those are two very different things.) The best thing you can do is help her talk through what is going on in a nonjudgmental way.

Widow(er) Tips

Relationship changes. Almost all relationships change in some way because of what we've been through. I felt like I had to "raise" my parents all over again until they came to terms with the "new me." This can sometimes be painful, but many times the outcome is not such a bad thing. Most widow(er)s find that the people they were closest to before have a hard time maintaining the friendship they've had for years (for various reasons) and the people they weren't close to become their greatest champions. Remember that friendship changes are something that everyone goes through in life—whether they've experienced a loss or not. These "growing pains" take time, but in the end, we usually end up with friendships we know can stand the test of time and hardship.

Be patient. Everything in our lives changes so rapidly that it's hard for us to keep up—and we're living it every day! Imagine how our friends and family feel when we call them and tell them the many things we're thinking about doing or changing. Remember that everyone is doing the best they can at coping with your new life, too.

Communicate. Upset that you don't hear from your friends enough? Feel like they never ask you over anymore? Tell them! They don't know…they think they're giving you space or being a burden. Starting to feel lonely and want to be with people? Remember that your friends are not mind readers. *You* call *them* and set up a plan.

Milestones

i'd rather pass a kidney stone than a milestone

Tips for Supporters

The date doesn't matter. Most widow(er)s begin grieving over a milestone well before the actual date. If your friend seems a little "off," ask her if she needs to talk or if you can take her kids for an hour...something to try and ease the burden of what's going on. Many times *we* can't even explain why we're feeling the way we do, which is frustrating. Often things that we've never thought of before may set us off, such as back-to-school time or family days like Labor Day. Basically any day when you feel grateful for your family, we're mourning the fact that ours has changed forever. Be sensitive to that.

Perform a random act of kindness. Is the anniversary of her spouse's death approaching? Send a card or some flowers—even if it was years ago. Is it holiday time? You and your kids can go over and spontaneously shovel her driveway just to let her know you're thinking of her. Nothing hurts more than feeling like our spouse or our loss has been forgotten. Never be afraid to acknowledge what we might be going through. We appreciate it more than you know.

Widow(er) Tips

Take care of yourself. Many of us have a "cluster" of milestones. Anniversaries, birthdays, and holidays are often gathered together on the calendar, making a couple of months out of the year seemingly unbearable. Acknowledge this. Clear your calendar as much as you can during that time and then maybe give yourself something to look forward to a month after they're finished—a trip with a friend, a nice dinner with your mom, a spa day. Dangle that carrot in front of yourself so that you have something to get you through that rough time.

Look at your calendar. It took me years to figure out that the reason I'm always emotional at the end of January is because I missed watching the Super Bowl with my husband. Getting emotional about milestones doesn't have to make sense—it will happen whether it makes sense or not. Forgive yourself for it. And if several weeks have gone by and you still feel like you're in that hole, it may be time to call your therapist. Take the time to feel what you need to feel, but don't spend too much time wallowing in agony.

Dating

mom...don't read this part

Tips for Supporters

Don't push in either direction. Hearing that we're young and we'll find someone someday is not what we want to hear right after the funeral. It could be ten years before we can imagine trying to find a new companion—or it could be a month. Our timeline is our own, and either being pushed or dissuaded from dating makes us feel alone and misunderstood. This is a good time to practice your listening skills.

Don't judge. Believe me that no one is judging us harder than we are. We are flooded with so many feelings when we decide to date, no matter how long it's been since our spouse died. Listen without judging (or if you feel a judgment coming, keep it to yourself). When we know you're judging us, we quit talking to you. That leaves us alone and vulnerable, which is a dangerous place to be when we're thinking about dating. Remember: asking for your support doesn't mean we're asking for your approval.

Widow(er) Tip

Take your time. Sometimes it's tempting to commit quickly when we think we've found a person who might be able to fill that sudden void in our lives. And that can happen no matter when we start dating. Remember that dating is a *process*. We carry many things with us from our previous relationship—both good and bad. It's important to take the time necessary to find out if this is a good fit. It's not as simple as it might seem in the beginning, but if you really pay attention to the process, chances are you'll end up with an amazing and lifelong relationship.

It's okay. It's okay that you feel guilty sometimes. It's okay that you compare the new guy to your husband a little. It's okay to love your husband *and* someone new. It's okay to miss the intimacy of marriage and then be grateful when you find it with someone else. All of these feelings are part of the process and will probably happen no matter when you decide to date. Give yourself the time and space to feel it all and work through it with the new person in your life.

Be a friend. Remember that your friends and family lost your spouse, too. And while you know that they ultimately want to see you happy, it may be hard for them to see you with someone new. Again, you're living with your loss and the outcome of it every moment of every day and adjusting as you go, and the people around you are doing it in fits and spurts when they see you. Be patient with them.

Moving Forward

time to pull on your tights
and become your own superhero

Tips for Supporters

A part of us will always be grieving. Four years later, we may look like we have it all together, but there will always be a part of us that is grieving our spouse. After all, we thought we would be together our entire lives, so it makes sense that we grieve a little for them our entire lives. Don't hesitate to really ask how we're doing.

Help us talk through transitions. As we start to imagine our lives differently, we begin asking ourselves so many questions about what comes next. We need people to brainstorm with and bounce ideas off. Remember that as we're talking to you, we're not asking how you would live your life. We're trying to figure out how to live our own.

Widow(er) Tips

Be patient. Once again, it's important to be patient with yourself, with others, and with the process in general. It may seem like others are getting on with their lives, and the hard truth is… they are. They're not living your life day to day so it's unrealistic to expect them to be with you for every little step of this journey.

And remember: sometimes when you're feeling low, you may be going through your own growing pains. Be patient with yourself and pay attention to the journey. You won't regret it.

Spread your wings: So many people find developing a new life completely overwhelming, but it doesn't have to be. This is the right time to dig deep and figure out who you are. And if the journey gets tough, seek resources to help you. Feel like you need a new path in life? A life coach could be perfect for that. Possibly thinking about going back to school? Make an appointment with a guidance counselor at your local college. Feel like you just need to get out more? Volunteer. It's a great way to network and possibly find a new passion you didn't know you had.

Identify your support system. Figure out the people in your life who are your greatest champions. It's important to know who those people are so that you can truly absorb what they have to say. Like hanging out with your neighbor but notice that you feel depressed after a conversation with her? Pay attention to that. It doesn't mean you can't meet her for a glass of wine…it just means you shouldn't give her advice the weight that you might to suggestions from another friend.

What to Say

(and what not to say) after loss

Many of us have found ourselves in the awkward position of not knowing what to say when a friend is going through a loss or transition. We all know how it feels: our mouths go dry, our palms get sweaty, and we leave feeling like we have said the absolute wrong thing.

Here are a few helpful tips that might get you through those moments.

1. *I know how you feel.*

   Hmmm…not really. I know you can sympathize, but until you've lived my life every day, there is a good chance that you don't.

   Instead: *How are you feeling?*

   Ask with sincerity and be prepared to practice active listening.

2. *This was part of God's plan.*

   That may very well be, but it really wasn't part of mine. Hearing that right after a loss usually doesn't help to make it "okay." There may be a time for that, but that is something that you should wait for the person going through the loss to say. Even the most spiritual person may not be ready to digest that quite yet.

Instead: This is one I do not have a "blanket statement" for. You need to assess where your friend is in their grief process. Loss can change feelings about religion in so many ways, and this is not the best time to go into detail about your own beliefs. If this is a person you have known to be a spiritual person, it may be appropriate to *gently* ask how things may have changed in that department. And, whatever they say, *do not judge*.

3. *It's been awhile. Shouldn't you be over this by now?*

There is no expiration date on loss. Actually, there is no expiration date on anything we might feel. Any major life transition comes with feelings we may very well carry with us always.

Instead: *I know this may be a difficult time for you. I just wanted you to know that I'm here for you.*

Just because your friend seems to have "moved on," don't assume that he or she doesn't still carry those feelings of loss with them. Milestones and grief in general are something that we will feel and recognize for the rest of our lives. We feel cared for when you do an "emotion check" every once in a while, even years later.

4. *Everything happens for a reason.*

Again, that may very well be. But we can't see the reason right now. We may never see it. And if we do, let it be up to us to tell you about it.

Instead: *He (or she) was such an amazing person. Sometimes I have a hard time understanding why this has happened.*

Well, sure. *That* we get. Most of us can't understand why

this has happened either. And that feeling of shock will revisit us for a long time. It helps us to know that you recognize that.

5. *At least he didn't suffer.*

Anything along those lines is really not helpful. Truthfully, even if it was something instantaneous, most widow(er)s have visions of what the last moments were like for our loved ones. We are constantly wondering what they were thinking. And in many cases, you don't know for sure if they didn't suffer. So it's best just not to go there.

Instead: Most widow(er)s are open to talking about their experience during their loved one's last days. It's okay to ask questions, but truly assess how your friend is reacting. If you're getting one-word answers, they probably don't want to talk about it. If they start telling you the story, actively listen to what they have to say. Don't be surprised if you get a "robot-like" account of what happened. Widow(er)s are often surprised at how they can mechanically tell their "story." This doesn't mean they are not completely devastated by the experience. It's just a coping mechanism.

6. *He's in a better place.*

Again, that could be true. But most of us consider ourselves rather "selfish" and would rather have them here with us. And I can guarantee that if you say that to just about any widow(er), you'll be left with an uncomfortable silence. Because we really have no response to that.

Instead: *I really miss when he used to _____.*

Instead of asking the widow(er) to picture him someplace that's not here with us, maybe remind them of a good memory. Don't shy away from mentioning their name or sharing something you remember. This is a person we think about constantly. It's nice to be able to share and feel like a part of them is still here. We don't want to be the only people who remember our loved one who is gone.

7. *At least you didn't have children.*

Um. Yeah. Well, we could have been trying to have children and you didn't know about it. We could have been putting it off for one more year and now we're filled with regret. We could have decided we never wanted children, but the bottom line is: *Whether we had children has no bearing on how much we are grieving right now.*

Instead: This is a tough one and is really up to your friend to talk about what their plans were for family. Chances are, even if they look to the future and see themselves in a new relationship, there is a certain amount of sadness that comes with knowing that they will never have children with the significant other that they lost. And if they have never seen having children in their future, you should keep in mind that they have lost the person they thought they would be spending every major event with for the rest of their lives. They have lost their family. Be sensitive to that.

8. *You're so young/vibrant/such a great catch, you'll find someone else.*

But we don't want to. We don't want to start over from scratch. And we know that you mean well, but right now we're just trying to pick up the pieces of our lives and function. The idea of a new relationship (that comes with the possibility of going through something like this *again*) is a little much. When and if we get to that point, we will let you know. And that's when we can use that kind of encouragement.

Instead: *Let's set up a monthly girls'/guys' night where we can get together. We can stay in or go out...you choose.*

Most of us are lonely. We miss our mates. But the idea of dating is incredibly overwhelming. Friendly companionship may be the closest we can come to socializing for a while. Coordinating nights out or in can be really hard for a widow(er), especially in the beginning. Can you help us with that?

9. *I will never forget how hard it was when my grandmother/cousin/pet died.*

I have no doubt that that was difficult for you. But what we are going through is completely different. And please don't compare our loss to one that you've been through. We realize that you're trying to relate to us, but for some reason it doesn't come across that way. If your loss was similar to ours, look for a sign from us that we want you to talk about it.

Instead: Try not to be too invasive, but most of us would really like to talk to someone about our own experience. And we can tell when someone is sincerely asking and when they're just trying to fill the silence. Think of it this way: *Mentally draw upon your own loss experience to ask educated questions about ours: Were there a lot of people at the hospital? Was there a moment you knew they were gone?* These may sound like odd questions, but widow(er)s usually don't mind talking about the loss with people we know are listening with a loving ear.

10. *You're so strong.*

I know this sounds odd, but most of us don't want to hear that. Because most of us don't feel that way. We're falling apart inside, and for some reason, someone saying this in admiration makes us feel as though we need to keep up a brave front. It adds to the pressure we're already feeling.

Instead: *How are you doing?*

I know I've said it before, but truly and sincerely asking us how we are doing and taking the time to listen to the answer is always your best bet. I can almost guarantee you that no matter how "strong" your friend may look, they don't feel that way on the inside and they are just hoping someone asks them how they are really doing. Bring the tissues, look at them, and give them all of your attention. That means more to us than anything.

Reading Group Guide

1. Catherine talks about how sometimes losing yourself is necessary to find out who you are meant to be. Have you ever had moments in your life when you have let go of who you thought you were in order to grow? Was there a specific incident that inspired this change?

2. Evolving relationships are an ongoing theme throughout the book—changes with friends and family made Catherine examine who she wanted in her life and who she didn't. Have you ever experienced uncertainty concerning personal relationships? Have there been times when you've had to work hard at certain relationships and when you've known it's time to let go?

3. Catherine talks about getting pedicures as a frivolous but necessary coping mechanism. Do you do something that comforts you when you're down? Maybe something others might not understand?

4. At one point, Catherine says that the clothes her husband was supposed to wear home from the hospital sat in her

closet in a bag as if waiting for the call to come pick him up. Do you have any items from your past that you just can't seem to part with? Why are they important to you?

5. Do you believe in signs from those who have passed away? Why or why not?

6. Throughout this book, Catherine is very candid about how out of control she felt about so many aspects of her life. Have you ever felt that way? How do you cope?

7. Catherine talks about how she felt that the person she was before her loss was perfect for her husband, but the person she became would be perfect for someone else. Do you believe in soul mates—one person you are meant to be with your entire life?

8. What do you feel has been one of your bravest moments? Was it a career change? A parenting moment? A time when you stepped out of your comfort zone to try something new or change your life in some way?

9. Catherine talks a little bit about being confused by her faith after Brad died—that she had a hard time going back to church for years. When you go through trying times, do you cling to your faith or do you find yourself questioning it?

10. Throughout the book, Catherine experienced moments when people made comments that they thought were helpful but were really not. Have you ever had that happen? Did you say something to the other person, or did you let it go?

11. Have you ever done any retail therapy? What did you buy?

12. Catherine was somewhat surprised at the things others did that she found helpful and things that some people did that she didn't like. What is something you like to do for people you know to support them? What have others done for you that you appreciated?

13. Catherine found a lot of humor in her dating experience. Have you ever had a date that was so bad it was funny?

14. Catherine and her mom had a huge blowup right after Brad died. As she said, "That fight over nothing important allowed me to let go, get angry, and finally yell at someone, someone safe, because deep down I knew that I would never lose my mother." Have you ever lashed out at anyone because you knew they were your "someone safe"?

15. Throughout the book, there were many moments when Catherine reacted the way she did because she felt like that's what people were expecting of her—she hesitated to let her true feelings show. Have you ever behaved a certain way just to make others feel better?

16. Do you believe that overall happiness is a choice?

Acknowledgments

There is no way I could have done this without my family.

To my children: Haley, your talent, spark, and enthusiasm inspire me every day and I'm so proud that we have put this book together with your amazing sketches. I'll never forget our first "business meeting" when you were nine years old and I said, "Hey. Can you draw an urn for me?"

Michael. You are the best of your dad and me because you were blessed with his brains as well as compassion for others that's way beyond your years. I just can't believe that I am lucky enough to be your mom and I can't wait to see the man you will become.

Sarah…where do I begin? I could write a book a day with the material you give me. You light up a room when you walk into it and make me laugh harder than anyone I've ever met. The world will be yours someday, sweetie. Take it.

To my parents and my sister: What you have done for me cannot be put into words. You have taught me the meaning of the word support and have always been there for me even before I asked. I love you and I thank the heavens above for you every day.

To my friends who let me cry on their shoulders, drink their wine, and provided me with a laugh when I thought I'd forgotten how…you made it possible to move from one day to the next.

To Mike. Thank you for being a part of my story.

To the team who made my dream of publishing a book a reality: Erin Cox, my agent and the friend who now has to deal with me because we have a contract—I love you and I have no doubt that I hit the jackpot, both professionally and personally, the day you accepted this manuscript. And to Shana Drehs with Sourcebooks—you have been nothing short of fabulous to work with. Thank you.

To Caroline Leavitt who helped me find the story within my story. And to Julianna Baggott who was so generous with her resources at the beginning of this process. You have both shown me how important it is to "pay it forward" in this business.

And to all of the members of the club no one wants to join—theWiddahood.com. There have been days when your support and friendship were the only reason I was able to get out of bed in the morning. You have shown me that the byproduct of loss is kindness and generosity of spirit and that we *all* have important stories to tell.

Hugs.

About the Author

Catherine Tidd is a writer, mother, and founder of www .theWiddahood.com. She received a degree in English from Rollins College in 1998 and has since worked as a writer, editor, marketing manager, and event planner. Originally from Louisiana, Ms. Tidd currently lives in Colorado.

Since the death of her husband in 2007, Ms. Tidd has become a source of support for other widows through her own blog (http://widowchick.blogspot.com) and Facebook support page (under the name Widow Chick). Ms. Tidd is a motivational speaker who focuses on "finding joy in an unexpected life" and thriving after loss. She is also a volunteer speaker for the Donor Alliance of Colorado and Wyoming.

Ms. Tidd is a contributing author to the *Thin Threads* anthology focusing on grief and renewal (www.thinthreads .com), *Open to Hope: Inspirational Stories of Healing after Loss*, and *Open to Hope: Inspirational Stories for Handling the Holidays after Loss*. She is a writer for the *Denver Post*'s Mile High Mamas and her writing can also be found in the upcoming publication *The Widow's Handbook*.